Many Paths

Searching for old Tibet in new China

Many Paths

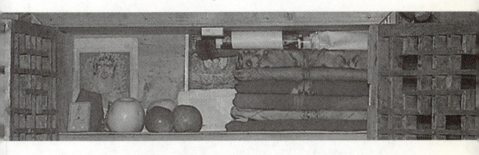

Searching for old Tibet in new China

MARK STEVENSON

Lothian
BOOKS

Thomas C. Lothian Pty Ltd
132 Albert Road, South Melbourne, Victoria 3205
www.lothian.com.au

Text and photographs copyright © Mark Stevenson 2005
First published 2005

All rights reserved. No part of this publication may be reproduced, stored in a retrieval system or transmitted in any form by any means without the prior permission of the copyright owner. Enquiries should be made to the publisher.

National Library of Australia
Cataloguing-in-Publication data:

Stevenson, Mark J. (Mark Jeffrey).
Many paths: searching for old Tibet in new China.

ISBN 0 7344 0585 5

1. Stevenson, Mark J. (Mark Jeffrey) — Journeys — China — Tibet. 2. Amdo (Tibetan people) — Social life and customs. 3. Tibet (China) — Description and travel. I. Title.

915.15

Managing Editor: Magnolia Flora
Edited by Stephen Grimwade and Sue Harvey
Maps by Ophelia Leviny
Colour reproduction by Print+Publish, Port Melbourne
Cover design by Michelle Mackintosh
Cover photograph courtesy of the author
Internal design and typesetting by Caz Brown
Printed in Australia by Griffin Limited

Cover image: simple shrine in a monk's cell, Rongwo Monastery — with ritual implements and Buddhist texts (wrapped in cloth)

Foreword

The title of this book is tantalisingly open-ended, evocative and enigmatic. Which paths? What destinations? On one level *Many Paths* is an absorbing story of Mark Stevenson's many journeys to the Buddhist monasteries of Rebkong. This story is told with a great relish for adventure, a generous open-mindedness and a cultural empathy for both the Chinese and Tibetan cultures he encounters. It is also told with great learning, lightly invoked, as Stevenson effortlessly weaves historical, literary and political allusions into his narrative.

This book is also a story of spiritual paths and destinations, as Stevenson encounters the all-encompassing Buddhist milieu that is intrinsic to the Tibetan world view. His aim is to study traditional Buddhist painting, but he learns to shift his emphasis from art to religion, from the particular to the universal. We go with Stevenson as he is confronted by those choices that shape one's destiny, the realisation that goals must be flexible, that there are universal truths that transcend restricted belief systems, and that there are limitations on his goals which are imposed by frightening political realities.

Just as the subtitle implies, we are all 'searching', all on a journey of sorts. We see what we want to see; we find what we want to. In a telling incident recounted in chapters Eight and Nine of this poignant, questing book, Stevenson tells how his painting lessons with Akha Yeshe showed him that we don't find things through looking, we find them through finding. No matter how much searching we have to do, eventually finding is just a matter of having our eyes open — or opened. His interaction with Buddhism, through the new friendships he makes with monks, and indirectly absorbed lessons, expose him constantly to the Buddhist reality of impermanence, that death is certain and the time of death is uncertain. The wisdom of Buddhist teaching is a refrain throughout the book.

The phrases 'old Tibet' and 'new China' are emotive: for Tibetans and Tibet-supporters, these two phrases conjure up loss of nationhood, autonomy and heritage, hand in hand with the destruction of culture, monasteries and artistic traditions and works of art of superlative accomplishment. Yet spiritual capital cannot be destroyed: it sustains individuals, and provides a sheath for cultural values.

One strength of this book is in the many paths it offers the reader towards opening our minds to the reception of other cultural values which will enrich our understanding of reality, and expand our spiritual world. Reading it reminds us of how much other cultures and their way of perceiving the world have to teach us.

Culture shock, that sense of disorientation and challenge to one's own value system, is more intense on returning to our own culture than on encountering a foreign culture; for the new culture has provided new value systems that augment those previously held. New paths have been opened and the accompanying realisations expose the limitations of one's own culture. To cite one more piece of Buddhist wisdom: every individual is constantly changing. None of us is the same person we were when we awoke this morning. It is the same with this book — you will not be the same after you have read it and made its journeys, particularly the personal and spiritual ones.

Jackie Menzies
Head Curator of Asian Art
Art Gallery of New South Wales

Contents

Acknowledgements   xi
Map of China and Tibet   xiii
Map of Rebkong   xiv
Map of Eastern Qinghai   xvi
Cultural notes   xvii

1
Introduction   1

2
Up in the air   11

3
New icons   27

4
One hundred thousand icons   49

5
The narrow path   63

6
First days in Rebkong   83

7
The wheel of life   107

8
Right livelihood   139

9
Painting magic   165

10
Ocean of sacred food   189

11
Cross-currents   209

12
Many paths   223

Epilogue   239
Glossary   243
Recommended reading   253
Bibliography   257
Notes   259
Index   263

Acknowledgements

Many people have helped in the process of bringing this book into the light of day. Many of them are of course part of the story that follows, and it is to them that I have the greatest debt. Their generosity and inspiration continues to extend far beyond the wonderful times we have spent together.

I have also benefited from the support of a number of institutions, both in Australia and China. My research in China was funded by two scholarships provided by the Commonwealth Government: an Australia–China Exchange Scholarship and an Australian Postgraduate Research Scholarship.

My postgraduate classmates and teachers in Anthropology at the University of Melbourne, my flatmates and teachers at Sichuan University, and my Asian Studies colleagues at Victoria University of Technology have all been instrumental, one way or another, in shaping the way I have come to understand the task of anthropology. In particular I would like to thank Elisabeth Stutchbury and Marc Askew for their good humoured, irreverent and sensible encouragement over many years.

The actual 'getting down' of this story has been made

Acknowledgements

far more pleasurable than it might have been thanks to the unwavering faith and commitment shown by Magnolia Flora at Lothian Books. I should also thank Stephen Grimwade for the patient editing of prose that was more mysterious than the actual mysteries warranted. I am also very honoured that David Templeman, a Tibet historian whose erudition is admired by so many international scholars, and Jackie Menzies, of the Art Gallery of New South Wales, offered their support to this project.

Lastly, I would like to thank Margaret and David Ford for their love as well as their advice on, among other things, opera and Polish Christian names. And in Armidale, Cuncun and Wufeng made sure I wrote with the right motivation.

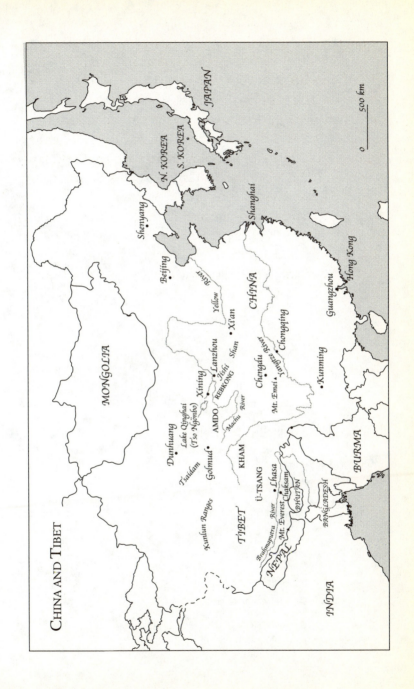

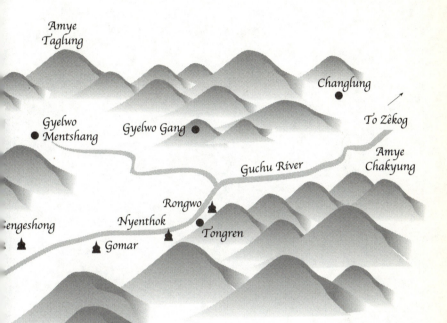

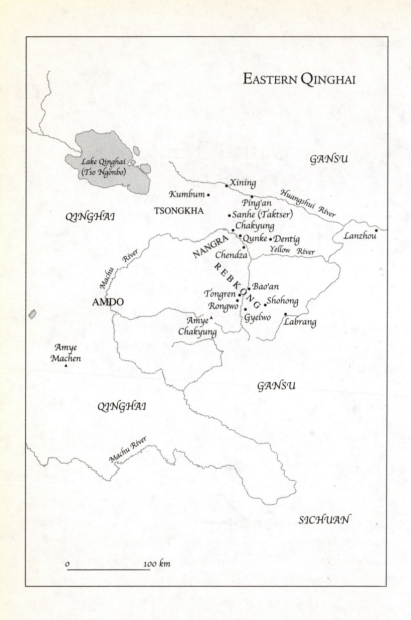

Cultural notes

Language note

Inevitably, many Tibetan and Chinese words, place names and personal names appear in this book. The representation of Tibetan words in romanised form for non-specialist readers remains an unresolved problem. The reasons behind this will become clear on reading Chapter Four. Like most other writers on Tibet I have taken the approach of approximating Central Tibetan (Lhasa) pronunciation. This is a somewhat artificial solution, since the Tibetans of Rebkong speak Amdo dialect, but any other approach would look unfamiliar for those readers already familiar with Tibet and its cultures. Furthermore, there is no easily readable method for representing Amdo pronunciation. To maintain consistency where possible, I have based the romanised spelling of Tibetan place names and names of historical persons on those found in the indexes to Matthieu Ricard's *Shabkar: The Autobiography of a Tibetan Yogi*. In addition to its very useful indexes, this translation of the autobiography of a nineteenth-century Tibetan saint is a magnificent book, and I recommend it as a marvellous introduction to life in pre-modern Rebkong (and many other parts of Tibet). Chinese words are represented in Pinyin romanisation. A glossary of Tibetan and Chinese words is included at the end of the book.

Geographical note

Rebkong is a traditional Tibetan tribal region focused on Rongwo Monastery, in Tongren county, Qinghai province. It appears well inside the boundary of maps of Tibet prepared by the Tibetan Government-in-Exile, as do many other parts of the western Chinese provinces of Qinghai, Gansu, Sichuan and Yunnan. The Tibet Autonomous Region (TAR), proclaimed by the Chinese government in 1965, includes less than half of the actual Tibetan population of China. Traditional Tibetan sources speak of Tibet having three provinces: Ü-Tsang, usually translated as Central Tibet (and including the capital, Lhasa); Kham, usually translated as 'Eastern Tibet'; and Amdo, usually translated as 'Northeastern Tibet'. While I would argue that it would be more accurate to speak of a concentric model where Kham is 'Inner Eastern Tibet' and Amdo is 'Outer Eastern Tibet', I have maintained the customary usage. Rebkong is located close to the centre of the traditional province of Amdo, but for the present-day traveller Tongren and Qinghai are the names to look for on most maps.

Orders of Tibetan Buddhism

The teachings of Shakyamuni Buddha (c.541–c.461 BCE) were practical, representing an open-minded inquiry into what is truly meaningful in life rather than a doctrine that would bind together a group of followers. Because of his insistence on a practical purpose, it is said that the Buddha taught in a manner that accorded with the level and disposition of his audience. The result, over his fifty-year mission, was a vast store of wisdom, compassion and insight that has since undergone further growth and development. Considering the variety and scope of the Buddhist canon it is remarkable how consistent the world's Buddhist traditions have remained.

In its long history, Tibet has produced and preserved a large variety of innovations in the Buddhist path to enlightenment. Some were imported from India, China and Central Asia, and others were developed locally. Centres of innovation rose and fell, but a number of lineages — transmitting their teachings through generations of masters and disciples — have survived. Today, as a convenient generalisation, there are said to be four orders of Tibetan Buddhism: Nyingma, Kagyu, Sakya and Geluk.

The name of the Nyingma order means 'old school'. Its heritage reaches back to the eighth-century Central Asian mystic Padmasambhava and it is the oldest of the Tibetan orders. A century after Padmasambhava was active in Tibet the ancient Yarlung Dynasty of Central Tibet collapsed, and a two-hundred-year 'dark age' is said to have followed. Only after this time did the Tibetan centres of Buddhism begin to flourish once more, inviting teachers from many corners of the Buddhist world, and giving birth to what are called the Sarma, or 'new schools'.

The Sakya and Kagyu orders had their origins in this new fluorescence of Buddhism in eleventh-century Tibet. The Geluk order was founded much later by followers of Tsongkhapa (1357–1419) in the early fifteenth century, but it also inherited the monastic mantle of the Kadampa order, whose roots could be found in the eleventh century. Each of the orders, old and new, has a distinctive approach inspired both by Indian Buddhist philosophy and by the example of their own great masters.

All of the orders have enjoyed political influence at one time or another, and historically they have also been associated with specific regions within Tibet. Territorial conflicts and doctrinal controversies involving differences between the orders were not unknown. Yet, within the broad spirit of Buddhism, they are each understood to provide authentic entry into the path to enlightenment, and it is not unusual to find them located side-by-side in the same valley.

In Rebkong, the Nyingma and Geluk are predominant. In the nineteenth century Eastern Tibet witnessed the rise of a non-sectarian movement, the Rimé, possibly as a response by the other orders to the influence that the Geluk order had gained through the political ascendency of the Dalai Lamas in Central Tibet. The non-sectarian movement continued to influence all of the orders in the twentieth century, particularly following the forced exile of Tibetans after the Chinese invasion in 1949. All of the four major orders accept the Dalai Lama as the spiritual and temporal leader of Tibet.

1
Introduction

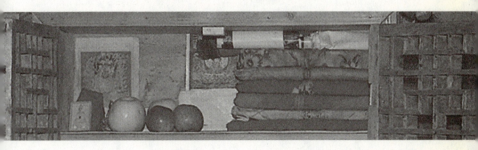

*E*arly one morning in late January 1992, my visa nearing expiry, I boarded a bus out of Rebkong and began my journey home to Australia. As the Tibetan valley disappeared behind me, I reflected on the changes I had witnessed in the two years I had been visiting Rebkong and I wondered what the future held for the people I had got to know. Although the journey from Rebkong was still nauseously death-defying for much of the way, I felt a sense of relief that the bus now took only five hours to cross the 200 kilometres of mountain passes. At an average speed of 40 kilometres an hour we approached the 'outside world', giving me time to collect my thoughts.

I had gone to Rebkong hoping to study its unique traditions of Buddhist art. There had been, at the time, nothing known about Rebkong's painters in any of the published surveys of Tibetan art outside China. Quietly I had imagined being apprenticed under one of the master Tibetan painters, learning everything I could of his art and the philosophy that it brought alive. I knew that the art and the artists had survived to re-emerge; yet I also knew that their world had changed, and that their lives and art must also be changing.

I had wondered how the Rebkong tradition of painting

had survived. I learned some of the answers to these questions, but not quite in the way I had expected.

Leaving Rebkong, I had no idea what was going to happen in my own life. Research under the watchful eye of the Chinese authorities had not been easy. I wasn't sure I had gotten all I needed — emotionally, or in terms of the research I had recorded in Rebkong — to go home, write a thesis and become an anthropologist. A born dreamer, I had wanted to be an anthropologist from the age of five, but the reality had been quite different to the romance, and I was heading home half expecting to be labelled a failure, completely unprepared for the next step in my life.

My experiences in Rebkong had forced me to wonder about the future of isolated communities. What does it mean to live in an 'out of the way' part of the world? In once-isolated places television is now everywhere; children in even the most remote towns of Rebkong are 'surfing the net', playing the latest digital games or contacting friends they've made in chat rooms originating halfway across the world. How 'connected' do people in places such as Rebkong want to be? How 'connected' can they really be? To what extent do they now feel disconnected or left out, rather than isolated?

With a prefabricated image of the world flooding into a place such as Rebkong, what does it feel like to know that your home does not reflect that image? How does it feel to realise that your world will never be like the 'real world', the 'modern world'? I was coming to realise that this may be one of the biggest questions the world will face in the twenty-first century. To what extent will the world's most isolated communities be allowed to realise the same dreams and expectations that they clearly know the 'developed' world — the rest of us — enjoys? For me there is no more urgent question.

How does travelling to Tibet help answer this question?

I don't for a moment believe that Tibet is a spiritual storehouse for the world's wisdom, the one place where humanity might find its ultimate cure. I would like to tell a bigger, more human story than that. The danger of the 'spiritual storehouse' version of Tibet is that it becomes a mirror for our own hang-ups, so that the story ends up being more about ourselves than the Tibetans or their Buddhist traditions. Coming up with stories that are not ultimately about ourselves is a trick anthropologists are still working on.

I read an article in an Australian newspaper recently about a colourful old football coach who had the Buddhist mantra *Om Manipadme Hum*[1] tattooed in Tibetan letters on his arm. According to the curious reporter, the coach said it was hard to translate, but it meant something like, 'You can achieve anything in life, so long as you put your mind to it.' I have no idea where he might have gotten such an interpretation, for in Tibet this mantra is associated with boundless compassion rather than egocentricity. This story is a reminder that the flow of ideas in the last century has not been in just one direction.

In this new century — and millennium — many people are searching for new relevance in ancient messages about meaningful living. Often such messages are still preserved by people living in traditional societies. We tend to twist those messages to hear what we want to hear, believing what we want to believe and what makes us more comfortable. Buddhism points to the mind as the key to happiness, and for that reason it asks us to be careful how we 'put our mind to things'. But there is nothing in Buddhism that asks us to ignore life's most gruesome or blissful realities.

When I had first stepped off the bus in Rebkong in January 1990, I had found much to remind me of the devastation, blow upon blow, that Tibetan communities in China had experienced in the forty years since the People's Liberation Army (PLA) had taken charge. It was all around me: stark piles of rubble, monastic life in disarray, fear in people's eyes. Located in an isolated valley system on the far northeastern edge of the Tibetan world, Rebkong had, until 1949, been the domain of successive reincarnations of the seventeenth-century Buddhist scholar Kaldan Gyatso, traditionally supported by a confederation of twelve tribes. The 'Twelve Tribes of Rebkong', each with its own headman (*pönpo*), included myriad upland valley villages growing wheat and barley, as well as highland yak herders and their encampments. At the heart of this area was the famous Rongwo Monastery.

Through Rongwo Monastery and its eighteen smaller 'offspring' temples, which all belonged to the 'reformed' Geluk order of Tibetan Buddhism, the people of Rebkong had strong links to the major monastic universities of Lhasa, Tibet's capital, as well as to the Dalai Lama's government. Many upland villages also maintained small groups practising an older order of Buddhism, the Nyingma, as well as the indigenous Tibetan Bön religion.

Despite the intense devotion the Rebkong Tibetans had towards their spiritual practice, life was not always peaceful. There were often feuds between nomad tribes over access to highland pasture, and over the centuries local rulers were caught up in wider conflicts between Tibetan, Chinese and Mongolian armies. In the first half of the twentieth century many Rebkong village and nomad communities also fell victim to marauding militias under the command of the Muslim warlord Ma Bufang. But none of the violence of the past, primitive and sporadic as it was, could ever compare to the scale of destruction that occurred following the arrival of the PLA.

On the far northeastern edge of the Tibetan world, Rebkong had been one of the earliest Tibetan areas to be 'liberated' — earlier, in fact, than the liberation of the Chinese capital, Beijing, in October 1949. Then, in September 1951, vanguard units of the PLA marched into the holy city of Lhasa, shattering any opportunity Tibet had of participating in the modern world as an independent nation. Despite Chairman Mao's promises that Tibet would be spared immediate revolution, the Chinese Communist Party (CCP) quickly began to reorganise Tibetan life, and hundreds of thousands of troops were mobilised to enforce Chinese control. Traditional communities in outer provinces of Tibet, such as Amdo and Kham, were redefined as their incorporation into Chinese provinces was consolidated. And when the warriors of Amdo and Kham resisted, in a series of revolts between 1956 and 1958, Chinese military reprisals struck hard. Many of those who fought in the resistance lost their lives, as did many ordinary Tibetans when their towns were bombed. Over 6,000 Tibetan monasteries and temples would eventually be destroyed; only a small handful were spared. Religious leaders were rounded up and those who were not executed as 'counter-revolutionaries' were thrown in prison, many later dying after decades of resisting communist 're-education' and torture. Perhaps the heaviest blow for Tibetans came in March 1959 when the mounting tension between the Chinese army and Tibetan

Introduction

resistance forced His Holiness the Fourteenth Dalai Lama, the twenty-four-year-old temporal and spiritual leader of Tibet, to traverse the Himalayas and flee to the safety of India. The Dalai Lama and his government remain in exile in India today, along with many other great Tibetan religious leaders.

Those *lamas* who remained in China often suffered the worst abuses as life was turned upside down, particularly in the ten years of protracted ultra-leftist chaos the Chinese called the Cultural Revolution (1966–76). During this period even more religious leaders were thrown in jail, and monasteries were once again torn down. It has been estimated that the Chinese 'liberation' of Tibet resulted in the death of 1.2 million Tibetans — one-fifth of the country's population. Re-emerging after Deng Xiaoping's reforms in 1978, Rebkong's communities gradually began to rebuild. Yet even now, after more than twenty-five years of 'liberalisation', there is little today that could be said to have returned to normal for Tibetan communities in China. These are themes and events that I will touch on again in the chapters that follow.

Much of Tibetan tradition survives in exile, largely in India, but also with strong communities in the United States, Switzerland, Canada and Australia. With the dedicated effort of the Dalai Lama and many other learned teachers, Tibetan Buddhism has been able to take root in the major metropolitan centres of the world, finding followers from all backgrounds and walks of life. In China it is mainly Tibetan grandfathers, grandmothers, parents, uncles and aunts, and an attentive younger generation, who keep the flame of the Buddha's wisdom and compassion alive. With their great teachers in exile, most of the monasteries can only remain as a focus for the community's devotion and hope. Unlike 'the rest of China', where most people have regained some semblance of direction and progress, for Tibetans the future remains unclear. Without political self-determination life for Tibetans hangs in a form of suspended animation.

When I left Rebkong in 1992, I had become certain of one thing: that supporters of the Tibetan people must not portray the Tibetan situation as genocide. Such a conclusion might be effective in wiping out the Tibetan people more easily and quickly than the act of Chinese colonisation itself.

A conclusion of genocide would allow the rest of the world too easily to slide into resignation, to see the fate of the Tibetans and their nation as a *fait accompli*, a lost cause. There would be nothing worse than for the world to say, 'Ah, the Tibetans, what a pity. They're finished.' Tibetan communities continue to live in China, and in many places they are succeeding in reviving their traditions. One of the best things I can do with what I have learned, I believe, is to show how the spirit of the Tibetan people lives on in their homeland. This has nothing to do with capitulating to China's colonisation of Tibet; it has more to do with broadening the vision of Tibet's future. In the story I recount in the following chapters I want to share as much as I can of what I have learned about Tibetan life in China today, and also, as an anthropologist, what I have personally come to learn from my journey and my Tibetan friends.

There tends to be a lot of confusion about the word 'anthropologist'. For many it conjures up men in khaki shorts standing victorious atop jungle-covered ruins, or brushing dirt from the skull of a newly unearthed member of the human species. But these men — and they mostly tend to be men in both fact and fiction — are archaeologists or palaeanthropologists. Archaeologists record and interpret the material remains of human activity, usually from prehistory, while palaeanthropologists study the fossilised remains of human ancestors. Both archaeologists and palaeanthropologists contribute to the branch of knowledge called 'anthropology', but today someone in the English-speaking world who refers to himself or herself as an 'anthropologist' is using the word to mean 'social anthropologist', someone who is interested in understanding people today, their living cultures and their diversity.

When I thought I wanted to be an anthropologist at the ripe old age of five, what I actually had in mind was the study of fossilised human remains. Sometimes I think life would have turned out much better if I had continued with that idea, because what a social anthropologist does is much more difficult — if not intellectually, then at least physically and emotionally. It is expected that an anthropologist should live in the society she is studying for a long period, immersing herself in their culture through a process called 'participant-observation', or, more popularly, 'fieldwork'. While this practice has changed over time, it is still the case that an anthropologist must make a career out of a daunting act of self-creation, a 'test of fire' as it has been called. The initiation into the tribe of academic anthropologists down through the generations was won through the drama of fieldwork in a far-flung corner of the globe. And an anthropologist's main tool, in effect, continues to be themselves: personal resources such as determination and empathy, and social skills such as those needed to access other people's lives.

The dismantling of the colonial world after World War II (1939–45) brought an end to an age when European powers governed and exploited distant territories in the name of 'progress'. It also changed the nature of anthropology — it has become increasingly difficult to arrange entry into the far-flung corners of the world and then access such remote communities. The obstacles are twofold: local regimes have continued to be wary of anthropologists and are certainly not as helpful as the colonial governments and their field officers once were; and anthropology itself has been undergoing a kind of open-ended inquiry into the profession's practices and foundations. Instead of being 'handmaidens of colonialism' (as they were labelled by intellectuals of the radical left in the 1970s), anthropologists today are more or less successful in revealing local and global inequalities of power. Instead of cataloguing cultural traits in the manner of a lepidopterist (a butterfly collector), increasingly we have been expected to be 'heroes' of the oppressed and marginalised (a proposition that has its own problems).

I try to return to Rebkong whenever I can and I am always startled by the rapid rate of change in the valley. I am also inspired by the determination and courage of Rebkong's traditional inhabitants as they come to terms with changes over which they are allowed little control.

2

Up in the air

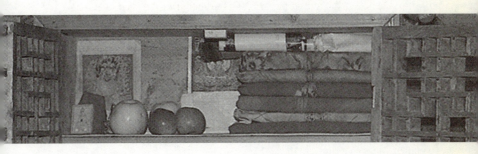

About twenty-five people had gathered in a poky fourth-floor seminar room at the University of Melbourne. We were there to hear a lecture, part of a regular series organised by the Melbourne–China Studies Group; we were a loose collection of academics and students from around the city's universities who met perhaps once a month.

It was late June 1989 and something catastrophic was on our minds: a couple of weeks earlier Chinese troops in Beijing had moved in on protesters massed at Tiananmen Square. Over the first half of the year I had been watching political developments in Beijing fairly closely. The mobilisation of popular protest — mainly students and workers — had been an impressive sight on TV. Month after month the largest public open space in the world had filled with hundreds of thousands of young men and women rallying to support the pro-democracy movement. In the end their protest — a broad call for reform ranging from objections to official corruption to accusations of political backwardness — was too great a challenge to the authority of the Chinese Communist Party (CCP). Government troops were marched from the edge of the city to the square where they opened fire, killing over 2,000 unarmed protesters.

At our meeting someone proposed that, as a response to these events in China, Australian universities should boycott educational and cultural contacts. Purely out of self-interest I argued against the proposal — and my views were carried.

At the time, I was approaching thirty and should have already found my feet as an anthropologist, but I had been away from anthropology and academia. I had spent two years in China as a language student from 1984 to 1986, and then a year working in Canberra at the Australian Bureau of Statistics. In 1989, as the centre of Beijing erupted into turmoil, I felt that I needed to move quickly into fieldwork so that I could finish my postgraduate degree. What had begun with a proposal to study Tibetans outside the Tibet Autonomous Region (TAR) had soon been narrowed down to a project that would investigate Tibetan painters in the western Chinese province of Qinghai. I hadn't been very sure about the procedures for setting up fieldwork access in China, but the best course of action had seemed to be getting into an official student-exchange scheme that relied on an arrangement between the two governments. This would ensure me a student visa for two years, the approval and support of the two governments, and a base at a Chinese university. I would also receive guidance from a local professor and a living allowance on top of my postgraduate scholarship.

My application for an Australia–China Exchange Scholarship had been successful. But I was told to keep in touch with Foreign Affairs and warned that if the situation in China worsened the exchange might not take place. I was also waiting for my placement within a host university in China to be confirmed. By early June there were deep concerns for the safety of Australian students in China and reservations about sending a new group.

Immediately after the Tiananmen Square massacre, everyone who was interested in China — from foreign ministers to trade unions, from corporate executives to academic commentators — could only express deep shock and disapproval, if not condemnation, at the violence of the Chinese government. I held my breath. No one had any idea what direction China would take: not in the next few days or the next week, let alone in the months and years ahead. My anxiety was largely self-centred. In Beijing a solid, impenetrable front combining China's military and propaganda might was gathering to lead a massive nationwide crackdown on all forms of dissent. The full oppressive power of the party and military machine remained intact. Horrified at the display of power, many dissidents escaped overseas or went underground.

Back in Melbourne a memorial service was held in the Town Hall for those who had been killed in Beijing and other Chinese cities. Chinese students in Australia — supporters of dissidents who were trying to escape — stepped up their fundraising efforts. My own travel plans were looking bleak. It was early August before I heard anything: I was informed that none of my preferences to study Tibetan language were 'available', but that the Australian embassy in Beijing was continuing to negotiate on my behalf. It was suggested that I consider an alternative course of study. My original plan had been to head to either the Central Nationalities Institute in Beijing, or the Northwestern Nationalities Institute in Lanzhou. I needed to study Tibetan (or more specifically the Amdo dialect) for a year, and then I could move on to fieldwork. I had also been told that

Sichuan University was a respected 'key university' that offered Tibetan language classes. For some reason I had put it down as my first choice.

Eventually I was notified that the Chinese education authorities 'can only enrol Stevenson if he changes his proposed area of specialisation'. Was that a hint that I should tell them anything, then do what I like once I got there? On 14 August the Department of Foreign Affairs kindly mailed me photocopies of cable communications between the Australian embassy in Beijing and Canberra. The most important paragraph read:

> SEDC [the Chinese education authority] confirmed that, at least for the 1989–90 academic year, it is not possible for a SEDC-funded foreign student to study courses relating to Tibet (i.e. language, culture or sociology).

This was becoming quite an interesting situation. It seemed as though the Chinese government was not prepared to support any study of Tibet by foreign students. Such a stance made a lot of sense: few foreign social scientists have been prepared to praise China's 'liberation' of the Tibetans, and there had been a series of incidents involving Tibetan dissent through the first half of 1989.

Overshadowed by the unfolding crisis in Beijing and complicating matters further, other events were making the Chinese authorities even more nervous about all matters Tibetan. His Holiness the Tenth Panchen Erdeni (more popularly known as the Panchen Lama) had died in late

January 1989. After the Dalai Lama, the Panchen Lama was probably the most influential religious leader in Tibet; both men are incarnations of the two closest disciples of the founder of the Geluk order, the great scholar and reformer Je Tsongkhapa (1357–1419). Many people are surprised to learn that it is not just each Dalai Lama who is identified as returning after death, taking birth again in the form of a child, but that many other 'lineages' of important *lamas* also need to be identified in much the same way (using pre-death notes, personal objects and shamanic visions) after they pass away. Each of the four separate orders of Tibetan Buddhism has its own hierarchy of 'emanation body' *lamas* (*trülku*), as does each of the hundreds of larger monasteries. There are thus thousands of spiritual leaders incarnating across the generations. This makes sense when we remember that from a Buddhist point of view we are, every one of us, a beginningless series of rebirths. What *is* unique about the *trülku* is their ability, through successive rebirths, to continue as spiritual guides.

With the re-opening of many of the major Tibetan monasteries in the 1980s, there had been an opportunity to take advantage of the slightly more liberal political climate in China. So had begun the process of identifying the incarnations of those *lamas* who had been executed or who had died in prison. To some extent this had continued all the while outside China, but there were a number of limits to what the Tibetan diaspora could do in this respect. The search for child 'candidates' was hindered by a lack of access to the Tibetan homeland. Also, knowledge of the whereabouts of, and therefore fate of, many *lamas* under Chinese rule was unclear; and there was a danger that if too many *trülku* were identified outside Tibet's borders, the

Tibetan population in China would be further isolated from their most venerated teachers.

Initially the resumption of the identification of *trülku* inside China proved unproblematic. Candidates were found and the incarnations were identified, often with the assistance and confirmation of the Dalai Lama. But such a state of affairs could not continue, for not all *trülku* were simply religious figures. Like the successive Dalai Lamas, the Panchen Lamas also held considerable political influence. For the Panchen Lamas such influence was mostly within their own domain of Shigatse (the second largest urban centre in Tibet after Lhasa), but could also extend to Tibetan affairs generally. In the early part of the twentieth century the predecessors of the two incarnations had been involved in political machinations that included competing visions of China's role in Tibetan affairs. Again, this was not unusual, since international politics was a player in the early formation of the *trülku* system in Tibet — it is for this reason that both the title of the *Dalai* Lama and the Panchen *Erdeni* contain Mongolian words (*dalai* means 'ocean'; *erdeni* means 'treasure').

When the Dalai Lama had fled to India in 1959, the Panchen Lama had remained behind. Initially he had continued the strategy of avoiding open confrontation with the Chinese. At times it even appeared as if he had sold out the Dalai Lama in order to further his own influence over the future of Tibet. Before long, however, it became impossible to stand by and say nothing about the devastation his people were suffering, and in 1962 the Panchen Lama spoke out in a long, measured but scathing report of the consequences of the CCP's policies in Tibet. The report was confiscated and the Panchen Lama finally felt the full force of the socialist dictatorship, eventually entering nine years of solitary confinement in 1968. Released in 1977, shortly after the death of Mao Zedong, the Panchen Lama continued an uneasy balancing act between a kind of 'going with the flow' (he married and started a family), and resuming his role as a leader of his people, albeit from the safe distance of Beijing.

On 23 January 1989 the tenth Panchen Lama died suddenly, allegedly from a heart attack. His death fell suspiciously soon after he had made a speech at his traditional estate of Shigatse, where he had dared to announce that 'since liberation there has certainly been development, but the price paid for this development has been greater than the gains.'[2] There were rumours of poisoning and speculation that the Chinese authorities would interfere in the process of identifying his incarnation. And eventually, in 1995, they did: the communist leadership in Beijing forced a group of monks to reject the advice of the Dalai Lama and identify their own child candidate; then, to top it all off, the government 'disappeared' the boy favoured by the Dalai Lama.

My research plans seemed small and insignificant beside the historical events that were taking place around me. I could also understand the Chinese government's nervousness: with everything else that was going on, foreigners meddling with things Tibetan would have rung too many alarm bells. And why would the Chinese government want to share in funding someone, particularly an anthropologist, who was likely to make problems for them at some later stage?

Slowly negotiations for my participation in the exchange continued, and thanks to the hard work of the cultural attaché at the Australian embassy in Beijing, I was offered a place at Sichuan University, my original first choice. Tibetan language classes were no longer offered there even though they had been listed in the handbook, but I would be able to enrol in Minority Nationalities History with the noted scholar Professor Meng Mo. It appeared that I was going at last, and although it wasn't turning out quite as I had hoped, it seemed to be my only choice. In the meantime I had another lucky break.

Until August 1989, Rebkong had been closed to foreign nationals. When I had first gone to China to study the Chinese language in 1984, the country had been divided into three kinds of places for 'foreign guests': places that could be visited freely, without the need for a special permit; places that could possibly be visited, subject to application and the awarding of a permit; and the rest of the country, which was prohibited. The Tibet Autonomous Region (TAR) had been on the 'permit required' list. In 1989 the first category was expanded and the 'permit required' category was cancelled. This change was almost certainly made to rein in the confusing situation where local Public Security Bureau (PSB) offices were making ad hoc decisions, or worse, decisions that made a mockery of cases already decided in Beijing. This was especially the case in places around the edge of Tibet where unsuspecting law officers cowered into submission under the intemperate remonstrations of 'foreign devils'.

I can claim to be one of those 'foreign devils' who wore away at 'the system'. My first and only trip into the TAR was in 1985. I travelled as a tourist while a student in

China, taking my mother during the northern summer vacation by land to Lhasa, the Tibetan capital. Travelling in China, outside organised tours, is never easy. On that trip I was in a hurry, trying to fit long trips into a short break before returning to classes at Liaoning University. We had made a non-stop crossing of China from Beijing to Golmud, a railway terminus perched between the Gobi Desert and the Taklamakan Ranges, and hovering temptingly on the map above Tibet.

In China in the 1980s, train travel was crowded, seats were not always easy to get, and little effort was made to ensure the comfort of travellers. The trains moved the masses, and the discomfort of the journey was in all likelihood a part of China Rail's management strategy, making anyone think twice before queuing for a ticket. The length of the queue seemed to be well designed to make you think a third time. Twenty years later the increasing number of aircraft flying China's skies has long relieved the trains of all those travelling on official business; today no enterprise would risk the shame or resentment of asking an employee to rough it like they used to. Also in those days, wherever we foreigners (*laowai*) went we were constantly stared at — except when we arrived at a hotel looking for a room, in which case the receptionists rolled their eyes and looked the other away for as long as they could.

The authorities in China's far-flung provinces must have mixed feelings as they watch a foreigner approach. Certainly they would be puzzled as they wondered why people with all the choices in the world choose to end up in their neck of the woods. They probably also have a right to get a little annoyed when young, scruffy travellers who can't speak Chinese turn up on their doorstep and ruin what

Up in the air

might otherwise be a fairly placid day. And as if those *laowai* who couldn't speak Chinese weren't bad enough, often those who did speak Chinese were worse.

Golmud was, and must still be, a place offering nothing for anyone other than a staging post and a place to find a bus into Tibet. Our train got in at some ungodly hour and we woke up next morning in a concrete and plaster hostel (*zhaodaisuo*) full of dazed travellers from all ends of the earth. I remember a miserable-looking rabble that made the place feel like an army hospital ward. Some of them must have been recovering from the bus trip over the Tibetan plateau, and those heading towards Lhasa may simply have been alarmed at where they had ended up.

Outside there were potholed streets, unpaved sidewalks and block after block of transport depots. There was not a shred of shade and under the clear summer sky the town was blinding. In those days there were only two roads out of Golmud that foreign travellers were allowed to use: one east and one south. The first and only thing on the traveller's mind was to get out of town as quickly as possible. This aim was certainly shared by the three groups of people I would later identify among the foreign travellers. First there were those who had been to Lhasa and were on their way east — either to return to 'China proper' or get to Lanzhou, where they could depart for other western provinces. Then there were two groups of people heading to Lhasa: those with travel permits for Lhasa issued elsewhere, mostly Beijing, and those who needed to arrange them through the local PSB. During that August in 1985 there was soon to be another group: those who had failed to get transport because of a snap ban on foreign visitors to Tibet.

That morning in the hotel, breakfast was *mo* with salted vegetables and a bowl of rice gruel. In the western provinces of China, *mo*, or *momo*, are baked round flat buns of unleavened bread. Like their northern Chinese cousins the *mantou*, or steamed bun (definitely not the delicious roast-pork filled buns known as *char siew bao* on the *yum cha* table), *mo* quickly become like sticky paste once they are combined with the moisture of the mouth. They should be eaten with a large bowl of mutton broth or noodle soup, but I have always been amazed, and even a little envious, to see workmen on building sites bite into them without any accompaniment at all, not even a glass of water. The floor of the canteen was covered in bones left over from dinner the previous night.

After breakfast a rumour began to circulate around the Golmud Hostel foyer: no more foreigners were permitted to travel to Lhasa except on organised tours. A small crowd of a dozen or so soon gathered. Someone spoke of having gone to the bus depot and been refused a ticket. Someone else had bought a ticket the night before, and had been refused a seat. Amazingly, a young driver from the bus company turned up to apologise; he explained that the PSB had notified all the bus companies that foreigners would be refused entry to the TAR, and that none were to board buses in Golmud. Because of the celebrations planned for 9 September to commemorate the 'liberation' of Tibet by the PLA in 1951, travel to Lhasa was absolutely forbidden to foreign travellers not supervised by the China International Travel Service. Anyone who had bought a ticket with his company could have it refunded. 'No way!' the swelling crowd replied. They had a ticket and they were getting on the bus, ban or no ban. Then the bus company rep said something that turned the crowd's anger into action. He identified the common enemy: if we could get permission from the local PSB he would take us to Lhasa. 'Let's go!' went up the cry, and we practically marched the two blocks to the PSB compound. This was revolution and suddenly we had the fervour of a swarm of Red Guards.

We must have looked like we meant business as we passed through the gate and headed towards the Foreign Affairs Office of the Golmud PSB. Spotting our approach, one officer went inside and came out with reinforcements. Whenever they are unsure of a situation, security officers in China ask, or demand, 'Where are you going?' Taking into account the tone in which it is delivered it should probably be translated as 'Where do you think *you're* going?' In fact, we didn't appear to be going anywhere. At that moment I became more determined than I have ever been. I was not going to let this deteriorate into a comedy of miscommunication. I had dragged my mother halfway across China, and she was already miserable enough after roughing it for several nights on a hard sleeper; it would be too heartbreaking to be turned around here in this dustbowl of a town. I decided to stand up to them. Calmly and reasonably I made every argument I could think of for allowing us to travel to Lhasa.

'We'd already come this far — isn't it unfair to turn us around now? We had permits issued in Beijing — didn't that mean anything? Couldn't we go just for a few days and leave before the liberation anniversary?'

'No. No. No,' the answer came. The order had come from higher up, from the *provincial* PSB, and that was the end of the matter. 'We understand what you are saying, but orders are orders.'

I had an idea.

I spoke to the officer again, 'What if I spoke to the provincial Foreign Affairs Office and they said it was OK?'

'Fine,' said the officer who had taken charge; his shoulders back and his hands on his hips.

'OK then, where is the telegraph office?'

The officer waved his hand half-heartedly down the street, and I noticed a frown on his brow. But he wasn't the only one who was unhappy with the way things were going; I also had a feeling that the band of foreigners were looking at me somewhat suspiciously. Unable to understand what I was saying, they must have wondered whether or not they were included in any deals I was making. And I could tell they weren't impressed with the way I had taken control of the situation without consulting them. I was making decisions on my own, decisions that might have them travelling to Lhasa that day or might have them not going at all. I went out onto the street and headed for the telegraph office.

I was fairly sure I didn't need a telephone number for the Foreign Affairs Office in Xining, the capital of the Qinghai province. The operator would arrange all that and I just had to fill in the form. 'Just a small disagreement with the PSB,' I explained to the young woman at the counter. A short wait and the connection was made. She pointed to a small booth; I picked up the receiver and explained my position. I was an Australian student studying at Liaoning University, I was in Golmud, and I had a permit from Beijing that said I could go to Lhasa. The Golmud PSB was refusing to let me travel to Lhasa. I wasn't the only one, there were about a dozen foreigners, all with permits. I appreciated that a decision had now been made not to allow foreigners to travel independently to Lhasa, but I wondered if it might reflect badly on China that permits had been issued in Beijing just a week earlier and were now being revoked. There were foreigners from many countries, and such an unreasonable action might cause an international incident.

'Could you hold on a moment?' was the response.

'Yes,' I replied.

The phone went dead for about five minutes, and as I was debating whether or not to hang up they returned.

'Did you say you all had permits for travel to Lhasa issued from Beijing?'

'Yes.'

'Okay, go back to the PSB. Do whatever the Golmud PSB decides!'

Click, the line was cut.

What did it mean: 'Do whatever the Golmud PSB decides?' As I passed through the gate of the PSB, a huge officer stepped down from the Foreign Affairs Office and we approached the group of waiting foreigners from opposite directions.

'Who called the Xining PSB?' he asked, almost shouting. In his flying jacket and riding boots he looked like a warlord from the 1930s. I owned up. 'Go!' he grunted in English, waving his hand fiercely.

'I'm sorry, I didn't mean to …' I started to say in Chinese.

'To Lhasa! Go! Now!'

'And the rest?' I asked.

'All of you go! Today only!'

By the time we got around to the bus company they'd had a phone call. The young driver was so delighted. He was almost skipping towards us. We would leave at eleven. I went back to the hotel to pack. Not one of the foreign backpackers expressed even a hint of appreciation for what I had just done.

Five years later, in 1989, things were quite different. Perhaps wanting to have a better hold on the movement of foreigners after the democracy movement had been crushed, everything was to be carefully controlled by the central office of the PSB in Beijing. No negotiations: a place was either on the permitted list or it wasn't. As it happened, this decision had been a lucky break for me. While I had already been planning to make Rebkong my research focus, the 'opening' of the region to foreign tourists made access much easier than would otherwise have been the case. As the plane made its way along the runway at Melbourne Airport, I reread a piece of paper that said, I hoped, that no one could stop me travelling to Rebkong.

3
New icons

*I*n September 1989 I flew via Hong Kong to Chengdu, the capital of China's far southwestern province of Sichuan, to begin my fieldwork. In Australia, during my research into topics for my doctoral thesis, I knew that I had stumbled onto something that was then unexplored and unrecorded in our knowledge of Tibetan culture. While I couldn't be sure what I would find on the ground, my reading of Chinese books and magazines uncovered tantalising descriptions of a Tibetan painting tradition that was not yet identified in any literature on Tibetan art outside China. The training in that art tradition had been institutionalised in five village monasteries in a remote valley on the northeastern edge of the Tibetan plateau. And there were even signs that, with the death of Chairman Mao in 1976 and the introduction of reforms by China's new leading statesman, Deng Xiaoping (1904–97), the painters and their painting tradition were making a return. I set myself the challenge of discovering what had happened to Tibetan art after 1949, and how the painters of Rebkong had managed to save their tradition.

I had fallen in love with Tibetan art the first time I saw it in books on Tibetan Buddhism. One of the 'fortuitous' outcomes of the Dalai Lama's escape from China in 1959

has been the flourishing of interest in Tibetan Buddhism in the West, and particularly in the United States. This may have much to do with the concurrence of the Tibetans' flight from oppression with the early years of the hippie movement. At first, young, mostly well-heeled men and women were running into *lamas* on their travels through India, but soon they were bringing the *lamas* home to stay, and Tibetan Buddhist centres were appearing all over the United States and Europe. As the centres mushroomed they became more sophisticated, and between 1969 and 1980 four new presses specialising in Tibetan Buddhist publications sprang up in the United States.[3] When I started at university in Melbourne in 1979 there was already a student-run Buddhist Society with a good selection of books on the *dharma*, the liberating teachings of the Buddha. As my mind devoured the stunning logic by which Tibetan teachers got to the heart of things, my eyes devoured the illustrations scattered throughout the chapters on meditation, patience, emptiness and compassion.

The illustrations I admired most often were not the traditional 'finished product' which would have been bursting with colour and gilt. Rather, they were the simple drawings of the Buddha and other wonderful saints — drawings based on the outline models that Tibetan painters and woodblock carvers used. I was also impressed by the fact that most of the illustrations were drawn by men and women from the West who had studied with Tibetan painters in the refugee camps of India. The use of images drawn in outline may have initially been a cost-saving measure to keep the prices of the books down, but this solution may have had an impact beyond anything anyone had expected; it was as if the drawings had been deliberately left blank so that the readers, mostly new to the traditions of Tibet as I was, could feel free to colour them in with a 'vision' of what they learned as they read. Some of the line illustrations were remarkably intricate, depicting enlightened beings as a fierce complex of fanged mouths, multiple eyes and myriad arms — all in clear detail that was solid and calm, and never clumsy. Each deity (in Tibetan Buddhism 'wisdom energy' takes many forms, both peaceful and wrathful) retained a lightly worn majesty. I was especially drawn to the clean accuracy of line that defines the deities and saints, as well as the sacred vision of the crystalline landscape in which they appear; it conveyed a sense of spaciousness.

As I touched down in Chengdu I pictured myself soon sitting beside an old Tibetan master on his verandah, grinding his pigment and listening meditatively as he passed on to me all he knew about his artistic tradition. I had made up my mind to fit in with the paperwork surrounding my visit and finish a year at the university, which would leave me a second year to spend in Rebkong. I would make a quick preliminary visit in the winter break after my first semester of classes.

Sichuan is reknown for its spicy Szechuan cuisine, the most famous dish of which must be *mapo doufu*, 'pock-faced matron's beancurd' — a fiery red fry-up of beancurd, Szechuan peppercorns, spring onions, minced beef and hot bean-paste, topped with sesame oil and a dusting of chilli powder. The capital, Chengdu, is hot and humid for half the year and cold and damp the other, and I mostly recall an overcast sky and drizzle. But I will never forget the sight of snow draped over banana trees in the grounds of Wenshu Monastery, first built by Chinese Buddhists in the seventh century. When I arrived in September it was hot, and I remember buying half-a-dozen bottles of ice-cold Lüye beer on that first day. The bottles were all empty by the end of the evening and by then I felt I had known my three new flatmates, students from France, Germany and Italy, all my life.

For some reason, perhaps because my fellow student flatmates and I had arrived later than the other foreign students, we had been placed in an apartment block outside the foreign student compound known as the 'Panda Garden' (named for all the pampering foreign students received). Because it was outside the supervised confines of the Panda Garden, our apartment block was supposed to accommodate older students or those who had previous experience in China. This arrangement seduced us with the illusion that we were allowed to get closer to the real China.

Classes for foreign students at the university filled the mornings from Monday to Saturday, but the rest of our time was free, so my flatmates and I spent a lot of time together. The four of us shared a kitchen and a living area. We had a refrigerator and a television, and also a balcony with two rattan armchairs. The balcony was a wonderful place to read and smoke without distraction. Looking out over the concrete rail there was rarely a distinguishable skyline through the murky Chengdu haze. Once our classes were over for the day, our afternoons were for homework, reading, smoking and chatting, or for exploring Chengdu and its famous cuisine.

As long as I could ignore the research I had come to

China to do, this was an idyllic existence, but it was also an artificial and isolated existence, offering little motivation. As with most universities in China at the time, foreign students were set apart from the rest of the university and local visitors were scared off by registration procedures. We were also locked in at night, with a curfew at 10:00 pm, which gave me plenty of time to introduce my friends to a 'hobby' I had learned on my first stay in China: drinking *baijiu*.

Available in 40, 50 or 60 per cent alcohol distillations, *baijiu* is a spirit, although on menus it is often deceptively translated as 'wine'. Distilled from various grains, usually sorghum, sometimes maize and sometimes a mash including peas, it is to China what vodka is to Russia. In many Chinese cities on payday the effect of *baijiu* is easily recognised by the boisterous crowds in dumpling inns, where men play *huaquan*, a finger guessing game designed to get tired workers inebriated as quickly as possible. We drank our way up through the 'concentrations', although my flatmates weren't as interested in this 'research' as I was. Indeed, one Italian student soon grew tired of all this and escaped to the Panda Garden, just in time for a newly arrived Polish student to take his place.

Bronko was, I think, part academic and part worn-out spy. Much older than the rest of us, he had family connections in Sydney, had smoked dope with hippies in Kathmandu, and had suffered gonorrhoea in Vietnam. He also knew a lot about Chinese history; he had written a book or two on the subject. Besides all this, he was an alcoholic who was never more excited than when a bottle appeared.

In the end, Bronko made two serious errors of judgement. The first was his habit of drinking outside the university on trips alone into town, probably in search of 'romantic' company, although I may be using the word loosely here. The second was joining drinking parties with the visiting Russian teachers where drinks were made from pure industrial alcohol accompanied by various mixtures of flavours and colourings that they added themselves.

Bronko's night-time adventures were, as far as we could tell, rarely rewarded, except if you count a regular relationship with the police who were bringing him home in the early hours. He soon became incapable of going to class, spending most days in a semi-conscious stupor. When he was eventually found unconscious in the street he was hospitalised and arrangements were quickly made to send him home. We missed Bronko, but my friends were good enough to point out to me the obvious comparison. It may be partly due to seeing Bronko's fate that I am still alive.

At the university I was paired up with Professor Meng Mo for one class a week. Professor Meng was a wonderful, patient teacher. He was a very old man, approaching eighty, but strong, with a square face that made him look both serious and kind. He was an expert in the ethnology and history of the minority peoples of China's southwest, but his interest in Tibet was not strong. We loved his classes, partly because they were taken at his home where he gave us so much of his time; and partly because it was inspiring to watch him make his way around the sprawling library that he had assembled in his living room, introducing us to the vast literature — both ancient and modern — on the life of China's border peoples, his special interest.

Although it was hard to imagine during the boom years of the 1980s and 1990s, Chengdu had until recently been considered a frontier region itself. This southwestern corner of China was once called Shu and had been fought over for most of China's history. It was also associated with some of the most famous of China's heroes and poets, including the third-century military strategist Zhuge Liang (181–234), the Tang dynasty (618–907) poets Li Bai (Li Po) and Du Fu (Tu Fu), and more recently, Deng Xiaoping (1904–97), whose leadership transformed China's economy in the 1980s and ended with the Tiananmen Square massacre.

Deng was something of a hero in Sichuan, one of the original guiding lights of the revolution; he had survived imprisonment and exile during the Cultural Revolution to return after Mao's death in 1976. He led China into a new era of economic modernisation and improved relations with the West, deliberately distancing China's fate from that of the Soviet Union. While his years at the helm of the Communist Party were finally marred by the massacre in Tiananmen Square, the peasants of Sichuan and the rest of China remain grateful for the transformation made possible in their lives under Deng's reforms. Indeed, his reformist agenda created the new interest in private enterprise that continues to drive the Chinese economy today.

Chengdu was often a place of retreat (or exile), and for this reason it was usually portrayed as somewhere at the ends of the earth, separated from the political hub in northern China by a series of impassable mountain ranges and ravines — tracts of landscape beyond the imagination. Such territory was made famous in Li Bai's poem 'The Route to Shu is Hard', by which he meant you might not make it all the way.

The earth cracks, mountains slide, killing mighty men,
Then there are the endless skyward steps of stone.
Above us at the highest point six dragons roll the sun,
Below us in the seething river are waves that roll upstream.
A yellow crane struggles to fly all the way across,
And agile gibbons climb halfway and chicken out ...
The route to Shu is hard, as hard as scaling the blue sky,
Hearing it described saps all colour from men's cheeks ...[4]

For much of its history, China's hold on places like Chengdu had been tenuous. No matter how long each dynasty lasted, its borders fluctuated as constantly as the tides on its eastern seaboard. And, of course, many of the dynasties were not exactly 'Chinese' but were established by conquerors of China like the Mongol and the Manchu royal families.

When Li Bai wrote 'The Route to Shu is Hard', Chengdu was a large frontier prefecture of over 100,000 households. Today Sichuan province has over 100 million people, around one tenth of China's total population. The province's reputation as 'China's rice bowl' is testimony to the productivity achieved through expanding the amount of cultivated land over several centuries and the intensification of land use; it may also be a warning that eventually the population increase can be expected to outstrip both. The history of the expansion of the Chinese into Sichuan also confirms the validity of Tibetan concerns over the inclusion of traditional Tibetan areas in Chinese migration programs. Today, China is suffering from population pressures on a scale that outweighs anything in the past, and the integrity of Tibetan cultural areas is increasingly threatened. China's majority population, the Chinese-speaking Han people (who we usually refer to in English when we use the word 'Chinese'), show little concern for the implications of population growth on the internal economic and political status of China's minorities, never mind the territorial claims of the Tibetans.⁵

The size of Tibet and the location of its boundaries is a matter of some controversy. Over half of what the Tibetan Government-in-Exile considers to be 'Tibet' lies outside today's Tibet Autonomous Region (TAR). Tibetans consider most of the territory west of Chengdu in Sichuan province as being part of their traditional province of Kham. And the southeastern corner of Qinghai, where I was heading, was part of the traditional Tibetan province of Amdo (as were the southern end of Gansu province and some northern corners of Sichuan).

I remember once, teaching later in Melbourne, how I made one of the Chinese students in my Tibetan History class absolutely livid, simply by displaying the Tibetan Government-in-Exile's map. This map shows the border of Tibet reaching within less than 100 kilometres of Chengdu, which just happened to be her hometown. Pointing out that her ire was mirrored in the experience of the Tibetans, who saw her people as invaders and colonisers, did little to calm her down, inviting rather an argument about history in which sentiment was more influential than historical fact — on both sides.

No matter how it is defined, Tibet is usually bigger than most people first imagine. Because it is considered 'hidden' it is imagined as being small, a mountain kingdom hidden beyond the Himalayas, or even a single broad valley, a Shangri-la. Yet even China's official TAR exceeds 1.2 million square kilometres and a map produced by the Information Office of the Dalai Lama states that the area of Tibet covers 2.5 million square kilometres.

National territory was not a clearly defined concept in Tibet before the beginning of the twentieth century, when suddenly Tibet and less suddenly China were forced by the incursion of the Western world and its 'international law' to rethink their own understanding of nationhood. Tibet had existed under a rather imprecise sense of national territory from at least the collapse of the ancient Tibetan empire in the ninth century, after which Tibetan political life remained highly decentralised, with local principalities competing to control regional power. It is possible that the development of Buddhism may have been partly responsible for this: as a sophisticated monastic culture evolved, monasteries and influential families often combined to establish kingdoms that had extensive regional authority. Indeed, in some ways religious, cultural and national identity came to overlap each other. Tibetans and Tibetan culture were more easily defined than was 'Tibet', for Tibetans shared a connection through Buddhism, through their language and script, through their art and architecture, through their highland life, and through Tibetan customs.

Nevertheless, from around 1400 onwards the centre of power in Lhasa was supported by a well-linked network of monasteries — particularly those of the Geluk order from which the institution of the Dalai Lama emerged. Indeed, perhaps the most important means of identifying what is 'Tibetan' is the deeply felt allegiance of Tibetans to His Holiness the Dalai Lama. Yet the title of the Dalai Lama, or at least the 'Dalai' part, was not originally Tibetan. In Mongolian, *dalai* means 'ocean' or 'oceanic', a reference to the extent of this great *lama*'s knowledge and wisdom.

The first Tibetan to receive this Mongolian title was the leading Geluk monk Sonam Gyatso (1543–88) in 1578. He was a missionary at the court of Altan Khan and was actually the Third Dalai Lama — the title was counted back through two 'predecessors'. The title emerged from the attempt by the Geluk order in Central Tibet to court the allegiance of the warrior Mongol nomads to the north, but the Mongol khans had already enjoyed a long period in running Tibetan affairs three centuries earlier, under the rule of the ruthless Khubilai Khan (who reigned 1260–94) and his descendants. Incidentally, the Tibetans were not the only victims of Mongolian expansion, for the hordes of Khubilai Khan also wiped out the Chinese northern Song dynasty (1127–1279). In the sixteenth century the Mongolians seem to have interpreted the new arrangement between Altan Khan and the Dalai Lama as an invitation to return, and, in 1642, the army of Gushri Khan conquered Lhasa and placed the Fifth Dalai Lama (1617–82) in charge of a unified, militarily reinforced and much expanded Tibet.

With the help of the Khoshot Mongols, the Fifth Dalai Lama presided over a unified Tibet, but the influence of external powers still tended to be disruptive. Powerful monasteries and principalities within Tibet competed for Mongolian support, and the Mongolians' own factions were not always patient with each other. Around the same time the Manchus had become a mighty power in China's northeast, and after 1644, when they became rulers of all China, the Manchus also began to meddle in Tibetan affairs. The Manchu emperors of the Qing dynasty (1644–1911) were the last rulers of imperial China and by the end their hold on Tibetan affairs was negligible. As the dynasty came to a close, Tibet should have emerged as an independent nation.

In the nineteenth century, the vulnerability of the Tibetan regions was obvious as Western powers began to surround China, annexing concessions along the east coast and surveying the western borders. But the British invasion of Lhasa in 1904 had a greater affect on China than it did on Tibet, and soon Chinese frontier officials had imperial support and funds to consolidate the Tibetan–Chinese borderlands. Chinese warrior-officials like Zhao Erfeng tried at first to seduce the 'fiercely independent' Tibetan tribes in Amdo and Kham, the eastern regions of Tibet closest to China, using persuasive gifts of titles, stipends, education and infrastructure. But soon it became clear that far more sweeping political changes were in the offing, changes that would undermine every form of local control, and this realisation set off a series of bloody uprisings.

The Khampa warriors had long been suspicious of both the Dalai Lama's court in Lhasa and the Chinese, but over time many of the indigenous leaders (the Tibetan *gyelpo*, or kings) had accepted titles from the Chinese emperors; in return they were expected to guard the interest of the Chinese empire. When the Thirteenth Dalai Lama countered this Chinese expansion by declaring the independence of Tibet in 1913, he immediately sent an army into Kham to wrest the region from *both* Chinese and Khampa control. But the resistance from the Khampas was every bit as ruthless as the Chinese attempts at expansion, and to this day the citizens of Chengdu point nervously to the Khampas who regularly visit the city, knives suspended from their waists.

The Thirteenth Dalai Lama's declaration of independence in 1913 was in part a reaction to the fall of the Chinese empire in 1911. With a new republic and a nationalist government, China was not only reinventing itself politically, it was also redefining itself geographically. In the dying days of the Chinese empire, the Qing dynasty court attempted to revive proposals from regional officials to create a series of new provinces around China's ill-defined western borders. Of five planned new provinces, three were in the north and would later become part of the Inner Mongolia Autonomous Region, and two were in the west – Qinghai, which incorporated most of Tibet's Amdo, and Xikang, formerly a province that annexed the entire eastern half of Kham.

The incorporation of large parts of Amdo and Kham into Chinese provinces in the 1920s was an effective way of subverting the formation of a strong, modern and unified Tibet. The communist victory in China and the Red Army's subsequent march into Tibet through 1949–50 meant that the rest of Tibet increasingly came to resemble a province of China, despite the misleading title of 'Tibet Autonomous Region'.

For me, one of the true ironies of Tibet's unhappy fate in the twentieth century has been that most Chinese I have met see the Tibetans as a threat to themselves and the 'inviolability of the motherland'. In China there is simply no debate about Tibet's status, or none that a foreigner would ever be invited to hear. Even in our class on minority nationality history with Professor Meng this was an issue best politely left alone. There is not even the slightest awareness of Tibetan dissent, but how could there be when any show of Tibetan nationalism is quickly and brutally nipped in the bud, characterised in the state media as the activity of 'criminal elements' or 'splitists'. In China any overt support for the Dalai Lama can attract accusations of 'splittism', the crime of working for the splitting of 'the motherland'. In Chinese newspaper cartoons His Holiness the Fourteenth Dalai Lama is portrayed as an insane, knife-wielding butcher, blood from his 'victims' dripping from his hands.

Because of the 'barbaric Tibetans' mentality prevalent in Chengdu, the 'violent' Tibetans are seen as a threat to the 'peace-loving' Chinese. Barbaric and uncivilised, the Tibetans are said to be ready to cut your throat at any time; they are certainly not considered worth studying. I heard these opinions everywhere: from university students to restaurant owners and government employees to businessmen; none had ever met a Tibetan, but many had stories of a friend or relative being attacked by Tibetans on Chengdu's streets.

Needless to say, Tibetans have a very different perspective on their own history, and that was something I was keen to get closer to. In Chengdu I was introduced to a number of Tibetan scholars associated with the university, but they were all connected to Khampa areas within Sichuan, and I had come to study Amdowas[6] much further away to the north, in Qinghai province. It occurred to me that I had a chance to shift my focus. I was based in Chengdu and most of the people I was meeting were from Tibetan counties close by in the west and in the north. I could have chosen to use these contacts to develop a new direction in research, but what I had learned about Rebkong and its painters from my research in Australia was just too alluring. I had my plan and it seemed best to stay with it. Meanwhile, I needed to begin studying the Tibetan language, but it was no longer available as a subject at the university.

I hadn't studied Tibetan before leaving Australia. It wasn't easy to find a teacher in Australia, and there was no course in spoken Tibetan available in any Australian university (there still isn't). There was also the problem of the different Tibetan dialects (*khey*) in Lhasa, Central Tibet; Kham, Eastern Tibet; and Amdo, Northeastern Tibet. I had decided that if I was going to Amdo, then learning the Lhasa dialect (which had become an unofficial standard, but which was incomprehensible to Amdo Tibetans) was a waste of time.

I was also faced with the difficulty of learning the Tibetan alphabet. Tibetan histories say that their alphabet was brought back from Kashmir by Thonmi Sambhota, a minister in the court of ancient Tibet. 'Sambhota' is Sanskrit and means something like 'good Tibetan', but from my experience of his alphabet I think he must actually have been something of a sadist. One of the biggest hurdles for anyone starting to learn Tibetan is its spelling, which involves something that still makes me quake — 'consonant clusters' — groups of consonants packed or piled together. There is a root letter to which may be added prefix letters, superscribed letters, subscribed letters, suffix letters and even secondary suffix letters. Using the transliteration system developed by Turrell V. Wylie to romanise a Tibetan word (transcribe it into the Roman alphabet familiar to English readers) can have alarming results, such as 'bsgrubs', which is the Tibetan for 'to carry out' (in the past tense). Most of these letters are not pronounced, and in Lhasa this word would be pronounced something like *drup*.

Clearly I had to find someone who could bring all this alive. Another anthropologist at Sichuan University introduced me to Nyima, a broadcaster for the provincial Tibetan-language radio station. Nyima was from Derge in the alpine forests of northwest Sichuan, a town located right against the eastern border of the TAR. I arranged to take language lessons with him.

Nyima was married, but his wife had just had a baby and had gone to their home in Derge. Their home in Chengdu comprised a couple of rooms in a brick apartment block on a leafy avenue, just around the corner from the radio station. With his wife away Nyima was happy to have company, sneaking me in so as not to cause too much curiosity among his neighbours. I brought along a Chinese textbook on Amdo Tibetan that I had managed to pick up in a Chengdu bookstore, and we attempted to work out how this dialect might be pronounced. The grammar of spoken Amdo Tibetan is very different to the written form; in fact, it is much simpler, but the textbook provided no systematic introduction. So we concentrated on memorising several dialogues, and I began to get some idea of the grunts, hisses and rolls of the tongue that the prefixed, superscribed and subscribed letters represented.

Nyima was an interesting man. He was concerned about the Chinese government's portrayal of Tibetans as backward, as well as the way such portrayals were so readily accepted at a popular level, and he felt an urgent call to let China and the outside world know more about the beauty and sophistication of Tibetan culture. This personal mission had been inspired by a *lama* who had come back from Europe with a small documentary team, and Nyima had his own plans to make a film about Tibetan life in Derge. The woodblocks for the Derge Parkhang, Tibet's most renowned printing house, had come from Derge's forests in the heart of the traditional Tibetan province of Kham. And the town was also one of several centres in eastern Tibet involved in the dynamic revitalisation of Buddhist practice and scholarship in the eighteenth, nineteenth and twentieth centuries. Unfortunately, as a result of suspicion about my visits from Nyima's *danwei* (work unit), we had to call our classes off.

Back at the student block, I was reading and smoking on the balcony, whiling away time before the end of the semester and my first trip to Rebkong. Interrupting this lazy schedule were occasional, short excursions through Sichuan that the Foreign Affairs Office of the university would arrange to save the foreign students from dying of boredom. I mostly avoided these on the excuse that I had serious research to do, but occasionally I ended up attending some interesting 'evening entertainments' in Chengdu. One of these was Mozart's *The Marriage of Figaro*, in full costume with fancy wigs, and sung in Chinese!

By some miracle the *Figaro* experience didn't prevent me from attending further cultural experiments, and it turned out that one of these was of some relevance to my own project. I was taken to see an opera rendition of a Tibetan folk story performed by the Sichuan Provincial Song and Dance Theatre Company. The performers were all Han-Chinese who sang in Chinese in the style of 'European' opera. What follows is a loose translation of the program notes, without which, of course, any new opera is largely incomprehensible:

> *In* The Highland-Barley Prince *we see, recreated in opera, the story of Prince Kelsang roaming across the Tibetan plateau in search of ney, highland-barley, so that his kingdom might be saved from famine. On his quest he first falls*

in love with Drolma from the Kingdom of Farmers, whereupon he is guided by a mountain-god into the lair of the Serpent King. There he will find the barley, but the Serpent King turns him into a dog. In the form of a dog he escapes and takes the barley back to Drolma, who then takes the dog and barley back to the kingdom. Then, just before Drolma is wedded to one of his friends, the prince miraculously reappears in human form.

The Highland-Barley Prince was not an artistic triumph, but it provided me with some insights of value into my own research. Sitting in the bus on the way back to the university, I began to question the absence of references to Buddhism in what I had just seen. The 'Tibetan' opera performance, when I put it together with other material I was reading, had led me to notice a trend. Tibetan dramatic performances, which traditionally included rich references to Buddhism, were being rewritten by Chinese cultural workers to ensure that religious themes were either reduced or completely deleted. *The Highland-Barley Prince* extravaganza was a perfect example of how Chinese writers and artists, under the supervision of the Communist Party, had to find or invent examples of Tibetan culture distant from the Buddhist themes that pervaded almost everything that was Tibetan.

My sojourn in Sichuan was bringing in more material than I had expected, but my next find came as a shock. In one of the specialist bookstores along Chengdu's main avenue I picked up a remarkable art book.[7] This slim volume was printed throughout in Chinese and Tibetan, and the title translated as *Tibetan Paintings from Kantze*. Kantze was an important monastic centre in Eastern Tibet, another important part of traditional Tibet that was now part of Sichuan province. A quick flip through the book's full-colour pages revealed assorted attempts to transform Tibetan painting or, as the introduction put it, 'create works of art that reflected contemporary reality'. Various elements of Tibetan culture were rearranged as socialist propaganda. One of the paintings was in the style of a Tibetan carpet out of which walked a happy Khampa herdsman pushing a motorcycle, his wife walking beside him with a new umbrella. Around the border of the 'carpet' were scenes from a street-side market, which surrounded the new family with all the promised trappings of socialism within China: cassette recorders, sewing machines, televisions and mechanised cream separators. In another painting nomad children sat on rich grassland, drinking Tibetan butter-tea, surrounded by daisies and butterflies, and offering a bowl of tea to a fluffy white lamb. Scenes of festivals and dancing were in abundance, with doves of peace pictured flying in and out of all the paintings, just in case someone failed to get the message. But it was heroes from the past — warriors, statesmen, princesses and mythological characters — that filled the largest number of paintings. Buddhism was made invisible, and in its place a new iconology was being born. Large intricate tableaux depicted the sweep of Tibetan history in a universal and heroic 'public mural' style.

The book I had found identified these works as coming from a movement called 'New Tibetan Art', and also explained that they were mostly made by teams of Tibetan and Han-Chinese painters working together in Kantze in the early 1980s. While the 'movement' was based in Kantze, it was also identified as an initiative originating in Beijing, and it was clearly meant to catch on more widely — to set an example. Like the traditional Tibetan operas, Tibetan painting was undergoing a makeover and Buddhist images were being erased from the new, official version of Tibetan culture.

Traditional Tibetan paintings of Buddhist deities or saints are known as *thangkas*, an art form used exclusively for religious subjects. Most traditional *thangkas* use space in a very interesting way, dividing the surface of the painting into zones representing different manifestations of the sacred. The main deity usually occupies the centre, then above the main deity is a buddha representing the highest embodiment of enlightenment, and in the upper section of the painting there might also be ancestral teachers. Flanking the main figure there are typically a pair of attendants or close disciples. Beneath the main figure appear a number of 'lineage protectors', wrathful deities protecting the purity of the Buddha's teachings. Sometimes monks might also be pictured in the lower part of the painting presenting offerings, and occasionally in one corner are found figures representing the sponsor of the painting. However, the new paintings reproduced in *Tibetan Paintings from Kantze* made use of this traditional division of the *thangka* in rather ingenious ways.

In one of the reproductions I found a famous *lama* pictured with a Chinese general. They were the main 'deities' and were depicted seated on the lotus base of a Tibetan statue as if the original deity had been moved away to make room for them. There they were, chatting as friends, monk and military man. In the lower part of the painting, traditionally reserved for the protectors of Buddhism, the general's troops were depicted lined up in parade in front of the *lama*'s monastery. Daubed across the monastery wall was a Chinese slogan that read: 'Han and Tibetans are one family. Head northward to oppose the Japanese.' This depicted an actual event when the Tibetan *lama* Getag *Rinpoche* (an honorific title meaning 'precious one'), who was later assassinated, had indeed played host to the Commander-in-Chief of the Red Army, Zhu De, in 1935. In the upper part of the painting, the part traditionally reserved for the highest expression of Buddhist enlightenment, was New China's most sacred monument: the memorial stele in Tiananmen Square that commemorates the martyrs of the revolution. Similarly, every part of the traditional *thangka* had been adapted exactly to a corresponding symbol from New China's revolutionary mythology. I had to admit it was quite an achievement, but at best this was ersatz art — propaganda — a pastiche of styles from Tibetan art to Russian book illustration, with some of these paintings approaching the fantasy of *Batman* comics.

State-run arts organisations had no compunction in regarding Tibetan literature and art as their own to change as they saw fit. I was beginning to wonder what I would find when I got to Rebkong.

4

One hundred thousand icons

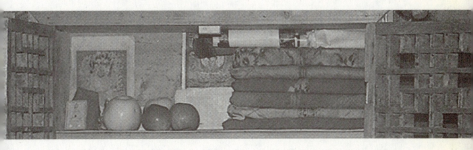

The first semester at Sichuan University ended in mid-winter and I was free to travel. Before heading for Rebkong I felt duty-bound to make a detour and visit old friends at Liaoning University, where I had been a student in the mid-1980s. Taking a series of trains I crossed China from the southwest to the northeast, alighting in Shenyang, the former capital of the Manchu emperors. Occupied by the Japanese in the first decades of the twentieth century, Shenyang is now China's most important city for heavy industry. In January 1990 it was a strange winter wonderland, with ice covering the city and its streets painted black with coal smoke. Shenyang in January is so cold that you can feel your eyelashes stick briefly as you blink.

I spent Chinese New Year with old friends, one of them a teacher still undergoing interrogation over the student protests the previous year. Then I made my way back through Beijing to Xining, traversing China again, this time from the northeast to the northwest. Xining is the capital of Qinghai — one of China's very poorest provinces — and it had much the same colour scheme as Shenyang: black ice. The winter freeze had pared existence back to a bare minimum. Xining's citizens, predominantly Han and Hui,[8] shuffled on the ice, rugged up against the sharp winds that came over the mountains looming above the city to the north. Bunched tight along the banks of the Huangshui River, Xining appeared to be a city that could not make up its mind. Situated in a broad and fertile valley it should have flourished, but perhaps the centuries of defending itself against waves of raiding 'western hordes' were just as much responsible for leaving it huddled and alone.

It was late afternoon and the winter night was already falling when I stepped onto the platform. I headed straight for the Xining Guesthouse: a large, stately three-storeyed hotel surrounded by struggling gardens just south of the centre of town. From outside it looked like a mansion; inside it was standard hotel decor, along with the standard winter 'extra' of musty air — every single window was sealed up against the cold. The heating *was* working, and it was just warm enough to make cold hands burn.

In Chinese hotels it is usually forbidden for foreigners and Chinese to share rooms, so if you opt for dormitory accommodation, especially in out of the way places, there is a good chance you will get a room to yourself. Walking into the ten-bed dorm I found it had a single occupant, a large young Dutchman who was in Xining while he waited for a parcel containing his ice-skates to arrive from home. Travelling alone through China, he had come up with a unique challenge for himself: to head up to the sacred Tibetan lakes of Kyering Tso and Ngoring Tso, the twin lakes at the source of the Yellow River, where he would be the first person to cross them on skates. As we talked into the night I also learned that he was a professional pickpocket, taking advantage of the portability of his profession, you might say, to travel the world. Six months later I ran into him on a quick visit to Hong Kong. Walking up Nathan Road I heard a voice behind me, turned around, and there he was! He offered me his copy of the Lonely Planet guide to Hong Kong: 'I lifted it from Swindon's, take it.' Swindon's was Hong Kong's largest English language bookshop. He hadn't ice-skated on the twin Tibetan lakes, making for Afghanistan instead.

For me Xining wasn't just a stopover: I had a contact I should find. Using up my meagre supply of good karma I had run into a man from Xining in Melbourne, a Chinese 'student' working in factories while he searched for a new and better life for himself and his wife. And he wasn't just 'from Xining'. As a photographer, he had travelled the length and breadth of Qinghai, and it was on his advice that I first picked up the Rebkong trail. He also had a brother, Mr Kang, working at the Qinghai Provincial Museum.

I found the museum in a busy alleyway not far from the Xining railway station; it has since been relocated to new premises, a move bankrolled by a Japanese philanthropist. Originally the private residence of the Hui warlord Ma Bufang (1903–75), the premises of the Qinghai Museum were surrounded by a five-metre high wall. The original glazed-tile entrance to Ma's mansion was still intact, and just below the plaque identifying the museum I could make out the faded characters *Xinlu*, 'Cottage of Spreading Fragrance'. A stunningly poetic, even erotic, flourish from one of the most brutal and volatile figures of modern Chinese history.

The French scientist and explorer André Migot, whose expeditions through Kham and Amdo concluded at Xining in 1947, notes in his memoir *Tibetan Marches* that 'General Ma was the best type of Chinese Moslem, an administrator as well as a soldier.' A strange description for a man who may have equalled Europe's dictators in brutality, but perhaps the Central European 'Fathers of the Sining [Xining] Mission' failed to inform the explorer of certain facts of which they could not have been unaware. Or, alternatively, maybe there was something in Ma's military style that would impress a European colonialist.

The Ma clan produced warlords in the northwest for three generations before the communist victory in 1949, each generation becoming more brutal and imperious than the last, until, in the 1930s and 1940s, Ma Bufang practically ran Qinghai as his own domain. For twenty years Qinghai's political, military and commercial affairs were locked up in the iron grip of this one man — then, the Red Army approaching, he packed up and fled to Taiwan. The slaughter he inflicted on Tibetan tribes was still a living memory for some of the old men and women I would meet in Rebkong.

Stepping inside the museum grounds I found the sprawling arrangement of ageing wooden halls and courtyards not unlike the small palace of a 'frontier emperor'. As I walked from hall to hall searching for Mr Kang I could picture the mansion seventy years earlier, rows of packhorses bringing in the spoils of General Ma's 'taxation drives', an array of officials further inside the courtyard haggling over how to divide it all, and finally, in the inner court, a struggling garden oasis with well-wrapped children playing in the snow.

For the museum staff living at the rear of the complex, the reality in 1990 was a set of small brick buildings, little more than sheds, filling one of the old courtyards. Here Kang, his wife and their little girl had a single room apartment to make their home. Their kitchen was a makeshift shack over the outside of the front door (the only door).

Inside, a curtain separated 'living-room' and 'bedroom'. If only the museum had the budget 'Old Ma' had; but sadly it was so poor, and the original buildings were so run down, that it wasn't even open to the public. Occasionally the provincial government funded research expeditions or special in-house exhibitions, but most of the time the museum workers were employed with cleaning and cataloguing. Kang's wife had just been laid-off on half wages by the automotive spare parts plant where she worked, and she was now labouring over a knitting machine set up in the 'kitchen'. This was a family in limbo; in Xining, Deng Xiaoping's entrepreneurial brand of capitalist-socialism, 'socialism with Chinese characteristics', operated in slow motion.

The slow pace of life in Xining and the virtual shutdown at the museum meant that Kang could spare a few days looking after me. He showed me around the museum, and I met the director. The museum director arranged a jeep, and we all went out to the famed monastery of Ta'er Si.[9] (In Tibetan, 'Kumbum Jampa Ling', which is roughly 'One Hundred Thousand Icons Abode of Maitreya' in English.) Just 26 kilometres south of Xining, Kumbum should have been a relatively easy target during the Cultural Revolution, but it remained intact, reputedly under the protection of the urbane Premier Zhou Enlai (1898–1976). As the jeep made its way up a valley crisp with new snow, Kumbum soared above us, a mix-and-match complex of Tibetan and Chinese-style halls curling up a small creek on the side of a hill. Today the monastery is both a pilgrimage centre for the Tibetans of Amdo and a worldwide tourist attraction.

Kumbum exists because it marks the birthplace of the monk-scholar Je Tsongkhapa (1357–1419), a figure looming large in Tibetan religious history as the founder of the Geluk order. The Geluk became distinguished for their methodical approach to mind training, their strict application of monastic discipline, and an emphasis on compassion. It is said that at the spot where Tsongkhapa was born, blood fell from the umbilical cord onto the ground, causing a sandalwood tree to shoot from the earth. As the tree flourished it was found that icons of the *bodhisattva* Manjushri, the embodiment of wisdom, appeared on its myriad leaves, and this is why the monastery is called Hundred Thousand (*mbum*) Icons (*ku*): in Tibetan *kumbum*.

By the time the miracle occurred the teenage Tsongkhapa had already made the trek to Lhasa in search of enlightenment, and the strange behaviour of the tree moved his mother to miss him all the more. She had a letter prepared telling him of the unusual happenings in their little valley, and also had the scribe write down her wish to see her son once more. When it was finished she plucked a strand of white hair from her head and attached it to the letter. Tsongkhapa, however, was in so much demand as a learned and enlightened teacher that he was never able to return. Instead, he sent his mother a small self-portrait and a small statue of Manjushri, along with a mysterious instruction: 'If you use these to set up a small *chorten* at the spot where the sandalwood tree has grown, it will be just like seeing me in person.' This may also explain the other element in the monastery's name, Maitreya, the Future Buddha whose name means 'loving-kindness' or the tender love a mother feels for her child.

So Tsongkhapa's mother set up the small *chorten*, showering it every day with prayers for her son's happiness and the happiness of all creatures, for in Tibet it is believed that all beings throughout the universe have at one time, in the beginningless time of the past, been one's mother and one's child. Her son went on to accumulate a circle of supporters in Central Tibet who together gave birth to one of the most remarkable systems of monastic education the world has seen, the Geluk, or Way of Virtue. Soon the small *chorten* was encased in a large silver one over 10 metres tall; around that, between 1560 and 1577, the inheritors of Je Tsongkhapa's Geluk tradition built the core of the monastery that still flourishes there today.

As the museum director led us quickly through the array of snow-dusted temples and halls it was clear he had been to Kumbum many times. The Tibetan halls, he pointed out, faced east, while the Chinese halls faced north. We went straight into the courtyard of one of the Tibetan halls, the Medicine College, where the monks seemed suddenly to freeze. The director asked for the abbot, his 'old friend', who was not in. Instead of leading us back out again, the director suggested they should offer us tea and be nice to the 'foreign guest', and one of the monks courteously led us into a sitting room and brought tea flasks and a box of *tsampa*. I was in a very embarrassing position. The director was being, as far as I could tell, really rude towards the Medicine College monks, but he had been nice to me and was insisting on a show of hospitality on my behalf. He helped himself to *tsampa* and insisted we do the same. I sensed it would destroy his display of 'command' if I didn't.

Tsampa, a staple food in Tibetan communities, is an instant snack or meal made from the flour of roasted barley. *Tsampa* is not a food that should be prepared by amateurs. All sorts of embarrassing things can go wrong. As you mix it with a dash of tea the powdered barley can puff up out of the bowl and coat your clothes. Or it can stick to your fingers if the mixture is just a little too moist. Or as you eat, it can powder your nose. And worst of all, if it is too dry, a whiff of flour can go close to choking you to death. We displayed all these shortcomings in the abbot's sitting room as the monks stood in the doorway, glaring. I sensed it was an inconvenience they had witnessed many times before, and which they would likely suffer many times more. In that spotless room of golden glowing timber, crisp paper windows and cotton awnings in pure primary colours, we were an unwanted stain and disruption.

During the visit to Kumbum I began to feel as if I had entered a kind of diplomatic freefall. And indeed I had: my fate was clearly in the hands of my Chinese 'connections' and I had little choice but to go along for the ride. It was a strange kind of gamble where I had no choice, and no idea of what might happen next. In the evening, back in Xining, I went with Mr Kang's family to have dinner with the family of Mr Ren, a middle-school English teacher. He was married to the sister of Mr Kang's wife, and it had been decided that he would come with Kang and I to Rebkong in case I needed a local interpreter.

The next morning I was taken to have an interview with the provincial director of the Bureau of Culture, the government department responsible for the museum. The director's office could only be described as 'spacious', being about five times the size of the room that was Mr Kang's 'home' at the museum. The size of the office indicated his importance. We sat bolt upright on the edges of leather sofa chairs as Kang explained who I was, where I was studying, and what I wanted to do in Rebkong. I took out a list of innocuous research questions, suitably fitted to the historical-materialist model of social history that prevailed in China, where the social sciences where still based on a fundamentalist version of the theories of the founders of communism, Marx and Lenin. I had picked up the basic style from Professor Meng back at Sichuan University, and had set out questions relating to the production, consumption and function of Buddhist art in the painting traditions of Rebkong. It appeared to go down well. He waved his hand and soon a researcher with the Culture Bureau appeared. I took notes as the bureau director made sure I was familiar with all the basic facts of Rebkong art.

In outline, the story went something like this:

The origin of Rebkong art reaches back to the late fourteenth century. Most of the painting families are descended from Han-Chinese who settled and married Tibetans in Rebkong in the early years of the Ming dynasty (1368–1644). Most of the villages that are the home of Rebkong art go by old Chinese as well as Tibetan names. For instance, the 'Wu' in Wutun, one of the 'Five Villages of Rebkong Art',[10] refers to the Lower Yangtze region near Shanghai. Later, with a 'construction boom' in the seventeenth century, and a burgeoning of Tibetan Buddhism associated with the spread of the powerful Geluk order's monasteries, Rebkong art flourished and its reputation spread throughout the Tibetan-speaking world.

Over the centuries, painting and sculpture became an integral part of the curriculum in the monasteries of the 'Five Villages of Rebkong Art'. When they reached the age of fifteen, young artists could choose to remain as monks or return to lay life and set up their own workshops. Both professional and monk-painters travelled extensively, accumulating influences from other regions of Tibet, Central Asia and Nepal, and in particular they became skilled in the meticulous (gongbi) style of Chinese painting.[11] The most refined skills and techniques were transmitted down the family line. Rebkong artists became famed for their skill in painting, sculpture, ornamental design, appliqué and butter sculpture. Today, with the new atmosphere of reform and openness, a new generation of artists is re-establishing the vitality of the tradition under the encouragement of the government's enlightened nationalities policy. The emphasis is on replacing old and neglected icons with new and fresh work that reflects the Tibetan masses' desire to revive their traditions. This made it very easy to purchase old paintings, because the Tibetans do not treasure antiques.

Apart from the very last comment, I had read similar reports on Rebkong art in various publications from Qinghai, available in research libraries at home in Australia. Coming from the director of the Culture Bureau, however, the statement on antiques was both curious and worrying. Was there something in it? Could it be that for Tibetans a *thangka* that is worn and cracked is not as meaningful as one that is fresh and intact? In some heritage projects, in Tibetan areas outside China, certain forms of restoration work — where the antiquity of cracked murals is preserved by work that only fills in the 'gaps' — have been rejected as unsuitable for sacred icons. In such cases the expectation of the local community had been that restoration would restore the icons to their *original* condition, not leave them as a patchwork of antique and restoration. I could not imagine anyone ever giving up a *thangka* lightly. The Tibetan icon is *kuten*, a 'support for the body', or a 'ground' in which a deity is actually invited to reside. As we have seen from the example of the statue Tsongkhapa sent to his mother, and as one American scholar of Tibetan Buddhism recently put it, 'The consecrated image of the deity thus is not a symbol of the deity but, effectively, is the deity, and there are numerous stories in Tibet of images speaking to their devotees.'[12]

I wondered if perhaps the Cultural Bureau director's comment was aimed at testing me, making sure I hadn't come to smuggle away Qinghai's art treasures? Or was he trying to lessen the tragedy of wanton destruction that had left Tibet's holy places in ruins? Maybe I would find clues to help resolve these problems once I got to Rebkong. The director prepared a letter of introduction for us to present to the local officials there.

Red tape completed, we moved my things from the hotel to the museum, where I would stay the night so we could get the early bus to Rebkong. Then we went to the bus station to get our tickets to Huangnan. Why, if I was going to Rebkong, would I want a ticket to Huangnan? The traditional Tibetan region of Rebkong has been given a new Chinese name — actually several new Chinese names! In the 1950s minority areas were given a new system of administrative districts, which were, from smallest to largest: township, (autonomous) county, autonomous prefecture and autonomous region. Huangnan ('South [*nan*] of the Yellow [*huang*] River') is a large Tibetan Autonomous Prefecture that has its government seat in the county of Tongren. Tongren county is roughly equivalent to the territory of the Twelve Tribes of Rebkong. The upshot was that at different times the 'former' Tibetan territory of Rebkong could be referred to as Huangnan or Tongren, but rarely did it ever appear in public usage as Rebkong (Regong in Chinese), except in relation to Rebkong art. For official use Chinese names replaced old Tibetan ones. On the timetable displayed on the bus station wall it was 'Huangnan', and that was the ticket we wanted. By the time I worked this out we were at the ticket window itself.

There was then a problem at the ticket window. Apparently foreigners could not travel on the Huangnan route because of the risk of accidents and the absence of adequate insurance. Something was said about a recent incident, the death of a foreigner that cost the bus company and the province a large sum in American dollars. I had heard about places where foreign travellers had to pay extra insurance, 100 *yuan* or so — could we buy insurance? No provision for extra insurance had been made. We tried a change of tack — I wasn't a tourist, I was an advanced student at Sichuan University with research responsibilities. Our persistence got us into the manager's office, where, pleading our special case, we assembled our various letters of introduction on his table. Under the weight of our paperwork he relented. We walked away with the three tickets we needed.

Now all I had to do was survive the *baijiu* and finger guessing games Kang and Ren had planned after a dinner of juicy pork-filled dumplings. By one in the morning I was blissfully unconscious.

5
The narrow path

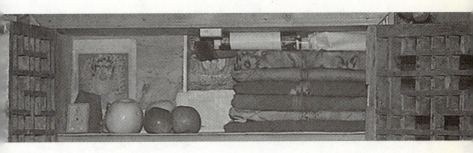

*I*t was still dark as we stepped out a small hatch door in the museum gate and headed down the lane towards Xining's bus depot. The pre-dawn sky was clear and just beginning to pale. My beard quickly turned brittle in the icy air and my eyes began to water. Heavily dressed hawkers had already set up shop, and we picked up some pears and apples to take on the bus. There was still about half an hour before the 7:30 am coach to Tongren was due to leave, and this left us time for a quick breakfast from one of the stalls near the station.

My favourite breakfast in China was hot, sweetened soybean milk served with golden, freshly fried dough sticks (*youtiao*), but this morning I had a bad attack of the butterflies and felt a pressing nausea feeding through my veins. Someone once told me *baijiu* did not cause hangovers, but they were very, very wrong. Or were they? Kang and Ren sat there happily downing their bowls of steaming mutton soup; there were no signs they were any worse for wear after our binge the night before. I kept turning to check the time on my watch; we needed to hurry, but the thought of what I was doing had made me dizzy. My head was spinning and suddenly I needed a toilet. Putting down my chopsticks I suggested we head for the station.

It was either a panic ritual or a panic attack. This was it: a bus was about to take me to my proving ground, and I was either going to make it as an anthropologist or not. Everything had to be right, and that included things I couldn't control, like passing water. My will was shaky, and it began to show as panic messages raced through my body. A circle of doubt spun around my nervous system, confusing my bladder, and the more I thought about it the longer it seemed to take. I began to get annoyed with myself.

When I came back Kang and Ren were waiting at the 'boarding gate'. The other passengers were already on board. The engine was warming up, failing, and warming up again. A *keche*, literally 'passenger vehicle', sounded promisingly like a 'coach', but was in fact more like a school bus. We checked our tickets with the boy at the bus door. 'What do we do with the luggage?' I shouted. The boy stuck his hand out the door and motioned upwards.

It had been years since I had taken a long-distance bus in China. Of course the luggage was all piled up on the roof. With a full pack on my back I grabbed the ladder that hung from the back of the luggage rack. My woollen driver's gloves slipped on the steel bars and I had to take them off. My hands burned as the icy metal bars stuck momentarily in my grasp. Once I was up on top of the bus I remembered to take out my day-pack, which had my camera in it. The luggage rack was a mess of netting and rope. There were spare tyres, toolboxes, candy-striped bags, canvas bags, packing cases and a jack. None of it was secured beyond being thrown under the rope net. 'They must know what they're doing,' I said to myself, and slid the pack under the net. Just in case, I looped one of the pack's straps through the netting and clipped it.

Kang and Ren managed to make sure the seat numbers on our tickets were honoured on what was a quickly over-filling bus. We were in the middle, the warmest seats, and also the most immune to the shudders of dirt-road travel. Kang and Ren sat together on the left-hand side of the bus. I joined a very unhappy looking Tibetan woman on the right-hand side of the bus near the door. Her family were just outside the bus window. My Tibetan was still at a beginner's stage, but from the pitch of their voices I knew they were saying farewell, offering some quick instructions and trying to reassure her. As the bus started to move I got my first lesson in the Amdo dialect as they beckoned *demo kyi*, 'Go safely!'

Barely before we were on our way we came to a stop. The alley outside the depot was blocked with buses trying to get in and buses trying to get out. The sprawling stalls along the sides of the alley didn't help either, using as much of the pavement as they could get away with, awnings sheltering their customers as they ate at tables on the edge of the lane. Bus drivers shouted at each other, and store holders joined in.

Thirty-five minutes sitting in a freezing bus and we hadn't even left town yet. The sheepskin cloak enclosing the woman I was sitting next to doubled her size and left me with a quarter of the seat at most. At first I thought sitting right up against her might make her move in a little. She didn't budge. Was she being deliberately unco-operative, or even rude? Or didn't I know the rules?

My thoughts went back to an encounter with Amdo Tibetans in Chengdu the previous October. The provincial authorities had 'invited' foreign students at Sichuan University to attend the city's celebration of National Day, the pre-eminent celebration of the Communist Party's victory in 1949. In 1989 the event took on a much greater significance than usual: it was the fortieth anniversary of the founding of the People's Republic of China. And besides marking four decades of the Communist Party's leadership, it was crucial, after the massacre in Beijing earlier in the year, that the celebrations should have all the usual signs of the CCP's firm hold on national life. The presence of 'foreign guests' was an important part of the administration's effort to create an atmosphere of normality. Many students refused, but given the difficulties I had been through before leaving Australia I knew, cynically, that I would be doing myself a big favour if I made the Foreign Affairs Office at the university happy. So a dozen of us, including four or five semi-retired teachers from Japan, were bussed to the centre of the city where we joined other official parties on a platform alongside the central podium, and where we would be recorded for state television admiring a long parade of school children and assorted military units.

It was a rare sunny day in Chengdu, and a soft breeze made us feel a lot more cheerful than we perhaps wanted to be. Flags were flapping and balloons were bobbing, then just as the parade was starting there was a small commotion on the benches behind us. A dozen Tibetans were arriving, their coats filling the air with the odour of sheep. My nostrils twitched with a distinct and familiar Australian memory of sitting in a car while passing road trains crammed full of sheep on outback roads. The Tibetans moved to their place on the same bench as our party, sitting right alongside the group of Japanese teachers, who already had their hands over their noses. Five seconds later the Japanese teachers stood up in unison, looked for a spare spot, and moved away. The odour was too strong and too strange. The Tibetans were puzzled by the reaction they caused among the Japanese. I slid along the bench towards them, across what now seemed like a gaping hole. A German and a French student followed. The Tibetans were from Ngawa, a Tibetan region in northern Sichuan province. They had travelled two days to represent their autonomous prefecture at the National Day parade. Perhaps, like the 'foreign guests', they were part of the symbolic array, as we took our places as altar pieces dedicated to China's prosperity, unity and international credibility.

When Ren leaned across the aisle of the bus to give my bulky Tibetan 'travel companion' a push I stopped him. I was happy with my memory of that balmy, late autumn day in Chengdu, and I was suddenly happy that our bus was on its way. Nor did it really matter if I had to sit on the corner of the seat; and I had noticed, when she finally turned to look at me, that the Tibetan woman's face was quickly losing colour. It was in my own interests that she be allowed as much comfort as possible.

From Xining we first headed east to Ping'an, a county township, where we took on more passengers. I noticed that the Tibetan woman next to me had a large jar hidden away in her coat, and from time to time had been spitting into it. Before long, as the amount of liquid in the jar increased, its contents had turned bright green, not unlike the thick coolant liquid that fills car radiators. With the contents of her jar turning greener and greener the colour of her face turned increasingly ashen. When the bus pulled up at Ping'an she slid the window open and turned out the jar, 'painting' the side of the bus and almost tipping it over a boarding passenger (at one later stop I think she did manage to baptise someone's coat sleeve). From Ping'an we turned south, and following a broad valley we began to leave behind the flood plain of the Huangshui River. The bus started to slow as the neck of the valley narrowed and we climbed through hills dotted with farmhouses. In the villages we passed there was usually a simple mosque, which in this part of the country was a small Chinese temple topped with a crescent. Set in compounds behind pisé walls (made of earth or clay and sometimes mixed with straw) the mosques were just visible from the vantage point of a bus window.

As the woman beside me kept spitting into her jar I remembered the bus trip I had taken with my mother in 1985. I think Mum had let out a loud groan when she had taken her first look inside the Golmud–Lhasa bus. It was, as I had expected, nothing more than a school bus with bench seats and backrests that were bolt upright. There was no heating and the window next to our seat would not close properly. We were travelling at the height of summer, but we were also crossing the hump of the world's highest plateau. I think what finally did Mum in, however, was travelling without rest for thirty-six hours. Sitting for such a long journey on a relentlessly hard seat, ramrod straight, was, for someone not used to it and nearing fifty, simply a torture worse than death. Add to this the diesel fumes and cold air coming through the window and the combination of fatigue, discomfort and nausea from the high altitude, and you have a recipe for disaster. By the first afternoon Mum had had enough and she nudged me to let me know something was up, or more accurately 'coming up', and in a flash I scrambled for a big enamel mug I carried on my travels. These mugs were ubiquitous throughout China for most of the twentieth century, and a convenient way to make a cup of green tea. My other new habit of carrying a moist handtowel now also came in handy. As the bus climbed higher Mum became convinced she was done for, and our customary roles were reversed as I nursed and tended to her for the rest of the trip. It took two days resting in Lhasa, revived on a diet of fried rice and a constant supply of orange soft drink, before she was able to venture out and explore the holy city. Back on the bus to Rebkong my heart went out to the woman suffering next to me as she leant her head on the window — I had a good idea of what she was going through.

I put in my Walkman earplugs and played the latest Patti Smith album, *Dream of Life*. As the part-biblical, part-political anthem 'People Have the Power' kicked in, as we moved through bare fields and naked poplar groves, song and sight gradually came together. Patti sang of the meek of the earth rising up from their shining valleys of pure air, and suddenly I knew she was singing about just the kind of place I was moving through. Now, every time I see images of Central Asia's hotspots, from Afghanistan to northern Iraq, the cold highlands always remind me of northern Tibet — a vast tract of alpine wilderness running through Asia and shared by a multitude of ethnic and religious cultures.

Seeing this kind of country for the first time, I shouldn't have been surprised by the lack of colour. In winter it was a palate of pale yellow and grey, for we were still travelling on the loess plateau of northern China. From the bus I could see that the earth was soft and loose. Walls surrounded each household, stamped from the same soil on which they stood. Houses, too, were a combination of stamped earth and timber from nearby forests. Gone were the straight lines of the city. Here families built side-by-side, huddled close but still making the best of the warming sun. Each small settlement seemed to be alone, self-contained, and the only precise or regular feature was the road our bus was taking. Yet the road hardly seemed relevant — men, women and children all ignored the traffic. Whether it was children playing or a tractor carting hay, it was the impatient buses and jeeps that had to stop or swerve to avoid an accident, a collision between two worlds. In late autumn or early winter the entry to each hamlet was covered in low piles of sun-dried sheaves of wheat; passing vehicles contributed to the work of threshing as they first slowed and then rushed over each golden mound.

The villages along the road might have been home to an assortment of China's Muslim minorities, but in the mountains less than 30 kilometres west was Shadzong Hermitage, near the village of Sanhe (Taktser in Tibetan). The small Tibetan village of Sanhe was where the search party discovered the boy who would be enthroned as the Fourteenth Dalai Lama. It was his birthplace. And it was near Sanhe, at the retreat centre of Shadzong Hermitage, that His Holiness was first given his tonsure after the search party from Lhasa confirmed his identity in 1938. These are scenes now familiar to many viewers of Martin Scorsese's 1997 epic retelling of the Dalai Lama's story, *Kundun*. The film speaks of the Dalai Lama symbolically taking birth on the very edge of Tibet, as a sign that the full extent of Tibetan territory would not be forgotten. What the movie could not depict was that the territory between the Huangshui River and the Yellow River to the south, where the Dalai Lama was born, was once populated by large numbers of Tibetans, or how Chinese armies and settlers had been displacing them southward since the eighteenth century. Gradually Han-Chinese, Hui and other Muslim ethnic groups came to dominate the agricultural land south of Ping'an.

The Hui are the third most populous of China's fifty-six officially recognised minority nationalities, and are certainly the most widespread, living in 2,308 of China's 2,372 counties and cities.[13] Sharing a distant heritage of foreign origin but without their own language, they are a diverse group because of the way they are closely assimilated with the local cultures within which they live, maintaining their identity as Muslims but speaking the local language (usually together with the local variant of Mandarin, but not always). Numbering over half a million, Qinghai province has the second highest concentration of Hui per population among all of China's twenty-three provinces and five autonomous regions.[14]

As we continued south there were clear signs of a stronger presence of mixed Hui and Tibetan communities. Open hill country gave way to the steep valleys of the Tsongkha Range, a series of mountains that jut between the Huangshui and Yellow Rivers. The road zigzagged its way up the mountainsides, thick grass-stubble still slightly green under a light cover of snow. Turning another bend a *lhatse*, or cairn, came into view, marking at once a tribal boundary as well as the spot where our long ascent became descent. The driver switched off the engine and let the bus coast for the next few kilometres. A plaque in Chinese fixed to the cairn read 'Blue Mountain Pass, 3,650m', and as I peered through the iced-up window at the jagged peaks that closed in around us I began to be thankful I had chosen somewhere on the 'low' end of Qinghai for my field site.

The stone *lhatse*, its rainbow of flags and streamers flapping in the wind, marked a cultural as well as physical watershed. Behind us the streams flowed north to the Huangshui — ahead to the south they ran more sharply down into the Yellow River. From its headwater north of Lake Qinghai (Tso Ngönbo in Tibetan) until it enters the Yellow River, the Huangshui irrigates the richest arable territory in Qinghai. In Tibetan it is known as the Tsongchu, or Onion River. The region around it is known as Tsongkha, 'the part (*kha*) around the Tsong'; it was because he hailed from this region that Je Tsongkhapa was known by that name during his studies in Lhasa.

The Yellow River carves a deep cliff through the loamy layers of its own ancient flood plain. And our bus would cross it approximately 90 kilometres south of Xining, at the northern boundary of the Rebkong tribes. The mountains of Rebkong are an extension of the Jishi Shan Range; these and other mountains force the Yellow River west, back on itself, before it finds a way north through some of the most jagged ranges in the whole of Amdo. The awesome landscape through which the Upper Yellow River flows has worried and preyed upon the imagination of Chinese mythmakers from time immemorial. Jishi Shan, or Mount Pilerock is, in Chinese mythology, the creation of the demigod Yu, left in a mess after he had taken it upon himself to quell the world flood.[15] The twisting waters of the Yellow River are the 'trickle' that remains. The mythical western paradise of the Kunlun Ranges, or Mount Offspringline, a plateau that in Chinese myth allowed deities to travel between heaven and earth, is located just west of the source of the upper Yellow River, high in what is now called, unpoetically, the Qinghai–Tibet Plateau.

Out of sight, hidden behind a massif southwest of the bus route, was Chakyung Monastery ('Garuda Monastery'). Like its namesake, the roc-like *garuda* of Indian myth, airborne symbol of the freedom of awakening, it is perched on a mountain ridge towering above the Yellow River. Chakyung Monastery was founded in 1349 by Döndrub Rinchen (1309–85), who is remembered in Tibetan history as the first preceptor of Je Tsongkhapa. Döndrub Rinchen came from the heart of Rebkong; he was born at the foot of its mountain power centre, Amnye Chakyung.

About 60 kilometres to the east of our road, even closer to the Chinese heartland, there was another monastery that has a central place in the history of Tibetan Buddhism. Dentig is perched among cliffs in the Lesser Jishi Mountains and is linked to Buddhism's survival in Tibet. Dentig is said to have appeared through the magical activity of the eighth-century charismatic master of *tantra*, Padmasambhava. The 'Lotus Born Guru', as he is also known, was invited to Tibet during the time of King Tri Songdetsun (reigned c.756–97), in order to deal with local deities and spirits obstructing the royal patronage of Buddhism.

To some extent Padmasambhava succeeded, allowing the construction of Tibet's first Buddhist monastery, Samye, to proceed. Yet, according to the Tibetan histories, about a century later the conflict between supporters of the foreign tradition of Buddhism and the local spirit cult of Bön continued. An anti-Buddhist king gained the upper hand, only to be assassinated by a monk. The chaos that followed brought the Tibetan empire to a close. Three monks — the 'Three Learned Men of Tibet' — fled north and met up at Dentig. It was from this vantage point that the religious 'refugees' began to attract new converts among the Tibetan villagers in the surrounding Amdo countryside. Dentig became know as a 'second holy land', or 'second India', honouring its role in the preservation of the lineage of monastic discipline (*Vinaya*) in Tibet. The edge of Amdo was a long way from Lhasa, but we were passing through country that has produced some of the most important men in the Tibetan Buddhist tradition — including the present Dalai Lama, whom the whole world has come to honour as a great scholar and a tireless worker for peace.

As the bus descended from Blue Mountain Pass the country changed back into the round, bare slopes of the loess plateau. Soon the land opened into a broad, tree-covered flood plain that filled the valley as flat as a table. Across the other side was the Hui town of Qunke. The river cut itself deep into the flat and we negotiated a 10-metre drop, forded the stony riverbed and climbed up the opposite side of the cutting. When we stopped for lunch at the town centre, everyone rushed to find somewhere to relieve themselves and then rushed to place their orders; it was strictly a thirty-minute stop.

The strong Hui identity of the town was visible from the line of *qingzhen* ('pure and true', or halal) eating establishments, and also in the green and black veils hung out for sale in front of the sundry goods shops, hardware stores, wholesalers and kiosks that spread down the street. The kiosks offered neat stacks of *nang*, or *mo*, the flat bread of Muslim North China. Only the buildings on each corner of the crossroads were standard socialist cement-covered brick. Down the street it was all jerry-built — brick and muddy mortar — before melding into household walls that were the same stamped earth found throughout eastern Qinghai.

Mr Kang from the museum recommended I order *ganban*,

pointing to a plate on another table that looked surprisingly like spaghetti bolognaise. *Ganban* means 'dry tossed', one of the few fast-food alternatives to soup in these parts. Other fare on the menu included mutton soup — *zacui* (the original chop suey, a soup made with sheep offal and cabbage), *fentang* (a clear mutton soup with thick, glassy bean-starch noodles), *mianpian* (mutton soup cooked with squares of pasta) — and *shouzhuarou* (boiled mutton on the bone, eaten with the hands).

Facing another couple of hours in the bus, I wasn't sure if I wanted to fill up on soup, even if I could soak it up with a couple of *mo*. And feeling worse for wear anyway, I chose the comfort option of the spaghetti look-alike. Little did I know that these hearty home-made noodles, covered in diced mutton and celery, spiced with coriander and pepper, would become a tried and trusted raiser of my flagging spirits over the next two years. Always coming in huge serves, a plate of *ganban* was magic for the homesick soul. It wasn't Italian, but it was heart-warming all the same. I added some oil-marinated chilli flakes, a dash of vinegar and tucked in.

Outside, the weather was turning gloomy. The clouds had come in low and it was snowing. Everyone stamped their feet and patted their shoulders as we waited to get back on the bus. I was beginning to feel grateful that it was so crowded; all those rugged-up bodies kept the air inside the bus warm. The floor of the bus was freezing, and my hands and feet stung. The left-hand side of the bus came with 'heating', a metal pipe connected to the engine and passing under passengers' seats. My seat was on the right-hand side, which had to go without a heating pipe because of the door.

By now I had completely given up my struggle with the poor woman and her jar of bile, and perhaps the buddhas

Looking south from Sakyi Village towards Rongwo Monastery.

▲ Detail from 'The Buddha's passing into Nirvana' *thangka* painted by Shawo Tshering.
▼ A new *thangka* of Tsongkhapa, outdoors in the debating ground, Rongwo Monastery.

▲ Winter sunrise, Rongwo Monastery, Rebkong Valley.
▼ Nyingma temple at the village of Gyelwo Gang.
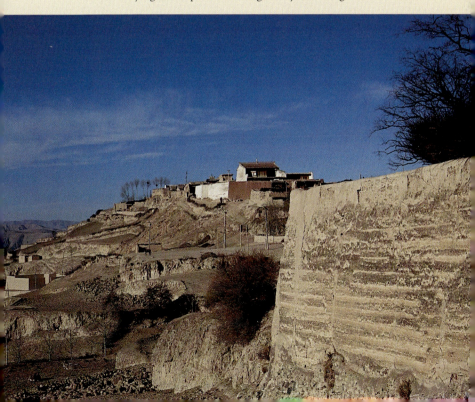

were smiling on my compassion, because I was beginning to find that sitting on the corner of the seat was quite comfortable — my back naturally straight and relaxed, not unlike sitting on a meditation cushion. Everyone in fact seemed pretty comfortable, and not a few were dropping off to sleep. Perhaps the heating contraption was sedating us with poisonous exhaust fumes? The warm air of our combined breaths turned to frost as it hit the windows, and soon it felt like we were enclosed in a crystal ball.

As the road reached the Yellow River we turned east, heading downstream and cutting a path perched halfway up the river wall. The frozen river was 20 metres below and it seemed not so much to flow as ooze, pale silver filled with white swirls of ice gliding in the centre of the stream. This part of the river changed each time I passed. In another month or two it would be a churning brown mass as the melting snow tore down mountain gullies and washed away the icy slush. Then the water level would slowly recede and long grass would take root along the banks. By the middle of summer each bend would reveal a pile of washed, round river-stones — stones gathered to reinforce the walls of the monasteries of Amdo, or to pave the *chöra* (monastery debating grounds). Lately there had also been a craze for 'Yellow River Strange Rocks' (*Huanghe qishi*), which poetically-inclined Xining gentlemen would collect and show, giving them names like 'Goddess of Mercy', 'River Goddess' and 'Mother and Child'.

Across the river the southern bank alternated between stony sandbars and sheer red-loess towers. Beyond, on ridge tops and in gorges and narrow valleys, were the Tibetan hamlets of the Nangra tribes, whose leaders put up some of the fiercest resistance against the People's Liberation

Army in 1949. For several years Nangra's warriors terrorised Chinese army outposts until the most recalcitrant of all, the *pönpo* (village head) Wangchen, finally surrendered in 1952. Their struggles have been neatly and efficiently erased from history by the Chinese government's use of the phrase 'Peaceful Liberation of Tibet'.

Occasionally, through the frosty bus window, I could see signs of the thick forests where the bands led by Wangchen had their hideouts. But in truth, I was more worried about the progress of our bus. The road was rudimentary at best, and we constantly had to skirt close to the cliff edge as we inched past rock falls. Or worse, we had to lurch down and up huge dips where the road was eroded by gullies. Each time I peered down at the icy river it seemed to run that little bit swifter.

Our next drop-off point was at Chendza Bridge, which crosses the Yellow River into the northern-most county of the Huangnan Tibetan Autonomous Prefecture. The discomfort of vehicular travel had finally come to an end for the Tibetan woman next to me. She and her jar made it to their destination without serious mishap. I moved in beside the window and a young man, who had so far been standing without a seat, moved to take up the spot next to me.

South of the Yellow River the proportion of the population that are Tibetan jumps from less than 10 per cent to more than 60 per cent. Across the bridge the township of Maketang, the seat of the county government of Chendza county (Jianza, or Jainza, on Chinese maps), looked frozen and deserted. Behind the town lay the long river flat that brought prosperity to the Tibetans of this county. It also brought water to the Yellow River via alpine streams. The falling snow was beginning to cover the dark brown earth of the bare fields. Lines of stunted poplars marked boundaries between terraced fields, and here and there walnut trees stood in the fields like gnarled hands reaching out from within the cold ground. In spring the ripening grain would change this spot into an emerald plain. As well as good harvests of wheat, Chendza county is a major fruit-growing district, producing apples, pears and apricots for the local markets. In the middle of winter the fields are hard and unworkable, and well-to-do farmers busy themselves with repairs and religious activities. The not so well-to-do hit the road to seek work elsewhere.

Just before arriving at the Chendza bridge it is possible to catch site of the monastery of Lo Dorje Drak, 'Vajra Rock of Lo'. Here, after assassinating the anti-Buddhist king Lang Darma in 842, the monk Lhalung Palkyi Dorje joined up with the 'Three Learned Men', taking up residence in nearby caves. Deeper into the mountains to the west of Dorje Drak, in the shade of Khamra Forest, is Achung Namdzong, a 'citadel' where bands of Buddhist exiles gathered during the persecution of Buddhists in Central Tibet. It remains a centre for the ancient Nyingma order of Tibetan Buddhism, and belongs to a group of monasteries known as the 'four citadels of Amdo', a set of isolated retreats favoured by yogins from all the Tibetan Buddhist traditions.

This countryside was truly a 'second holy land', as has so often been pointed out in Tibetan history and folklore. The devoted communities throughout the hills and mountain ranges of Amdo have created a *mandala* (a sacred circle) array of sacred and blessed places. In some ways my destination —

Rebkong — is the centre of the Amdo *mandala*, surrounded as it is by a 'pinwheel' of mountain ridges and river valleys that radiate within the arc of the Yellow River. Rebkong is a *gakhyil*, a 'whorl of delight', with famous monasteries and wild peaks surrounding it on all sides.

The bus crawled for half an hour from Chendza along the steep channel of the Yellow River, and we approached what looked like an impenetrable wall of shale and sandstone. Gradually the stone cliff face parted as the road found the entrance to the Guchu Gorge.

It is said that paradise is reached through narrow passes or through the eye of a needle. The Guchu, for reasons that remain its own, had prepared a blizzard to welcome us. Snow whipped around the bus, the temperature dropped and ice thickened on all the windows. The bus was a bubble of crystal, a space capsule, a little world of its own. The sides of the ravine were barely visible as we were carried along its passage by the grace of our collective merit. Looking on the bright side I wondered if the snow was not a convenient means for me to ignore the ugly precipices that hung above and below the road. The driver guided the steering wheel, juggling a cigarette between mouth and right hand, using his left hand to wipe the ice off the inside of the windscreen. I knew things were not going well when I noticed that the Tibetans in the bus were, almost to a man, busy telling their prayer beads and muttering mantras under their collective breaths. Except for the occasional hum of prayers that rose above the whine of the bus, we had all turned silent, each attending to our personal fears.

What I could see from the frosty window was at once fascinating and terrifying and my mood changed. Tibet has inspired multifarious responses from those hoping to discover its secrets, and the images we have painted in the West lurch between the realms of pure spirit and the gutters of superstition. Perhaps this love–hate relationship is not out of touch with Tibetan slants on psychology. Such theories would suggest that the mind never makes contact with what is real; instead it grasps towards an externally projected promise that slides away like a mirage. Not finding truth in our own projections we externalise our resentment. And so our involvement in our own apparitions repeats a cycle of grasping outwards and pushing away. Even when we get hold of exactly what we have wanted it still tends to turn into disappointment. We are very confused about our frustration and frustrated with our confusion. And in the West, having spun a story about progress, we are more confused than anyone else. That's my theory. Suspended in the ravine, perhaps driven by my own reserves of guilt, I could almost hear myself reciting all the different reasons I might deserve a grisly death on the rocks at the bottom. Death, or the spectre of death, conjured up both fear and expectation, the awesome and the fantastic.

Surrounded by towers of rock and ice, our bus crawled from one bend in the river to another. At one point we passed beneath a concrete aqueduct that spanned the ravine to feed a small power station. Completely encased by frozen water, long fangs of ice hung from the aqueduct above the Guchu Gorge. The bus slowed to a stop. We waited as another bus eased over and around a rock slide, and then we took our turn. Further on the bus stopped again. Part of the road had collapsed into the gorge. A pair of steel girders had been set in place to straddle the gap. The driver got down to have a look, made sure there was no ice on the girders, and got back in. I closed my eyes. The tyres of the bus eased into the girders' sleeves. It was only a small gap to cross, less than a metre, but one slip and we might topple sideways.

Another theory courted by those who aim to demystify Tibet is to explain their religious commitment as a result of the extremes of their environment; or as some Chinese analysts do, blame Tibetan superstition on the extremes that surround them in their homeland. If we think about this theory, however, it becomes clear that it is not a reflection of Tibetan fear. It has more to do with a projection of the visitor's own fears, which are then further dressed up in the garb of a weary anthropological theory — functionalism — that says cultures only have religions because they sustain or protect both the social and individual 'organism'. Why would Tibetans be afraid of mountains that have surrounded them like a cradle since birth? Yes, Tibetans have to be alert to dangers in the environment; yet like everywhere else it is carefulness that is the best protection, not panic and blind faith. Nevertheless, our journey in the bus kept reminding me of a teaching repeated by Tibetan *lamas*, 'Death is certain, the time of death is uncertain.' I was also reminded of a line from Samuel Beckett's absurdist play *Waiting for Godot*, 'What do you do when you fall far from help?'

After an hour my fears subsided and the sides of the gorge smoothed out, separating into a broad valley. Snowy lines picked out broad terraces on the hillsides, as well as mapping the spread of fields across the valley floor. Smiles returned to the faces of my fellow passengers, and the bus picked up speed. Approaching the village of Bao'an there were twelve cairns lined up along the mountain ridge: we were now entering the territory of the Twelve Tribes of Rebkong; we were nearly there.

6
First days in Rebkong

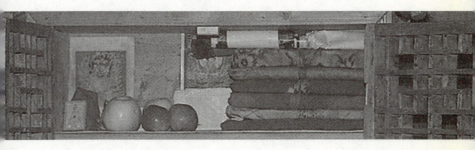

Our bus debouched from the Guchu Gorge and the valley opened up. Everyone brushed the ice from the inside of their window to look out on Sermojong, the 'Golden Valley' of Rebkong. Some looked out at the comforting sight of home; I was simply glad to see the dark walls of the gorge part and slide behind us. The blizzard had also eased. The Guchu river flat grew broader and broader, snow picking out the fields in bare outlines. Gentle treeless slopes rose on either side of the valley and were a dapple of white ice and grey earth; here and there terraced fields jutted through the snow.

Not long after leaving the gorge we stopped to let passengers down at a village on top of a rise. The air outside was well below zero and Mr Kang pointed to the hills rising behind the town. Stone and bronze implements uncovered by archaeologists had confirmed that this part of the valley had probably been settled by humans for around six millennia. It had also been constantly rebuilt as a Chinese military outpost for much of China's history, to prevent passage northward through the gorge and to protect the agricultural lands along the Yellow River from 'barbarian tribes'. More recently, perhaps only for the last four hundred years, this ancient village of Bao'an was also the home of one of

China's smallest national minorities, the Bonan, whose total population in China numbered just over 12,000 in 1990. They descended from an ancient Mongolian tribe that converted to Islam; only 170 or so still live in the town that gave them their name, the rest having shifted eastward over the centuries to join the Muslim settlements of southern Gansu province. With two small monasteries nearby, a small mosque and a few Chinese shopkeepers and their families, little remains of Bonan culture or language. Nothing remains of the early fortresses except for a few segments of crumbling wall.

From Bao'an onwards, the valley takes on an entirely Tibetan character, at least on the surface. Glowing white *chortens* can be seen on both sides of the Guchu River — white-domed monuments marking the influence of the Buddha's teaching in the community. Here the tightly packed villages nestled alongside their monasteries, as if huddling against the winter cold. In fact, most of these villages at the northern end of the Golden Valley are not as Tibetan as they appear. Kang explained that while the architecture of their homes and monasteries, as well as their religious culture, are all inherited from the Tibetans of Amdo, these villages belong to Monguor farmers and Chinese families who have been assimilating with Tibetans in the valley for over six hundred years; this is another reminder that Tibetan communities on the edge of Amdo shared ongoing contact with Mongolians, Muslims and Han-Chinese. In the 'Golden Valley', Tibetans were dominant and the other groups had, at least in the villages, gradually blended in.

On safe ground, the bus sped on. Soon we were crossing a bridge over the Guchu and making our way up its high bank into Tongren county, the bus putting its passengers down at a roundabout in front of the New China Bookshop and the Agricultural Bank. If Tongren actually had a town centre, this was it. Looking out on the street I saw a scaled-down model of Xining: grey, bare, barren and unkempt boxes of brick; a dust-covered road with smoking piles of rubbish; and failing attempts to line the cement landscape with trees. Down the road that led south out of town there were monastery buildings spread up the mountainside, organic, melting into the slope. It was every man for himself as the luggage was unloaded, and we made our way up the street to the hotel.

The driver had pointed us towards the biggest unkempt box of brick at the other end of the street. After a long bus trip, and with a fully loaded backpack, a mere walk of 500 metres was a killer trek. The altitude at Tongren is 2,500 metres — the air thin enough, I found, to dry my mouth out when I made even the slightest effort. A large red sign in a column of four Chinese characters stood over the Huangnan Hotel entrance.

Guests were not trusted with keys, and instead had to go up and find the floor attendant. By the time we found her and got into our room it was getting close to five in the afternoon. The sun was already disappearing behind the western rim of the valley and it would soon be dark. My guides were convinced that the first thing we had to do was report to the Public Security Bureau. We found the offices just around the corner but they had closed for the day. The gatekeeper told us to come around again in the morning. For some reason, the usual reasons, Kang and Ren did not want me to do anything until we had checked in with the PSB, a measure that was as much to protect themselves from suspicion as anything else, and so I just had to be patient. All I could do was look around town; I definitely shouldn't go to the monastery, not until I had seen the PSB.

So we kicked around for an hour in the black, slush-coated streets. There were a couple of the standard banks; a post and communications office; a Workers Cultural Palace with a cinema; several department stores; two hardware outlets; the taxation agency; an electrical goods store with repair shop; and a small door into a 'planned-birth' clinic. Close to the main intersection there was a corral for mules and horses. As we walked the monastery came into view, tantalisingly less than a kilometre just up the road.

We went looking for a place where we might get some food and restore our travel-weary bodies. Through a grimy curtain over a door we found an even grimier dive. A Han-Chinese man we had met on our walk had assured us that the old cook was a graduate of the postal service culinary training school, and that it was the only restaurant in town that served pork. The cook was Han, from Hunan province. Hunanese food is similar in many respects to Sichuan cooking, and old Bai did a pretty good job with some classic favourites like 'Pig Ears' and 'Prickly Hot Beancurd'. Pig Ears is often just a fancy name for cold cuts from a pig's head, but here we got the real thing, choice slices of pig ears with that special crunch between your teeth. The beancurd was cooked with chilli powder and prickly ash, that special Hunanese ingredient that sets your mouth a'tingling. More than a few ounces each of *baijiu* ensured a good night's sleep, broken briefly at ten o'clock by the crush of army boots on the snow below our window as a parade of soldiers made a circuit of the town.

The hotel heating was, as was the rule, turned off at midnight, and next morning our windows were completely iced over. Out on the streets, sweepers in their surgical masks were rugged up and already at work clearing dust off the black ice. Steam rose from two gaping manholes in the street. Our room had three iron beds, a table and a bare cement floor. Two thermoses of boiling hot water had been delivered to our door and we made breakfast with instant noodles in our covered enamel mugs.

We were at the PSB office when it opened. They were business-like, and to my amazement they helped us make some appointments for quick interviews. First stop was the Culture Bureau, where, as I had done at the provincial office, I presented my credentials and outlined the research I planned to do. They put us in touch with the 'Huangnan Tibetan Autonomous Prefecture Rebkong Art Gallery', which had not been open long. This was another brick apartment block, although it was set back from the street. The gallery's offices were on the first floor, exhibition space on the third floor, and apartments for some of the painters and their families on the floor in between. The gallery director was a large-framed Tibetan in his fifties, named Pema Gyel, who had held various posts with the government, including a recent stint with the Religion Bureau. It became clear during our interview that he had undergone many years training in the game of old-style communist aloofness. But it was all style, and I think he was more exited about the prospect of international interest than he was prepared to show. The gallery had already organised exhibitions in Honk Kong and Bangkok.

Pema Gyel called in the gallery staff and I was given a brief lecture on the history of the gallery and how it was financed. Originally it was established in 1977 as a 'research institute' at a nearby village called Sengeshong, which he referred to by its Chinese name of Wutun. Then it moved to another monastery famed for its artists, and later, after a travelling exhibition to Beijing, Shanghai and Guangzhou in 1981, it was moved to the Workers Cultural Palace in town. Eventually it was given a grant to set up a separate office and gallery in 1989. The building I was sitting in was a temporary base for promotion and exhibition (like many of the buildings around it, it looked much older than it should), and a newer and more lavish facility was planned once more funds could be raised. Pema Gyel asked one of the Tibetan gallery staff to take us on a quick tour of their collection.

The 'exhibition space' was a single large hall that took up half of the third floor. The room looked empty at first; the *thangkas* and paintings were tucked away in a corner. A painter named Kontar took out four *thangkas* mounted in the traditional brocades and hung them up on one of the display walls. These were the Four Guardian Kings: divine protectors of the Buddhist word, hands on their swords with their eyes bulging. There were also thirty or so *thangkas* mounted in Western-style frames behind glass: wrathful protectors with fangs and flaming hair, benign gods and goddesses, Shakyamuni Buddha, the saviouress Tara, and the great masters Padmasambhava and Je Tsongkhapa. Arranged on tables in a corner opposite the stacked paintings was a selection of gilded clay images glowing in warm raiment. There were also the standing forms of the Buddha Maitreya (the Buddha-to-come), the warrior king Gesar mounted upon his flying horse, and a graceful image of White Tara, the saviouress bestowing long life, carved from creamy birch wood. Most of the statues were made of unfired clay, and I could see in the cracks and breaks that had appeared on some of them that the clay used was deep red-brown, almost purple.

I took notes but was not allowed to take photographs.

Apart from one or two nods in the direction of Chinese folk themes, the exhibition was of all the most beautiful examples of traditional Tibetan art. Yet, in its gentle pastel hues, the painters of Rebkong had achieved something quite different to *thangka* painting anywhere else. At first glance I could feel relief that Rebkong art had apparently avoided the ideologically driven 'modernisation' that had taken place in Kantze.

Before we left the gallery the director informed us that the Culture Bureau had promised a car the following morning to take us out to Sengeshong, the home village of one of the most celebrated masters of Rebkong Painting, Shawo Tshering. It seemed that having my two 'guides', Kang and Ren, was paying off, making my arrangements much quicker than they might have been, and that the letters of introduction I had obtained in Xining were also doing their work.

After lunch that day we walked around the back of town and headed down a dirt road towards Rongwo Monastery. The back road, turning to mud with the melting snow, passed through the Tibetan village of Sakyi that spread between the monastery and the Chinese town. Excited children ran around us calling out *yinji yinji*, and *kase kase*. The first call I knew meant 'foreigner' (English). Later I learned that *kase* meant 'beard', which I have to say struck me as far more exalted than the 'long-nose' I was accustomed to hearing from Chinese kids.

At the edge of the monastery we saw two kinds of building. As one would expect in this part of Tibet there were low-roofed, stamped-earth pisé huts huddled together behind high, stamped-earth walls. Then there were rows of white-washed brick barracks in poor repair; these were left over from the Cultural Revolution and some still had slogans such as 'Long Live Chairman Mao' daubed across their walls. Having served as quarters for revolutionary youth throughout most of the 1970s, they had now been taken over to accommodate the return of monks to Rongwo.

Making our way through the monastery precinct Kang and Ren were just as lost as I was. Then, as we came out of the maze of alleyways running through the monks' quarters, we were met by a group of young monks. They were, until we had interrupted them, busy tidying the *chöra* (courtyard) of the monastery's Assembly Hall, or *dukhang*. The *dukhang* was one of the few buildings at Rongwo *gonchen* (large monastery) that was not razed to the ground to make way for the Red Guards. Nevertheless, it was in bad repair. Part of the cobbled *chöra* had been given over to a garden for medicinal herbs and vegetables, a necessity since the monastery had lost control of the surrounding land. The rest of the stones were covered in an accumulation of dirt and weeds.

Some of the monks working in the *chöra* could understand a little Chinese and we were able to let them know we were interested in looking inside the *dukhang*. In 'take me to your leader' fashion we were shown to the door of a small room just inside the monastery's main entrance. My Chinese friends insisted on going in first while I waited outside. They always seemed to be nervous about me doing any decision-making, or taking the initiative. After what was an unnecessarily long wait — a breakdown in communication? — I poked my head past the cotton curtain over the door. At that exact moment a monk opened the curtain from inside and met me face-to-face with the words 'Oh! How are you? Where are you from?' — in loud and passable English! I could see he was as excited to have an *yinji* visitor as I was surprised to receive an English greeting from the other side of the curtain, and my friends from Xining may even have suffered a greater shock. This surprising man was Sherab, at that time the *gonyer* (keeper of the keys), and he would later become my closest friend and adviser on all subsequent visits.

As he came out through the curtain, Sherab was holding open a notebook where he had written a number of English phrases, with Tibetan cribs below each line. Looking back I suspect that the original delay was caused by Sherab going over these phrases from his notebook, phrases he had learned very well from an earlier German visitor. Sherab has a wonderful sense of theatrical opportunity and from the moment we both reached for the curtain that day, until now, the two of us have been linked by *ley-wang* (Tibetan for 'the power of *karma*'). Subsequently, Sherab was to open many doors on each and every one of my visits.

Sherab gave us a guided tour through the main monastery buildings, first leading us through one of the four heavy yak-wool curtains covering the entrance to the *dukhang*, bending down to unlock the iron bolt at the bottom of the main door. It may have been cold outside, but stepping inside the *dukhang* was like walking into a commercial freezer. The stamped-earth walls were well over a metre thick at the base, and they kept the air inside the *dukhang* at least 10°C cooler than outside. A high skylight hardly illuminated the central pillars of the hall, leaving the outer edges in almost pitch darkness. As my eyes adjusted I could make out butter lamps flickering at the foot of a seated image of Je Tsongkhapa, seated like a buddha and rising three storeys high at the far end of the hall. The smile of the great Tibetan saint glimmered softly through the frozen air.

A nomad family on pilgrimage and clad in sheepskins came inside to join us, and Sherab led the way clockwise around the inside wall, acknowledging each mural of an enlightened being with a tap of his forehead against the dado below. With great pride Sherab pointed out the size of the *dukhang*: eighteen major and 146 minor columns, rising to a height of 12 metres, just over three storeys. It was entirely built in earth and superbly fitted wood, with not a single nail. The floor along the middle of the *dukhang* was lined with rows of flat cushions permanently laid out for the daily assembly of the monastic congregation. Chinese surveys made before their attacks on monasteries in 1958 record Rongwo *gonchen* as having as many as 1,669 monks enrolled within its several colleges and studying under the supervision of forty-three *trülku*. A congregation that once must have more than filled the *dukhang* had been reduced to about eight rows, and around three hundred monks.

Sherab took us to the central altar. The image of Tsong-khapa towered over us. There was a high wooden throne rising to chest height and piled high with cushions. On top of the cushions was a large, framed photograph of the late *gondag* (supreme head) of Rongwo, the seventh emanation of the seventeenth-century meditation master Shar Kaldan Gyatso (1607–77). Born in 1916 and in his early thirties when the communist troops arrived, the seventh Shar *Rinpoche* went out of his way to avoid conflict between his people and the new Chinese leaders after 1949, even assisting a peace delegation on its way to Lhasa. Yet in their suppression of the uprisings of 1958 the Chinese government was sweeping and relentless in its directives, and by 1959 the monastery was sealed up and its senior *lamas* were all in jail. Apart from a brief reprieve between 1961–63, the seventh Shar *rinpoche* was never returned to his people, dying in prison in 1978 at the age of sixty-two. His throne remained empty in front of us, awaiting the day his photograph might be replaced with his new incarnation.

To one side of the seventh Shar *Rinpoche*'s throne was another for the officiating *lama*. On the altar bench behind the thrones, among an array of old photographs, sat, unexpectedly, large framed portraits of the Dalai Lama and Panchen Lama. The former had been in exile since 1959; the latter had just died in 1989 after a lifetime attempting to balance the needs of his people and the arcane swings of Chinese politics. Both were symbols of the unquenchable hope for a return to Tibetan independence. It was understandable that the Panchen Lama's photograph was displayed so prominently on the altar, given his decision to stay in China and the many years when he was promoted by the state as an alternative Tibetan leader. But I wondered why they were allowed to display the portrait of His Holiness the Dalai Lama, whom the authorities regularly smeared with every kind of accusation and abuse. According to another monk, who had arrived to arrange offerings, each chapel within the monastery was allowed to display one photograph of the Fourteenth Dalai Lama, an act completely forbidden for individual monks.

By now my ears were starting to ring from the cold — it was so cold that I was getting dizzy and I wondered how much longer I could remain vertical. Sherab took us outside on a mini-pilgrimage, making a clockwise turn around the base of the *dukhang* and on to the residence of the Panchen

Lama, built for the rare and glorious occasions of his visits over the centuries. This, the *dukhang*, and a temple for the protector Mahakala — a fierce embodiment of wisdom-compassion — were the only three original buildings left out of the thirty-one major ritual structures that had made up the monastery before it was wantonly torn apart.

The next morning I waited outside the hotel with Kang and Ren for the car that would take us to the 'Painters' Village' of Sengeshong. It didn't arrive, and after waiting half an hour we decided to walk. I raised the question of the future of Tibetan culture. Both of my Chinese companions were in agreement that the future now looked good, and that the days of leftist excess were gone forever. The future for Tibetans would be better because China had finally found its true course. Since Deng's reforms in 1978, Qinghai, and indeed everywhere in China, had flourished under the relaxed political climate.

I wondered why they weren't as shocked as I was at the extent of destruction. The monastery had lost most of its major treasures — although the greatest treasure must surely be the precious *dharma*, the teachings of the Buddha and the unique Tibetan traditions of self-transformation. How well had the function of the monasteries survived? How many *lamas* were left who could guide the young monks we had met clearing up the temple grounds? I must have started to sound like a righteous white man. As far as I could tell, neither Kang nor Ren were dismissive of the Tibetans and their Buddhism, but the Tibetan practices and traditions of this part of China were seen by the state as dubious superstition, a smokescreen for class exploitation, or worse, the activity of 'splittist' supporters of the Dalai Lama. My two guides reminded me that the Hui warlord Ma Bufang's reign of terror in the 1930s and 1940s had been disastrous for the Tibetans, who were not equipped for modern battles and did not have the political networks of the Ma family. Rongwo *gonchen* might have been safe from the torch, but numerous encampments, villages and temples had been wiped out in the old days, and lackeys of General Ma had even had the supreme head of Rongwo dragged onto the street and beaten up, later holding his brother ransom in Xining under the pretext of 'education and training'.

The walk to Sengeshong was about 6 kilometres, heading back north along the road to Xining. The upper part of the flood plain was as level as water, and the mountains on each side were like a pair of hands cupping together to scoop us up. Our cheeks burned against the cold air and ice clung to my beard, but the sky was clear and the blinding sunshine warmed us as we walked beneath leafless poplars. Except for our chatter and footsteps, and the odd tractor passing by, the road was absolutely silent. And just as we had all agreed that walking was far more interesting than driving, two jeeps pulled up beside us. I could see why the Culture Bureau had been delayed: they had been busy arranging a mini-conference.

Sengeshong is a twin village, having two halves that are slightly set apart from each other: Sengeshong *Mago*, or Lower Sengeshong, and *Yago*, or Upper Sengeshong, the home of Shawo Tshering. Poor Shawo Tshering — I'm not sure he had any warning that we were coming, or at least that there were ten of us. The growling mastiff that greeted us as we opened the gate certainly hadn't been warned. Shawo

Tshering came out to greet us with his wife and daughter and one of his sons. He was a lithe, unassuming, snow-headed man in his late sixties. He had alert eyes and a grace in the movement of his hands — anyone could have spotted him as an artist.

Shawo Tshering's house, now that I can compare, was as simple and well organised as any Tibetan villager's. Clearly he was not flaunting his fame and popularity as a painter: there was a simple single-storey residence with two courtyards, one at the front for the family and another for Shawo Tshering's workshop. The only material sign of his success was the incorporation of brick into the architecture of the family residence, and the presence of glass in all the windows. The workshop was plain pisé.

Tibetan painting is done on cotton that is not stretched around a frame, but 'stitched' into it with cord, and a dozen or so such frames were spread around the workshop looking a little like animal skins pinned out to dry. There were smaller canvases for *thangkas*, larger ones for murals, all in different stages of assembly; stacks of fully prepared canvases were stored in their frames under the roof of one of the work sheds. Newly arrived wooden poles and cotton, stacked up waiting for orders, spoke of a very busy workshop.

Shawo Tshering invited us into the family's living room. Tea was brought, but just as we were introducing ourselves a contingent of monks arrived to conduct a prayer-offering. We moved ourselves to another room annexed to the house. Our interview started badly, from my point of view, with the translator working through the points and sub-points of my research plan as if they were interview questions. I would have preferred to avoid the business-like official interview style, but had been caught by surprise when the officials from the Culture Bureau had turned up. I began to realise that from their point of view this was not meant to be a relaxed interview; rather it would be best if I got all I needed to know on that morning and never had to come back. The 'old master' looked pressured and confused by the 'questions' that hadn't been designed as questions. I was frustrated too, but Shawo Tshering may have noticed I was and he began to open up.

In his soft voice Shawo Tshering summarised what he had been taught about the origins of his tradition. Around the time the Chinese princess Wencheng was sent to marry the seventh-century Tibetan king Songtsen Gampo, a unit of the Tibetan army was stationed at the present site of Sengeshong. Among the soldiers who settled there, according to local tradition, was one who was skilled in painting. At that time Buddhist art was hardly known in Tibet and was just starting to be imported from India. There was no temple at Sengeshong, only a military garrison. But the association of this village with painting and other arts may go back to that time.

The characteristics of the early art and *thangkas* now made in Sengeshong, Shawo Tshering added, had not changed. The colours and formal arrangements are as they have always been. Based on detailed descriptions found in the Buddhist canon, artists use their creative ability to shape accurate representations of the deities. Objects like features of the landscape provide some opportunity for innovation, but sacred beings and their signature symbols and implements are not to be altered.

It was Shawo Tshering's view that the colour scheme in Rebkong was not as strongly hued as that found in the paintings of Central Tibet. Before 1958 there was not such a large difference in most paintings, but generally the quality of the pigments used in Rebkong had not been as good as those available in Lhasa. The best mineral pigments were imported from Nepal, at great expense. Before 1958 poster colours (mass-produced pigments) were avoided because of their inferior quality, and only very rarely used. The traditional colour scheme in Rebkong emphasised bold use of the primary colours and black and white, and also much use of gold leaf. Then between 1958 and 1977 the painting tradition was closed down entirely, revived again only when the state relaxed its policies on religious belief.

Traditionally, Rebkong painters aimed at creating a strong sense of living depth and form. More recently, great care has also been given to the use of line, with the same aim of bringing the images to life. Since the founding of the Rebkong Art Gallery, artists have been interested in exploring the limits of their skill in fine line work, and as a result the images are more decorative than in the past.

The painting of a *thangka* takes from three to five months — one of the secrets of the Rebkong painters must be patience. All of the monks of both the Upper and Lower Sengeshong monasteries are taught painting and other arts, and the old master had trained eighteen apprentices, nine of whom attended his workshop to assist in completing commissions. In the past, painters worked only for monasteries, but increasingly their work is sought by laypersons. Painting is a form of service offered to the monastery, and in most households the young boys have begun their introduction to the tradition by about eight years old. Sengeshong is most famed for its sculpture and *thangkas*, and some monks are also skilled at embroidering appliqué *thangkas*. In recent years examples of Rebkong art have been ordered from right across China, and it is gaining a reputation even among Chinese Buddhists for the way it brings the Buddha's teachings alive.

Shawo Tshering's own oeuvre includes all the major deities and saints of the Buddhist tradition, but the subject he feels most at home with is Buddha Shakyamuni, the historical Buddha.[16] The paintings of *Jataka* tales, or stories from the life (and previous lives of) the Buddha, allow him relative freedom to employ his individual talents. The same applies to historical figures such as the king of ancient Tibet, Songtsen Gampo. As one of the more renowned painters of the early twentieth century he is also involved in passing the tradition on to the next generation. When he was a child it was still possible to study painting in the monastery, and he had been a monk until forced to renounce his robes and marry during the Cultural Revolution. In the past the monastery was the only 'school'; it was the place where children first learned to read and write, and in the case of Rebkong, to paint. The tradition of painting instruction no longer exists in the monasteries, and the old master has taken on numerous apprentices, all of them relatives. There have always been secret techniques, which were forbidden to be passed outside the family line. Shawo Tshering himself studied painting from a paternal uncle who was one of the monastery's 'monk-painters'. Before they are considered ready to strike out on their own it is expected that apprentices first study under the master for about seven years.

What Shawo Tshering was saying seemed to pose more questions than answers, and that wasn't a bad thing. The more I heard the more I realised how much I needed to learn. But I found it hard to believe that Tibetan painting in Rebkong had not changed since the time of its earliest beginnings. I wouldn't have described his colours as 'bold'; from what I could see he favoured strong, deep hues — dark reds, browns and blues. Perhaps I was missing something in the translation. There also seemed to be a variety of styles existing side by side; certainly some of the painters whose works I had seen in the gallery favoured pastel hues, in contrast to Shawo Tshering's own style. Was that a recent innovation, I wondered, or had there always been such a startling range of variation? Perhaps, as a spokesperson for his tradition, he had wanted to stress what he regarded as the importance of accurate reproduction within the standards of iconological tradition, and that implied a resistance to change. Was he really as interested in themes from the *Jatakas* and national myth as he claimed? Or was that something he had learned to say, reflecting the view of government policy-makers that Tibetan painters should learn to reflect the 'real' world — landscapes, animals, and the labouring classes — rather than limit themselves to the merely 'metaphysical' — like buddhas and *bodhisattvas*? Other elements of his account, like the references to the Tang dynasty and princess Wencheng, suggested a similar attempt to fit in with Chinese versions of art history that had more to do with glorifying the role of China as a civilising power rather than acknowledging local traditions.

What I wanted more than anything else was to use the leverage I had that day to arrange study under Shawo Tshering, or at least to find some way of spending time at his workshop and with other painters at Sengeshong. That was the course I had mapped out for my research while still in Australia. But something inside me said not to push things, that it was too early and it may only result in an aggressive stance that might alienate Shawo Tshering.

Being pushy was just something I wasn't prepared to do. I had been very fortunate so far: meeting people in Melbourne, making contacts in Xining and then having those contacts snowball in Tongren. Just the interview that day seemed pushy enough; I didn't feel comfortable at all about barging into other people's lives.

At the end of the interview I was keen to get a photo of Shawo Tshering. I had in mind a shot that recorded the interview scene, but everyone else seemed to think it would be better to make a more formal portrait, at least with Shawo Tshering in Tibetan dress. And so the portrait I have has him sitting on a chair under the eaves of his new house. He is wearing a simple robe of heavy dark brown cotton, sleeves and collar bordered with deep blue silk brocade. Underneath he has the clothes he wore from day to day: a cotton shirt neatly fastened at the neck, a jumper, grey flannel trousers and black padded-cotton Chinese shoes. A simple 'maker of gods', *lhabzo*, and at the same time an important cultural representative, a quiet leader of his people.

Before we went to sleep that night I started to dream of all the possibilities that this first visit to Rebkong had begun to unfold. I knew my reading in Australia had led me to something that was very exciting: Tibetan culture in Rebkong truly was undergoing a revival. It was also changing. The next problem was to find a way to spend time with the right people, and to learn the language so that I could have more direct access to a wider range of voices.

As we rested on our beds, I was not the only one deep in thought. Something in the day's excursion had set Mr Ren, the school teacher, to mulling things over. He suddenly wanted to know if I thought human beings were born good or bad. And earlier in Xining he had asked how far behind the West I thought China was. Both questions were probably good ones to ask an anthropologist. Sometimes, I said, I thought that China might be our future, because eventually the West's affluence would become unsustainable and we would have to organise life much along the lines that China had. But sometimes, for example, when I was in Shenyang and confronted by the basic hardness of life for industrial labourers, I felt China was still in the middle of the Industrial Revolution (c.1750–1850). This seemed to get me off the hook, and it reflected my true ambivalence.

But what was he up to with this other question? It was a question I hardly felt qualified to answer, and it was one that went to the very heart of the Chinese view of the world. The problem of the innate moral orientation of humanity has a very, very long history in China, reaching back to China's great moral philosopher, Confucius (551–479 BCE).

Anything that smelled remotely like Confucianism was attacked by young democrats and communists alike in the first decades of the twentieth century. And not long afterwards, Confucius and all the old philosophers were attacked again by communist ideologues jostling for influence in the first three decades of the People's Republic. Yet by the late 1980s, some were starting to wonder if the wholesale rejection of China's cultural and moral roots had been such a good idea, especially since Confucian values were said to be behind the enviable success of the 'four little dragons' Taiwan, Hong Kong, Singapore and South Korea. But there were many others who thought that the Communist Party itself was beleaguered with feudal and other old-fashioned values, and they resisted a return to anything that hinted at cultural regression or inwardness. That these debates, in part, fanned the thinking that fed the student movement in 1989 indicates just how difficult it was, in the end, for Chinese society to get away from Confucian philosophy.

I got the impression from Mr Ren that a lot of soul-searching was taking place in the 'middle ranks' — among those who were not in a position to keep track of the latest philosophical fads imported from the West, but who were still concerned about where China was going. After 1978, television had brought knowledge of the outside world, and people like Mr Ren and Mr Kang seemed deeply disturbed that China was so far behind. Their day-to-day world seemed so different to how they expected it should be. I could see how a question like humanity's innate goodness or evil might serve as a safe way into what might otherwise be a suspect political debate for high school teachers. No doubt the events at Tiananmen Square on 4 June had also shaken them up.

That night we relived the 'showdown' between two early interpreters of Confucian philosophy: Mencius (c.371–c.289 BCE) and Xunzi (c.310–c.219 BCE). Mr Ren sided with Xunzi. That is to say, he believed human beings were born wayward, and that they required the heavy hand of guidance to shape and transform them into fully socialised, moral and cultivated people. Xunzi thought we were naturally interested in feeding, clothing and resting ourselves, but higher ideas, like accepting responsibility, needed a strong tradition of reinforcement. I wasn't as familiar with this territory as I should have been, but I threw my hat in with Mencius anyway. Mr Kang wisely sat to one side and assumed the role of referee.

Mencius was most famous for being optimistic about the human propensity towards goodness, citing the example of an infant falling into a well. Bring along any human being, he said, and you will find they are not only concerned and alarmed, but compelled to act. 'Ah,' said Ren, 'but that person is an adult who has at least had the benefit of some socialisation. Look at a child when it is born: it cries. Doesn't that prove that from the first breath a person is making selfish demands? A child is completely self-centred from the beginning, and soon it is proving that it is jealous of the mother's attention, impatient, and has no ability to regulate its desires or behaviour.'

'Okay,' I said, 'But doesn't your position also involve a contradiction? If human beings are innately selfish [which was beginning to sound like the evil of evils in Chinese philosophy], and if it is also true that human beings constitute society and shape its traditions, then where on earth does morality come from in the first place? How did ideals of responsibility come about in the first place?' The answer from the other side, of course, was that in ancient times there were sages, and they were special, and they established traditions (or objective standards) that would point the rest of us forward. They taught the way of heaven.

'Now,' I countered, 'Mencius claimed goodness was as natural to people as flowing downhill was natural for water. I would agree with Mencius in this way. All of us want to be good; it is just that, for whatever reason, some of us can't be. What I mean is, selfishness might not be all bad. All of us want to be somebody and get somewhere; even the hardest criminal is struggling for recognition, and deep inside may even be a little raw and tender. Indeed, without believing that whatever it is we are about to do from moment to moment is good, we just couldn't do it. It is only our judgement that is perverted.' I was unsure if this was actually what Mencius was getting at, but I wanted to clinch the argument and go to sleep.

Then, without warning, there was a great scream in the passage outside our door. Thuds and yells followed. Ren leaped across the room and made sure the door was bolted. Bang, a body was thrown against the door. Crunch, the same body was thrown against the wall. Where was the floor attendant? Squeals, hisses, screeching as if ghosts were at war. We sat in the dark and watched the door. Someone was howling; was he dying? Dire whining. Were they drunk? How drunk? Why had it suddenly gone silent?

About an hour later Mr Ren opened the door. There was not a sign of the commotion we had just heard, not even scuff marks on the walls. It was a timely reminder that next time I would be coming to Rebkong alone. My theory of innate human goodness wasn't all that reassuring.

7
The wheel of life

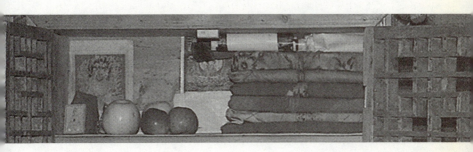

It was early summer when I returned to Rebkong, and the mountain valleys were covered by a patchwork of green wheat and golden rape flowers. Flashes of wildflowers painted the alpine slopes and leafy poplars shaded the road as we passed through busy villages. Inside the bus we struggled with the clouds of dust that passed straight through the shut windows and puffed up through the floor. Fortunately, like most of the Han-Chinese passengers, I had come prepared with a small surgical mask, which I hooked over my ears. Keeping a mask on me was a habit I had picked up from my days in Shenyang; few of the Tibetans on board had them. Instead, the men cupped the woolly opening of their sheepskin coat sleeves over their mouths, and women tied woollen headscarves across their faces.

Just as I was calculating how many hours of inhaling loess particles it would take to kill me, the bus halted at a hamlet on the approach to the township of Qunke. A road crew was taking advantage of low water levels to reinforce the ford. A detour took us through a maze of tight village alleyways more accustomed to the easy pad of donkeys. Predictably, we came face-to-face with another bus, and in a display of that eternal optimism characteristic of Qinghai's bus drivers, the two buses squeezed past each other, until both were jammed between the pisé walls on either side. We abused our driver, the two drivers abused each other, and the villagers came out to abuse everyone. Dogs, too, came out to give advice. Metal scraped against metal; metal scraped against earthen wall. A detour that was supposed to take two minutes took close to an hour.

On the bus I chatted with Wolfgang, a German traveller I had run into in the dormitory of the Xining Hotel. Wolf, a red-faced and slightly rotund man in his fifties, was an artist and practitioner of Tibetan Buddhism. It was reassuring for me to have somebody along because looking back, I was petrified at the immensity of the task I had taken on. In the months after my first visit my fears had grown larger and larger. The rough bus trip to Tongren would be one thing, but then there were the deep tensions and suspicion between the Tibetans and Chinese; the authorities were unlikely to leave me alone. Then there was the language barrier and, faced with the reality of a flesh-and-blood Tibetan community, I began to feel that my reading in Tibetan culture and history left me woefully ill equipped. Underneath all of these feelings lay my own deepest doubt: namely, that I just wasn't cut out to be an anthropologist — not just in Tibet, but in any part of the world.

Wolf was on his way to visit Labrang, a large monastery which, since the mid-1980s, had been gaining a reputation among international travellers in China as a 'little Tibet'; it was a large monastery town on the western edge of China that was relatively free of the heavy-handedness travellers came across in Lhasa. I had not yet been to Labrang, but in Xining I had suggested to Wolf that he might find Rebkong even more interesting, since it was an entire valley of monasteries, not just one large monastic university. When he had found out about the artists of Rebkong after some quick deliberation, he had decided to make a detour and come on the bus with me.

I don't think Wolf was quite ready for the discomfort of Qinghai bus travel, and as the dust floated around us he got pretty miserable, at least until we crossed the pass and entered 'Tibetan territory', when he came back to life. He was on an artist's travel grant, he told me, exploring western China in search of Tibetan images. In particular, one of the tasks set out in his grant was to search for signs of contemporary memory of the great Kagyu saint, artist and all-round 'renaissance man', Thangtong Gyalpo.

It is probably safe to say that Thangtong Gyalpo's life straddled the fourteenth and fifteenth centuries, and that he lived at the same time as Je Tsongkhapa. The precise dates of his life vary: 1361–1485 or 1385–1509 seem to be the most likely, which is a remarkable life span of 125 years. He was born the youngest of three brothers into a poor farming household in the region of Ngamring, about 400 kilometres west of Lhasa. When he was sixteen he was conscripted into military service in place of his older brothers, a fulfilment of local corvée obligations. Later he was forced to trade musk and yak tails to support his parents. On one trading expedition he came across a group of seven prisoners, including a nun, about to be executed. He took all of the musk, yak tails and other goods he had in his pack and offered them to persuade the local magistrate to commute their sentence. It worked, but when he returned home empty-handed his parents weren't so forgiving: after effectively being kicked out of their house he resolved to renounce the world and pursue a religious life.

Something had definitely awakened in Thangtong Gyalpo,

and in one source it is said that he trained under five hundred tantric masters in rapid succession, quickly developing unlimited insight. He was, all along, an extraordinary *siddha*, an adept at yoga who was fully accomplished in the esoteric practices of what was called 'secret-mantra'. Using the skills he had learned in his early years as a soldier and trader he wandered abroad in Ü-Tsang and Kham, as well as south of the Himalayas into India and Bhutan, offering teachings as he went, and even travelling to China. Wolf, my temporary German travel companion, was attempting to retrace his steps.

Tradition has it that while travelling through the Himalayas and Tibet, Thangtong Gyalpo soon realised that there were two major obstacles to the promotion of Buddhist practices and values. The first was the danger posed by the ravines and swift rivers of the region. The second was that many Tibetans were unable to read. To solve the first problem he is said to have built chain suspension bridges. His first bridge was built in 1430 near Chushul, where the Kyichu (Lhasa River) enters the Brahmaputra southwest of Lhasa. The Italian orientalist Giuseppe Tucci crossed the river at this point in 1948. Indeed, the exact spot was still known as Chaksam, or 'Ironbridge'. Tucci describes the spot in the river as particularly treacherous; he was in awe of the 'lurking rage of floods and sand storms [that] threaten life at any moment':

> At Chaksam ... we crossed the Brahmaputra on a thick raft. Once there was a suspension bridge from which the place draws its name, the wooden planks resting on two thick chains hooked on two pillars. Now the planks were gone.[17]

Tucci records finding a picture commemorating Thangtong Gyalpo displayed at a Nyingma *gompa* — a centre of religious life — overlooking the bridge, noting too that the monastery, located on a junction on the trading route south of Lhasa, had been the 'theatre of many battles'.

Thangtong Gyalpo also features in a traditional story relating to the First Dalai Lama, Gedun Drup (1391-1474). He had commissioned a large statue of Maitreya for the Tashilhunpo Monastery near Shigatse. He had wanted to employ a particularly renowned artist from the school of metal icon-makers in northern Latö, a mountainous region halfway between Shigatse and Kathmandu. The artist, one Trashi Rinchen, was unavailable because he was tied up in one of Thangtong Gyalpo's own projects.[18] It is tempting to believe that Thangtong Gyalpo had the metal workers working madly on his new bridge-building technology.

The great *siddha* has been called Tibet's 'Leonardo', an appellation that reflects his broad interests in not only engineering projects, but also painting, sculpture, temple building and even drama. Drama was partly his solution to the 'second' problem, the problem of literacy, as well as being a means of entertaining crowds with tales of the ancient Tibetan kings — a means for attracting donations and sponsors for his other projects. Thus *ache lhamo*, a masked drama also known as 'Tibetan opera', was born. Its Tibetan name is said to come from the seven beautiful daughters of the Béna clan, young women who Thangtong Gyalpo trusted would draw in the crowds. He wrote the plays and designed their costumes himself. Two of the sisters played hunters, two played kings and two played goddesses, while one accompanied them on a gong. Thangtong Gyalpo himself played the drum. The show was a hit, and the *siddha* got to build fifty-eight bridges. And the sisters? Since the opera is still called *ache lhamo*, or 'Goddess Sisters', we might say they were rewarded with lasting fame.

In my ignorance I suggested to Wolf that little trace of Thangtong Gyalpo was likely to be found in Amdo. He was mostly active in Central Tibet and Kham. The Tibetan name for Luding county, a large Khampa town in Sichuan, is still Chakzamka or 'The Iron Bridge Crossing', a legacy of this inventive and energetic embodiment of the Bodhisattva of Compassion. And Thangtong Gyalpo belonged in the Kagyu order, which had little influence in Amdo, let alone Rebkong. In Amdo, rivers were still sometimes crossed on rafts of inflated sheepskins and, apart from the occasional wood cantilever construction, in many parts bridges were unknown until after 1949. Still, Wolf was optimistic.

Our bus passed Qunke and soon it was travelling alongside a turbid, swollen Yellow River. In the intense light of late spring, red, purple and blue sandstone cliffs hung like a coloured curtain, hiding the sacred land of Rebkong beyond. I was surprised to see small farms dotted along the Guchu Gorge; these must have been hidden by snow on my first visit. Hui farmers followed their sheep along cliff-face paths.

The road through the gorge wasn't much wider than a sheep track, but that would change over the summer. As we went further the bus was forced to cross rows of gravel piled across the road, tipped there ready for grading. Not far from where the road had collapsed in winter the bus began to slow. A member of a road crew stood on the road holding a sign that read, 'Halt! Blasting'. We joined a queue of waiting trucks, buses and jeeps, and were advised to stay seated. Tibetans tolled their rosaries, Han cracked sunflower seeds in their teeth, and the bus filled with cigarette smoke. A blue jeep carrying half a dozen helmeted road crew appeared around the corner up ahead and stopped. There was a short silence. Crack! The mountains on both sides of the gorge gave a jump and dust shuddered into the air.

A brief wait and the lollipop man waved the traffic on. There was no sign of debris on the track, an indication that the blasting must have been down in the gorge below. This guess was right, I found out later: sections of the road were being widened, but the blasting was for tunnels that were being cut through some of the gorge's most harrowing bends. Perhaps Thangtong Gyalpo had returned to the world, this time armed with dynamite. As our bus crawled on through the gorge I couldn't help wishing they had rebuilt the road a year earlier. I also realised I was witnessing an important change. Rebkong was increasingly becoming part of the 'outside' world, the fame of the valley's painters was spreading, and the 'hidden valley' was being belatedly incorporated into Deng Xiaoping's modernisation drive.

As we left the gorge a more primordial change was visible. What a spectacular transformation the Golden Valley of Rebkong had performed before my return! The valley floor was an emerald carpet of ripening wheat. The whole colour scheme had shifted, or, more accurately, there now *was* a colour scheme. The yellow-grey loam I had seen in winter had turned pink under the summer light. The ice had gone from the Guchu River, replaced by a ribbon of water tumbling over pebbles and around sandbars. The sides of the valley had joined this summer concert, almost like a pair of mirrors reflecting the new life below, while the sky above was pure blue space.

There were more roadworks as we approached Bao'an township, and the bus made yet another detour. The temporary track was cut through a hill, and the traffic was taking its toll. Spinning tyres had turned the road into a long pit of pale yellow loess dust, and as we arrived several cars could already be seen slowly twisting their way through it and up into town. With each vehicle the road melted a little further and the dust deepened. The loess brought the wheels of our bus to a standstill. Our shoes disappeared in the powder as we got down to push. Each passenger took their station, heaving the clumsy weight of the bus from the back and sides. The wheels span vainly, sending jets of fine dust into the air and covering our every pore, clinging around our sweaty collars and clagging our mouths. We must have looked and sounded like ghosts when we finally arrived in Tongren, hair dusted white, and snorting to clear our noses and throats. I made a mental note to always keep an adequate stock of drinking water for bus journeys. But it was hard to be miserable. The water of the Guchu sparkled; the sunny streets of Tongren bustled with crowds of shoppers, carts and motorbikes and looking across the green valley I was filled with a sense of space and ease.

Wolf and I made our way up the street, watching out for the gaping manholes, and arranged beds in the hotel. There was a new arrangement with the PSB that foreign guests should wait in the hotel to have their papers checked. A young woman, Xiao Yang, arrived after about half an hour and was a little surprised to hear I would be staying a month. She advised me to be very careful to avoid the rougher types, or *liumang*.

While I was still in two minds about my own abilities, the three-day 'reconnaissance' in winter had convinced me that the project I had for exploring the life of Rebkong's painters should work. I still had a year up my sleeve, and I thought a month at this time was long enough to begin to explore Tongren and its neighbouring villages. I would get a feel for the place, and I would meet people who might be able to facilitate discussions with painters, and, with any luck, an informant who could guide me through the local traditions and politics. I felt I needed to very gently test whether I could become a part of the place. I needed to be swept up in the flow of life, to be carried along with it together with those around me. If I could start that process, I thought, I still had another year to come back for an extended stay. The dream scenario was for a painter to take me on as a student.

The afternoon sun was still high when the PSB officer left and I took Wolf down the road to the monastery. At the monastery's edge the old Chinese barracks were being pulled down. A start had also been made on a new *lhakang*, a frame of golden cedar already in place. We headed straight to the Assembly Hall, where I hoped I would find Akha Sherab. ('Akha' was a term of address for monks in Amdo, and it is also used like 'Uncle' before the name of a man senior to oneself.)

Akha Sherab was at home in his single-room residence by the Assembly Hall gate, and he was very impressed to see I had come back as I had promised. He was enjoying a relaxing cup of tea with some other monks. One of them, an old monk seated on the heated bed, suddenly became extremely agitated upon seeing the two foreigners, and his face tightened with fear. He began a loud, hissing diatribe in Tibetan and pidgin Chinese: 'Watch out! The Chinese will come! Worse than dogs! Completely rotten! Be careful, don't let them see you here ...' He spoke almost as if possessed. By this time he was standing up on the bed, reaching out as if to shoo us away, while the other monks in the room were trying to calm him down. He sat down, still agitated, cursing the Chinese under his breath. As he calmed down I noticed he had been busy decorating a small wooden writing table before we had entered the room. He picked up his brush and a small Chinese wine cup full of pink paint and started painting again.

It was quite a welcome. 'That is Akha Yeshe,' said Sherab, and, pointing to his own heart, he explained how his old friend had a problem called *nyinglung*, and that it made him prone to strange behaviour. By now Akha Yeshe was quietly engrossed in the pattern he was brushing onto the small table. From the lines in his face he looked liked he must have been in his sixties, but his arms were strong and wiry. His face was now soft, even cherub-like, but with a squint and a crooked nose. He looked embarrassed, in a cheeky sort of way, silently applying colour and line without hesitation, constantly straightening his brush between his lips. A peony, surrounded by arabesque tendrils and Byzantine leaves, was taking shape on the surface of Sherab's table.

From the little knowledge I had of Tibetan medicine, I knew that *nying* meant 'heart', and *lung* referred to 'wind', one of the three humours in Tibetan medicine, along with bile and phlegm. Jäschke's *A Tibetan–English Dictionary*, which I later checked back in my hotel room, provided the description 'low spirits, mental derangement' and 'heart grief, deep sorrow'. I wondered if it was a temporary condition, or a more permanent 'turbulence' within the heart. Did Akha Yeshe suffer from depression? Was he bipolar? Or could he have been one of the outlandish crazy-saints I had read about? As we tried to break through the language barrier, Sherab was reminded of something and fetched his notebook from a drawer inside the table Akha Yeshe was decorating. While I was there Sherab thought he might fit in some quick English practice. Wolf went off with some of Sherab's friends to explore Rongwo Monastery, while I spent the rest of the afternoon adding to Sherab's 'phrasebook'.

That night I reviewed my research plan. It was time for me to get out and about so I could start to fill out my picture of Rebkong. And after my visit to Sengeshong in winter I was convinced the best way to do that was to start visiting each of the villages famed for their talented *lhabzo*, or icon-painters. The next morning, after a piping-hot bowl of glassy *fentang*, beanflour-noodle soup, I set off through the new 'industrial precinct' north of town on a walk to the nearest of the 'Tibetan Painting Villages', Nyenthok, just 2 kilometres north of the Huangnan Hotel.

The monastery at Nyenthok began as a *gar*, an outpost or encampment monastery, built by Tsultrim Gyatso (b. 1587). Also known as the '*Siddha* of Danma', Tsultrim Gyatso was an important figure in the politics of Tibet, Mongolia and China in the 'troubled early seventeenth century'.[19] He was born at Danma, northeast of Xining and close to Gönlung Jampa Ling (also known as Jampa Bumling), one of the great monastic colleges of Amdo. Tsultrim Gyatso was the abbot there from 1637 to 1639. Gönlung Monastery had been built at the request of the Fourth Dalai Lama, and it quickly became instrumental in forging Tibet's relationship with

Mongol leaders, as well as the Manchu court of China's Qing dynasty (1644–1911). Then, in 1723, Gönlung Monastery became implicated in the anti-Manchu uprising of the Mongol nationalist Tenzin Ching Wang. Tsultrim Gyatso's successor and incarnation, the Second *Siddha* of Danma, was taken to Xining and executed. The monks of Gönlung rose up in protest — an action that resulted in Qing troops torching their monastery in the first month of 1724. In 1732 the Yongzheng emperor issued permission for the monastery to be rebuilt, renaming it Youning Si, 'Temple for Protecting Tranquillity'. As a meeting place for Mongolia, China and Tibet, however, the monastery was rarely tranquil, and it suffered again greatly in the twentieth century, eventually being reduced to rubble in the Cultural Revolution.

Nyenthok Gar had fared considerably better. Nyenthok village stands on a cliff above a tributary to the Guchu River. After almost getting lost in a maze of village alleyways I found the monastery by heading towards a large *thangka*-displaying platform lying on the mountainside behind it. Several old buildings survived, including a wondrous two-storey *lhakang* constructed mainly of latticed wood with its entrance under giant golden awnings woven from reeds. Its airy construction gave the whole monastery a light and spacious atmosphere. The Assembly Hall, Maitreya Hall and Tantric College were still standing, as was an ancient two-storey mansion belonging to the Khenchen Lama, one of the leading *lamas* at Rongwo Monastery.

Although many of its most important buildings still stood, Nyenthok Gar had not escaped attack in the 1950s and 1960s, and like Rongwo Monastery it was undergoing rebuilding and renovation. At the Maitreya Hall an old woman brought me a cup of tea while I joined a group of children watching an old sculptor repair a statue of the Lord of Wisdom, Manjushri. He had repaired Manjushri's broken limbs, had filled the cracks, and was sanding the clay to prepare it for gilding and the addition of colour. Gazing down at us from his lotus seat, his body covered with veins of new clay, the *bodhisattva* smiled sweetly.

In the courtyard of the old mansion I found the Khenchen Lama and a young understudy sitting under the shade of a large fig tree. Beside a garden flourishing with medicinal herbs, teacher and student had laid out long strips of paper, perhaps 10 metres long. Now dry, the strips of paper had recently been imprinted with thousands of prayers by the repeated application of an inked woodblock. The old *lama* and boy monk were rolling them up to fill silver prayer wheels.

The *lama* arranged for a monk, Dargey, to show me the Assembly Hall. Inside, it was in poor repair. The floor was dusty and many of the murals were sagging — the cotton paintings coming away from the wall. On the front wall there were a number of older murals that had been painted on plaster instead of cotton. Faded with time, they were crossed by cracks and, in some places, large holes. There were *mandalas*, their four quarters painted in staggering detail, and tableau narratives of the lives of *siddhas* and saints, *bodhisattvas* and temple-builders. In the middle of the wall there was an image taken from the famous Wheel of Life. Driving life's confusion, the pig of ignorance, the pigeon of greed and the snake of hatred chased each other's tails, and across them through the wall there was a gaping hole in the plaster — Dargey mimed out how it had been deliberately inflicted by a rifle butt. There was also crudely scratched graffiti, Cultural Revolution-era slogans such as 'Oxen Ghosts and

Snake Demons!' condemning Tibetan religious art as superstitious evil. It was my introduction to the full sacrilege of political extremism, a much more powerful history lesson than I had witnessed at Rongwo Monastery, where most of the now embarrassing evidence had been swept away. The damage I saw inflicted on these three-hundred-year-old murals somehow spoke more loudly than piles of rubble.

I think it was at that moment, gazing through dim light at the murals at Nyenthok Gar, that the image of the Wheel of Life, along with the Wheel of Time, seemed to take on an emblematic role in my imagination, symbolising the contrast that existed between the Tibetan world view and that of the Chinese Communist Party. A struggle had been, and is still being, played out between the 'Wheel of Time' and the 'Wheel of History', each turning around its own shifting axis. The Wheel of Time came to stand for the cosmic, psychological and metaphysical world view of Tibet that was derived from the Indian *Sri Kalachakra Tantra* and other important texts from Mahayana and Vajrayana (Tantric) Buddhism. By 'Wheel of History' I mean twentieth-century China's version of socialism — the 'real world' values of Marx and Lenin called 'historical materialism' — a theory of the relentless progress of history based on class struggle and the destruction of past social forms, and also, at least under Mao Zedong, a romantic dream of a classless future under socialism. In the Tibetan world view things changed, but at the same time the basic texture of life remained the same. There was little sense that history held to any direction; instead, life was played out within a small fragment of a great arc of cosmic time.

The contrast between world views based on 'cosmos' and world views based on 'history' is a fundamental one in world mythologies, and was first described at length by the great founder of comparative religion Mircea Eliade in *The Myth of the Eternal Return*. In the cosmic vision of life the world is regenerated from time to time, returning to a new beginning but repeating, or continuing, archetypal patterns. And within the great cycles there are lesser cycles within cycles. In the historical vision there is only one direction — time and man progressing ever forward. How much suffering had the collision of these two 'wheels' caused in the twentieth century? And how much misery and destruction was experienced as villages and monasteries were crushed between them? There seemed scant indication that natural cogs would form in the near future to allow them to turn in harmony.

Later I chased up a passage I remembered, from a speech given by His Holiness the Thirteenth Dalai Lama (predecessor of our present Fourteenth Dalai Lama) to an assembly of monks in Lhasa during the New Year gathering of 1930, just as China's revolution was building steam:

> *We should care for our responsibilities as much as we care for our eyes. If not, all we do is collect causes of a rebirth in one of the hell regions. The* wheel of time *continues to turn day and night as we continue to spend our time and energy just creating problems for people we don't like and favouring those we like. Meanwhile, our actual work never gets done. We cannot keep even our own house in order, let alone do anything useful for the country.*[20]

As it turned out, these were deeply prophetic words. The responsibility for the protection of Tibet in the race for imperial domination had fallen on the shoulders of the

Thirteenth Dalai Lama, and before he died in 1933 he had tried to initiate several plans for modernisation and reform. His passing away left Tibet far too vulnerable. Twenty-eight years after his speech encouraging monks to work harder for the future of their religion a Chinese ideologue in Xining would report:

> *When the socialist great revolution in the pastoral areas of our province was still in its primary stage, the diehards among livestock owners and counter revolutionaries in religious circles staged armed revolt against socialism, the people, and the Communist Party in an attempt to fight the masses of the people and stop the huge wheel of history. The result was their utter defeat. The religious and feudal power was completely burned away by the flames of revolution.*[21]

In Nyenthok I began to understand the ferocity of those 'flames of revolution'.

The pain for the people of Nyenthok must have been all that much greater, for, as I was learning, they had been caretakers of some of the most precious images in the whole of Rebkong. Tenpa Rabgye's nineteenth-century history of Amdo, the *Domey Chöjung*, links several painters with the development of Nyenthok Monastery, including a very important contributor to the flourishing of the Rebkong painting tradition, the artist Bithang Palden.

Active in the early eighteenth century, and perhaps even in the late seventeenth century, Bithang Palden was responsible for the construction of a large statue of Maitreya at Nyenthok Gar, as well as several murals, some of which were still visible in the upper level of the *dukhang*. According to my guide, the upper-level ceiling had not been touched since completion, and may therefore have been more than two hundred and fifty years old.

From what I saw of Bithang Palden's work, if it was indeed by this master, painting from this period still reflected early examples of painting from Central Tibet, with flat, quiet tones and minimal ornamentation. They are extremely reserved in style, reflecting the painter's careful measuring and modelling of his subjects according to strict iconographic rules. Even background areas were rendered with mostly plain colour, and with minimal landscape detail.

It is said in the *Domey Chöjung* that Bithang Palden worked with a large retinue of students, and on completion of their work for the new temple these early painters bound their used brushes together and secreted them inside the image of Maitreya as an offering so that their tradition might grow. The magic worked, but the tradition also evolved. The subdued colour scheme used by the early masters was replaced over the centuries by much busier images and much more intense hues.

Compared to Rongwo Monastery, the grounds of Nyenthok Gar were silent, almost deathly so. It had for some reason only re-opened in 1987 — Rongwo had been given permission to open in December 1980. The new Chinese government's survey in 1954 put the number of monks at Nyenthok at two hundred and ten. Dargey told me there were only twenty *gelong*, or fully ordained monks, and a rabble of *akha chungchung*, the tiny young novices that now almost outnumbered the adult monks in the monasteries of Rebkong.

The monk Dargey invited me to have tea at his home before heading back to Tongren. By the door of his private shrine-room I found a surprise. On a wooden panel there was a rough painting of Tibet's famous bridge-builder, Thangtong Gyalpo. It was faded, but unmistakable. A mildly corpulent yogin with shoulder-length hair, topknot and seated on a deerskin, he held a treasure-vase, and most importantly, a short length of iron chain.

I couldn't wait to find Wolf, but back at the hotel I found him in a bad way. His stomach had let him down. He had booked a taxi to take him east to Labrang in the morning, and would not be visiting Nyenthok Gar, or anywhere else in Rebkong. He was even thinking about abandoning his sojourn altogether.

A few days later, checking my notes with Akha Sherab, I learned that Nyenthok village was not in fact Tibetan, although I have come to wonder what that means in the context of Rebkong. Nyenthok's 232 village households were nearly all Monguor, a people known as 'Hor' in Tibetan, and 'Tu' in Chinese. Sherab explained that most of the people living on the river flat just north of Rongwo, the best part of Rebkong for farming, belonged to this mysterious ethnic group.

The Monguor of Rebkong had several stories about their ancestral lands. Some said they migrated south from other Monguor localities to the north, such as Huzhu, Datong and Minhe counties. Given that the founder of Nyenthok Gar was from Huzhu, that connection made sense. Other traditions suggested that they were among the earliest inhabitants of eastern Qinghai, and that the differences now experienced in various Monguor communities across the province only reflected the influence of cultures that migrated into the region much later. In the early part of the twentieth century European and American missionaries were fascinated by the question of the origin of their language, and concluded that it must be a distant branch of Mongolian.

Whatever their origin, the Mongour have shown a remarkable tendency to assimilate. Tibetan seems to have taken over as the language most widely spoken in the Monguor villages of Rebkong, whereas for their cousins north of the Yellow River, Chinese is increasingly displacing their mother tongue. Even in Rebkong there was considerable variation from one village to another, with Chinese influence stronger at Sengeshong.

I also found out that old Akha Yeshe, the 'crazy-saint' at Rongwo Monastery, was a Monguor from Nyenthok. Most monks in Rebkong continue to have close links with the surrounding villages, and are regularly needed to help with what in English-speaking countries is called 'pastoral care'. Sherab had invited me to join the two of them at a wake at the house of a Monguor man called Namgyal on the Tongren-Nyenthok road. One of the difficulties of fieldwork, I was finding, was that information and opportunities never arrived in any systematic way. I had quickly developed a haphazard way of deciding what I would do each day, because no matter what I planned there was sure to be something else that came up instead. Beyond my specific interest in painting I had to put what I was learning into a wider social and cultural context, and a small number of people were picking up that I was interested in anything that taught me about what they thought was important.

When we arrived at Namgyal's place there was no deceased laid out at the wake. His grandfather had already been cremated, but the family needed to have monks present to offer prayers on the twenty-first, thirty-fifth and forty-ninth days after he passed away. For the Tibetans and Monguor in Rebkong the passing of a relative presented two important tasks. The first was that the departing relative should die well, which meant calmly and without too much lamentation. Here the important thing was to preserve an atmosphere before and after the moment of death that emphasised the virtue and good heart that the deceased had shown in their life, so that their consciousness would move towards a positive rebirth. The second task was to ensure that the consciousness of the deceased found its proper way to its future birth, both for the sake of the deceased and for those who remained. Exaggerated expressions of attachment could distract the disembodied consciousness as it passed through the intermediate state between life and death (the visions of the *bardo*) or worse, they could end up condemning it to a lingering existence as a nearby ghost. While consciousness may migrate, as it is put in Tibetan, up or down on the Wheel of Life, no one life is eternal and it is better as the end approaches to recognise this primordial reality and let go.

The wake was really a quiet evening spent at home on behalf of the deceased. Akha Yeshe and Sherab recited prayers while I sat with the family, drinking the *baijiu*, eating the sweets and smoking the cigarettes they had prepared. Enjoying the family's hospitality seemed an important role for me to play and it was a good opportunity to find out more about the Monguor. But I was soon to find myself even more puzzled, because just as I was learning that not all that was Tibetan in Rebkong was simply Tibetan, I was to learn that not all who bore the label 'Monguor' were simply Monguor. Indeed, this family did not start off as Monguor at all, but had been classified as such by the local government.

They seemed to be just as confused as I was. They claimed to be what the Tibetans call *gya-ma-wö*, 'between Chinese and Tibetan' with mixed Chinese and Tibetan ancestry. But because they had to have an official 'nationality' they were given identity cards classing them as Tu (Monguor). The logic behind this re-categorisation, if I heard correctly, was that the authorities considered the Monguor to be on a 'cultural level' between the Chinese and Tibetans, so that the products of marriage between the 'lower' and 'higher' group would mathematically equal Monguor status. It was a neat solution, but it also raised questions about minority populations and their relation to powerful state institutions, the 'watering down' of Tibetan identity in Rebkong, and the fate of other 'combinations' that were living around Tongren.

Over the next few weeks I spent some time walking to each of the other villages said to belong to the 'Land of Tibetan Painting'. While I was learning how they were not exactly Tibetan, if they were anything like Nyenthok they promised to present me with further conundrums. As a group they were once known as the 'Four Fortresses', or even the 'Four Chinese Fortresses', and they still have walled precincts originally built during the Ming dynasty (1368–1644).

The village of Gomar, or 'Red Gate', so called because of its red clay wall, was just three kilometres further north from Nyenthok. Here village craftsmen and monks from Gomar Gar were building a large new Kalachakra *chorten* out of grey cement. Later they would paint it white so it would shine like a jewel in the Rebkong sun. Kasar village was about eight kilometres further on. Its name is said to mean 'New Ditch', because it was where riverside irrigation was first introduced to the valley. There was a simple bridge near Kasar which allowed me to cross over to the eastern side of the river to Sengeshong, the last of the Fortress Villages, and home of the painter Shawo Tshering. From there I could usually hitch a ride back to Tongren along the Xining road.

Nyenthok, Gomar, Kasar and Sengeshong were famous for their Tibetan art, but none of them were, strictly speaking, Tibetan villages. All of them, however, were completely integrated into the Tibetan religious traditions of Rebkong, and long interaction with the dominant Chinese and Tibetan cultures, perhaps over six centuries, had worn away at the Monguor language and traditions. Their villages were all known by Tibetan names, and their own families had Chinese surnames that have been handed down over the generations — despite the fact that they have been little used. Even the Tibetan word for this group of villages is a cultural conglomerate — (*Gya*) *treytse shi*. *Gya* is Tibetan for 'China' or 'Chinese', *treytse* is a Tibetan phonetic rendering of the Chinese word for 'fortress' (*zhaizi*), and *shi*, in Tibetan again, means 'four'. Hopping between the four villages I also began to suspect that even though they shared a similar history of assimilation each was quite different, and that each would eventually contribute something unique to the story of Rebkong painting. But again I was beginning to be overcome by thoughts of how complex a task it was going to be if I wanted to really find out what was behind it all. And the task of unravelling it all was at this stage incomprehensible.

―――

Staying in town I had got to know a group of three young Chinese guys, cabinetmakers from Xining who were doing the interior decoration for a set of luxury rooms at the back of the hotel. I had also become something of a curiosity about town, so it was hard to eat a meal or write my diary in one of the Hui teahouses without having to entertain someone by answering the same set of questions that everyone inevitably asked. Where was I from? How far away was that? Was it a Buddhist country? Was it a Muslim country? How much was an air ticket?

With Wolf evacuated to Labrang I had the whole four-bed room to myself for just four *yuan* a day (or AUD$0.80 cents), and the women at reception downstairs were happy enough not to send new guests in my direction. The problem with the four-bed room was just that four beds were all there was apart from a small table, an enamel basin and a thermos flask. It was a little depressing after a month. To wash I had to plan several trips to the boiler-room when it first opened in the morning, lugging the thermoses upstairs so I could take a sponge bath in my room using a small handtowel. The toilets on my floor were full of every kind of ugly disaster that could be caused by overeating and overdrinking. The days walking or just hanging out in the monastery were filled with brilliant sunshine and crisp air; the nights back at the hotel were surreal. I could watch drunken brawls out on the street or the army on their late night curfew march shuffling past under the moonlight; I could read my Tibetan–English dictionary on my bunk, write up my diary, or join other guests in the TV room to watch the late evening news. That's where I met the interior decorators, as well as assorted truck drivers, pilgrims, officials and various village representatives on business.

One afternoon, not long before my 'orientation month' was up, I ran into the interior decorators in the street and they asked if I wanted to walk up the mountainside with them. It sounded like a good idea at the time. But right from the beginning it was a race I could hardly keep up with, and we overtook villagers and yaks on their way to the next valley. I was a boy from Australia's flat mallee country and just not built for climbing at altitude. And no one was carrying any water, apart from what was in two jars of pears the other three had brought along. My companions imagined themselves as 'frontiersmen' and were in Rebkong looking for adventure, and when they couldn't find it, or got bored, they invented their own. I gave myself up to their whimsy and went with the flow. Resting on a knoll at the top of the ridge we could see across to small Tibetan villages hidden in distant valleys that opened up to the peaks in the east. For the first time I could also look down on the layout of the town.

I had come to see Tongren as three quite separate 'villages'. Down on the narrow lower river flat was the pre-1949 town of Longwu Zhen ('Lung-wu chen' on older maps), a single long street running parallel with the river, with shop-houses on either side. Next, on the upper flood plain, were Rongwo Monastery and a Tibetan village of about one hundred and fifty households. Then, just north of the village, there was the newest part of town, 'Tongren proper', set out on a neat grid of five streets, the post-1949 ('post-liberation') administrative and commercial centre, with residences for government employees and Communist Party functionaries.

Seeing the layout of the town I could also begin to understand something of the story of its settlement. The old town consists largely of dark, ramshackle two-storey wooden shop-house residences following the line of the riverbank. Some of the houses backed onto the river itself (for the usual reasons of sanitation) and on the other side of the road most backed onto the steep clay slope that led up to the upper valley floor.

Rongwo Monastery is situated high on the upper valley floor facing eastwards across the river to the opposite mountainside. Towering behind it stands an equally impressive backdrop, White Rock Peak, the steep, grassy slopes of which culminate in a huge granite bluff. Despite the destruction it had suffered, the monastery was still the most imposing site in all of Rebkong, occupying an area one kilometre long and half a kilometre wide, right along the post-Liberation north–south arterial road that traverses the town. From the view we had above it I could see how the monastery was an open space, not enclosed by walls or fences. It was built 'organically' — maze-like as footpaths and alleyways wound around a seemingly chaotic arrangement of chapels, colleges and monks' residences. When walking to the monastery from 'Tongren proper' I found it difficult at first to identify where the houses of the Tibetan villagers ended and those of the monks began.

The Tibetan village Sakyi was also on the upper flood plain and there were a number of rough alleyways to allow vehicle access, but again it was an irregular space fed by a spontaneous array of footpaths. Sakyi means 'middle-land', perhaps it was given this name because it was in the heart of Rebkong territory. Today it has taken on a new sense, a 'middle-ground' between the structures of the old monastic theocracy and a foreign colonial administration. At its northern edge there is a market street, its boundary against the new Chinese town.

The wheel of life

The market street was a clear line of division, there was little reason for the Chinese to cross south, and Sakyi's inhabitants could easily be made to feel like 'foreigners' when they crossed north. Heading north past the market street the streetscape was planned but sterile, and this was what I came to recognise as 'Tongren proper' — Tongren county, a fully fledged state town. It was wholly owned by the Chinese government and its various departments. Tongren's appearance duplicated newly established Chinese towns anywhere in China, from the coastal regions to the inner frontiers. Grey boxes of multi-storey residential apartments squeezed in between the grey, box-like provisions stores, department stores and office buildings, several under-used banks and a New China Bookstore. Lines of stunted trees spoke of forgotten attempts to green the streets, which were wide, considering the small amount of traffic that used them. Yaks strolled through town — safely and at their own pace. Unlike other parts of China, however, here there was no People's Park, or other memorial parks, or even an appropriately named equivalent; although there was a sports ground where a small group of old men played croquet and the army battalion went through their drills. The government offices and the army battalion's compound was nestled out of sight against the foot of the mountain behind Tongren proper.

For me the town often felt like the set of a western. Tibetan women coming down from the mountain valleys were loaded with meagre surpluses on their backs (there are never cart-loads and rarely enough to pack onto a mule). They looked just like the Native American women depicted in those western movies, who came to barter at the colonial trade stores. Groups of Tibetan men aged between fifteen and thirty would carry themselves aggressively out on the main street, with little else to do than make their presence felt. Few carried loads like the women. At night there were violent clashes shared by Han, Tibetan and Salar alike, occurring mostly on or near the edges between their separate parts of town.

Then there were the drifters — largely ethnic Han from neighbouring provinces wandering in and out of town — some shouldering bags of small items that they sold on the sides of the road, others looking for work as carpenters or watch repairers or cobblers. Others were heading south to Zêkog county where they said there was a minor gold rush, and some were looking for work in the lead mine at Tongren. Many were drifting because they had lost out and had nowhere to go — many minority communities in China's frontier lands accept a burden of ethnic Han losers and outcasts, people left out in the process of economic reform and rationalisation taking place in the eastern provinces. The government, however, would like us to think the dependency worked the other way.

We walked along the noiseless, bare mountain ridge, the town below us, until we were just above the provincial offices. The interior decorators decided that the quickest way back to town was not following the ridge and going back down the path we had climbed up, but rather to head straight down the mountainside. From where I was standing the ridge seemed to roll away into thin air. I couldn't see how going straight down wouldn't be a 200-metre dive to the death. There was no need to test me. Ever. I would opt for chicken every time. I tried to persuade the other three that they were making a big mistake, but these young frontiersmen said they'd done it before. 'Go ahead,' I said, 'I'll just head back the way we came.' But they talked me out of that too. We crept down towards one of the gullies that cut into the mountain, our steps gaining pace as the slope dropped away, and soon we were running just to stop falling, each footfall the difference between victory or injury. At the bottom I looked back and wondered how the impossible had become possible. The four of us were elated.

Back at the hotel the interior decorators organised dinner in their four-bed room. Canned meat, a jar of pickled cucumbers, peanuts, instant noodles and four bottles of *baijiu*. In China this was typical makeshift hotel-room fare.

When I woke the next morning I found my shirt beside me in the bed, torn into shreds. Images of some very strange occurrences flashed through my head. I had returned to my room blind drunk. There had been two other guests there, and for some reason I had been outraged. I had shouted at them to 'piss off', and when they didn't go I had begun to sing. Then, possessed, I had begun to perform Tibetan-style prostrations on the floor, shouting out at the top of my voice for the Dalai Lama to return to Tibet. The other guests in the room had tried to placate me, and I had swung a punch at one of them. Then my morning-after flashbacks trailed off ... There was a knock on the door, and a policeman walked in.

'So, you're awake.' In my confusion I stared at him. 'I'm with the police at Zêkog county. Do you remember what you did last night?' He pointed to a nasty graze on his face. 'You hit me when we tried to get you into bed.' For some reason, a mystery for which I will be eternally grateful, he was really excited that he had been there to witness a foreigner make a complete idiot of himself. Something to tell his grandchildren. As more flashbacks began to shoot through my brain I couldn't appreciate the joke. Just my luck, the one night I get stoned out of my mind and there's a cop in my room. I hit a Chinese cop!

'We called the Public Security but by the time they got here you were asleep.' I looked at the ripped shirt on the bed. Great, the local PSB must now have me listed in an incident file. The policeman from Zêkog gave me his address. 'Drop by anytime you're passing through,' he said. What a nice man. Was I not a complete idiot? In twenty-four hours I had been up to the top of the Wheel of Life, and then down again to rock bottom.

I was suddenly glad I was heading back to Chengdu the next morning, but I needed a place to hide my wounds for the day. I went to see Sherab, the keeper of the keys at Rongwo Monastery. Old Akha Yeshe was there too. As I arrived Akha Yeshe was looking at a fly on the wall. '*Nying-ma-jey*,' he announced. I had realised, after getting to know this strange old monk just a little, that this was one of his favourite words. It is perhaps untranslatable in English. 'Deserving of compassion, inspiring compassion, inspiring love, pitiful, lovely, cute' — at different times it could mean any of these. Akha Yeshe of course meant the fly, but in my poor condition *nying-ma-jey* sounded closer to 'wretched', and that summed up my feelings pretty well that morning.

Akha Yeshe then turned to me and asked, 'Thubten,' — this was the name I was known by in the monastery — 'Which has the bigger mind, the fly or you?' I knew I was being asked a subtle question of Buddhist philosophy, but I would have liked to have answered, 'This morning? Definitely the fly.'

But what is mind, and is it something we can quantify? If the mind is infinite, then are all minds equally infinite? There was more to Akha Yeshe, this gentle, mad old monk from Nyenthok, than met the eye.

8
Right livelihood

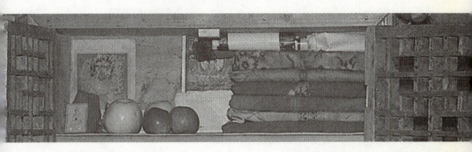

 I returned to Chengdu to prepare for the next stage in my research and was delayed there by protracted visa regulations. In the rigmarole of getting to China in the first place, it had completely escaped my notice that the education authorities in Beijing had only approved my studies for one year. Everyone else on the Australian scholarship got two years, and I hadn't realised that because I was studying Tibetans I was on 'parole'. With the first year nearly up, my work in Rebkong was only just getting started, and for a while it looked like I was going home empty-handed.

After managing the red tape in Chengdu it was a relief to get back to Rebkong again. I went to find Akha Sherab, and I made for the little room by the *dukhang* gate, but he wasn't there. I had begun to think of Sherab as my contact, my own 'keeper of the keys', and for a terrible moment I thought he had disappeared. One of the *akha chungchung* was dispatched to redirect me and I was led around the back of the monastery and through a maze of alleys; after summer Sherab had built a new house. And he was not the only one.

The demolition of the Cultural Revolution-era barracks in the previous year had made prime monastery land available for purchase by individual monks — via their community sponsors, savings and small monastery allowances. The scene was reminiscent of a real estate boom and new houses were springing up everywhere. Sherab's house had only just been completed. This was possible because monks in Rebkong maintain a fairly close relationship with their home villages and families. Although the monks are conscious of a slight incongruity with their status as renunciates, their own villages supply almost all of the monasteries' needs. In the case of Rongwo Gonchen, villages and encampments throughout Rebkong support the monastic community through donations of money, tea, butter, grain and labour. Teams of men and women, relatives and friends — Sherab's personal support group — had come down from his village in the mountains across the valley, and like those that were still building next door, had erected a simple house out of earth and pine. The building technique in Rebkong is one that is found throughout the Tibetan world. This technique is called *gyang* and earth is poured between wooden slats and then rammed hard with pounding sticks. Dotted around the monastery were teams of villagers standing on half-built walls; the sound of lift, pound, lift, pound, kept rhythm with their banter and song.

When I arrived Akha Sherab jumped up from his cushion on the porch of his house and welcomed me with a beaming smile; again he was pleased that I had come back as I said I would. He was also excited about moving into the house his relatives and friends had helped him build since summer, although it was still in a pretty raw state and there was a lot of work to do.

From the alley his gate opened into a walled compound. His small residence was at the north end, facing the gate. It consisted of two separate rooms joined by a space that, once he could afford to bring in carpenters, would become his shrine room. The room on the left was his kitchen, and would also serve as quarters should he bring in a junior monk for training. His own room was on the right. There was not much that differed between the two rooms: the floors were paved with house bricks and both had a heated brick bed surrounded by 'box windows' that fronted south on to the garden. Inside, at this stage of building, both rooms had a rectangular hole in one wall that would soon house a set of cupboards. These would be built at the same time the carpenters built the shrine, but for now the holes were big 'doors' that the local rats used with abandon. The heated brick bed in the kitchen was heated from the stove, and Sherab's bed was heated with smouldering straw stuffed into a hole that led under the bed from the wall under his window.

    I took a seat on his porch that faced south and was open to the sun, while Akha Sherab made tea. In one corner of the garden there was a shed, in the other a toilet pit, and between them by the gate a woodpile for firewood, dung and straw. Sherab pointed out two large building projects on the slope above his house. Work was going ahead on the Dünkhor Dratsang (the Kalachakra College) — the monastery's centre for tantric training associated with the Wheel of Time. The wall surrounding the college was already finished and now Chinese carpenters had been brought in from Gansu province and were working on the wooden frame that would support the college's main hall. 'Frame' is a western architectural concept and is a little misleading here because, like their Chinese counterparts, Tibetan temples were built around columns supporting carved brackets that in turn support the roof and eaves. The precision of the wood fitting was perfect. The pine shafts glowed gold against the blue sky.

A little further up the mountainside, with a view over the entire monastery and across the valley, earth-moving equipment was carving a large space for the rebuilding of the *shimkhang*, or mansion, that would become the home of the Eighth Kalden Gyatso *trülku*. There were many *trülku* lineages associated with Rongwo Gomchen, and most had their main residence, or *labrang*, within their own monasteries, usually one of Rongwo's branch monasteries spread throughout Rebkong. But a number of important *trülku* had 'mansions' within Rongwo Monastery itself. These larger residences were a lot grander than Akha Sherab's, but they shared nothing of the luxury of the old courtyards of well-to-do Chinese in the dynastic period, and paled into insignificance beside the aristocratic estates of Europe. Behind the high walls each had a simple 'villa' that formed a dynamic centre of spiritual activity, a function today most evident in the constant flow of visitors seeking to either contribute to projects supervised by the *lama*, or needing to benefit from the assistance the *lama* might be able to offer. Each had its own office, storage depot, workshops and kitchen-house; in the past they would have had access to an estate of farms and grasslands that allowed it to prosper.

I was coming to realise that Sherab was quite an extraordinary person. We had already discovered that we could communicate quite well; Sherab had more Chinese than I had expected, and we were slowly starting to develop our own unique mixture of Chinese, Tibetan and English. I think most of the monks at Rongwo had concluded that communication with the Chinese in Rebkong, their first and closest 'other', was difficult enough. Westerners were so many times more remote and rare and strange — they could be little more than an occasional curiosity and had nothing to do with the monks' own world. This, of course, was an impression easily broken by those *yinji* who could speak Tibetan with reasonable fluency, but I was not so well prepared. I later learned that Sherab was a natural anthropologist, and had an innate inclination to want to learn about other peoples, their lands, and their ways. I was lucky to have run into him.

I was going to have to rely on Sherab's hospitality, as well as his curiosity, and soon we were using one particular Tibetan phrase almost every day — *namkai ngami* — 'see you tomorrow morning'. One of the most contentious aspects of anthropology is the fact that the researcher is, no matter which way you look at it, using people. I was in Rebkong with my own project, my own ends and my own agenda. Everything I did pointed to my need to complete my research project and obtain my doctorate, the qualification I needed to become a 'real anthropologist'. Something like that colours everything the anthropologist does. In all of your relationships, with almost everyone you meet, there is this one fact existing between you and them. Fieldwork is always dependent on gaining 'entry,' making contacts and forming relationships that allow you to move about, observe, participate and record. None of this happens 'naturally'. We don't just walk into a community and find someone there to snap their fingers and make it all fold out neatly in front of us.

The people anthropologists meet in the field are not aware of these problems or dangers, at least not at first, unless the anthropologist has enough experience to tell them as much as soon as possible. Communicating your aims and a project's consequences (and possible personal consequences) is even more important when you suspect that a meeting with someone might be leading towards a closer relationship, and when they are likely to become a regular informant. Not all informants are going to be friends. Many anthropologists have made it perfectly clear how much they disliked the people they had to hang around with to get the information they wanted. But most are going to become involved in some quite intense friendships.

Thus the idea of friendship should be an important area of inquiry in anthropology in its own right, given its importance in the life of every human being. But there has been surprisingly little work on this topic, and it has not had much impact on the major debates that shape the anthropologist's view of human interaction. Perhaps it is so close to us that it is disqualified from the exotic requirements of ethnography; or perhaps it is too close for comfort, especially given its role at the centre of the participant–observation drama. Eventually this lacuna may be more thoroughly addressed by innovations in 'person-centred anthropology', an approach that has a surprisingly recent history in the discipline.[22]

I would venture to say that in all societies relationships called 'friendships' are established between people who have a mutual need for each other, and friendship itself may even be inconceivable without some 'instrumental' motivation there to maintain it. But I would also risk the generalisation that all societies also have another take on the basis of friendship, and that this points to a simple feeling of mutual understanding — without any reference to other ends. It is what the Chinese poets called 'one who knows my inner resonance', and what we today call 'someone on my wavelength'. And it is likely that it is the presence of these two poles — interest and disinterest, egocentrism and altruism — that allows us to form relationships at all.

Fieldwork friendships embody a fundamental inequality. They demand a lot from both sides, but it is the outsider who initiates contact and sees themself as 'finding' the local informant. Being found — the local informant, the local friend — starts off on the back foot as the 'passive' partner in a power relationship. Over time there might be a certain amount of seesawing and the local friend might use their knowledge to 'have it over' the anthropologist. But in the end it is the anthropologist who is going to leave and take their bundled up harvest of notes and images home, who is going to write about the local informant (anonymously), and who 'cashes in' on what has been brought home. And it is these last steps that drive the relationship from the beginning.

I can't say I went through all of this with Akha Sherab that afternoon at his new house. But I did tell him I was in Rebkong to research the local painting tradition and that I wanted to learn as much as I could about the valley and its people. I also told him I would write a book about it that would allow me to graduate, and hopefully become a university teacher. I also offered to help him paint his house.

'That's up to you,' he said. 'But I think there is a lot to write about, and people outside should know about it.'

'OK,' I said, 'But I think it is going to be interesting to paint your house.'

It was easy at this stage to throw my lot in with Akha Sherab. Sure, it was early days and I had no one else, but here was someone I was communicating with, and with far less effort than I had anticipated. Most reassuring of all was the fact that he immediately grasped what I was up to.

Perhaps surprisingly, by painting his house I began to learn quite a lot. Sherab expected me there for breakfast and we started work early each day. I got to observe his daily schedule and started meeting all the people coming by. I was often left there alone while Akha Sherab went about his daily obligations in the monastery, so I had to try and communicate with any callers in my rudimentary Tibetan. I got an idea of the social world he lived in as a popular monk, counsellor and 'spiritual friend'. I learned about things that I probably should have known already, like an avoidance of the use of black in the monastery's colour scheme because of its association with black arts and heretical sects. I learned about the reservation of bright yellow for the exclusive use of *lamas*, just as it was limited to the imperial court in old China. And then some things I didn't expect, like the association of window lattice designs with particular family traditions around Rebkong. Through Akha Sherab I also heard about rumours and monkish intrigue.

Sherab had to be very careful about not attracting suspicion, and even jealousy. And so did I. Hanging around with a foreigner was politically dangerous for Tibetans in China, but there were social difficulties too. Other monks would wonder, for example, if it meant that Sherab had plans to leave China. They may also have been asking themselves whether they might fall victim to suspicion by association.

At first Sherab would often suggest we walk separately

when we needed to go anywhere. But in the end public knowledge of our association was inevitable, and that always brought the occasional 'spy'. The monastery community, and the Tibetan community as a whole, was rife with all kinds of grudges left over from periods when China's turbulent politics spilled its way into this backwater. That is not to say that everyone got on prior to 1949 — the Amdowa were notorious for their inter-tribal feuding, often going to war over territorial disputes. Joseph Rock mentions coming across several feuds in his articles for *National Geographic* in the late 1920s; and these feuds are a regular theme in the biographies of local Buddhist saints, who were often sought as mediators. But since 1949, and especially after 1959, some families had become tainted with accusations of betrayal and 'collaborationism'. They were semi-ostracised making it easy, and also obvious, for the darker agencies of the Chinese state to recruit people for the purposes of collecting information. Most villages and larger monasteries had a handful of men or women who were thought — or often known — to be working for the 'other side'. In most cases everybody knew who they were. It was probably inevitable that my daily visits to Sherab's place would attract some attention, and we had irregular visits from certain monks who would come by for no apparent reason.

Of course the Public Security Bureau knew I was there, and they knew I was researching the painters of Rebkong. But perhaps they were curious to know why I was painting the house of a nondescript monk when I was supposed to be researching the painters of Rebkong. Perhaps they just wanted to keep a close eye on my activities because I was a foreigner in a Tibetan town. As it was, I learned later that there are two types of spies in monasteries. One group is recruited by the local PSB and the other is recruited directly by agents from Beijing, often without the knowledge of any of the local agencies, who apparently are not trusted. There always has to be more than one level of secret service.

How do I know informers were recruited directly from Beijing? Occasionally Tibetan dissent breaks out in Rebkong. In 1998 at least one news magazine in Hong Kong recorded protests, clashes and arrests in Tongren. Then early in 2001, about a year after my first visit, there was another incident. Posters were printed and pasted up around the monastery accusing the *nangso*, Rebkong's pan-tribal leader, of collaborating with the authorities against 'dangerous elements' in Rebkong's monasteries. The PSB was furious and a series of raids was made in an attempt to round up the 'splittist criminals' who put the posters up. A number of monks were taken in for questioning; stealthy reprisals followed and a number of houses in nearby villages were torched by Tibetan nationalists.

Those targeted by the fires were 'known collaborators', yet the story going around was that they had no connection to the local PSB, and that even the PSB had little, if any, knowledge of their activities. The collaborators, all from the same family, had fled Rebkong the night their houses were torched and they travelled to the safety of Beijing. Their connection to the central government authorities was made clear when agents from Beijing arrived demanding to know why the PSB was so ineffective in protecting national security, and why they had ignored the collaborators' pleas for protection.

Despite the mix of curiosity and suspicion, Sherab continued to have a busy social life. The monks at Rongwo weren't exactly party animals, but there was a lot of visiting between friends. Perhaps it was a special time; there was a cheerfulness about the place that may have resulted from the rebuilding that was taking place. There was also a feeling that life at Rongwo promised to become more or less normal again. As weeks passed I found I was being invited to lots of *donmo*, or parties. Perhaps someone who had just come back from a visit to Lhasa, or even India, was being given a welcome home party, or another monk was holding a big celebration on the completion of his house. Often there were ritual meals at the close of a religious festival, or monks from the same village simply got together to socialise.

The *donmo* at Rongwo Monastery, while sometimes described as banquets or feasts, were more about the get-together than the food. There was in Rebkong, at least among the Tibetans, no concept of fine dining as I knew it. Food was for eating your fill, keeping you active during the day and ensuring a good night's sleep. I was really surprised once to read that cooks from the Amdo region were in high demand in old Lhasa. Perhaps they conned their employers into believing they had picked up a few tricks from their Chinese neighbours. Outside of the monasteries cooking was women's work; while men took care of butchering and the preparation of carcasses they did little else in the preparation of food if there were women present. Yet, because boys are required to help in the kitchen at home, I have never come across a man who could not manage the basics. At Sherab's place his younger brother, Kunzang, had moved in so he could attend the teacher training school next to the monastery. In return it was his duty to do most of the shopping and cooking, and to fetch water from the spring by the river. He slept in the kitchen.

As I gradually grew accustomed to living in Rebkong, food seemed to be on my mind quite a lot, partly because of the plain diet and partly because I was also becoming involved in the everyday running of Sherab's 'household'. Mainly I think it must have been the former — my obsession with food sprang from the fact that Tibetan cooking was so dull, especially compared to the menu I had been getting in Chengdu, one of China's gourmet capitals. In contrast, the pattern of meals in Rebkong was the same almost every day of the year.

Breakfast was a thin porridge (*tuma*) made by adding hot water to *tsamkya*, a flour ground from roasted barley (which is also used to make the *tsampa* for which Tibetans are famous). This was a little like the mash I used to make with hot milk and cereal as a kid, but unfortunately the Tibetan version tasted mostly like sour peanuts. This gruel is washed down with cups of piping hot tea made in the same bowl — a way of 'washing' the bowl — and these helped my stomach settle a little.

At mid-morning we would break for more cups of tea, invariably enjoyed — summer and winter — soaking up sunshine on the porch. The tea that circulated in Amdo was 'brick-tea' (Ch. *zhuancha*, Tib. *janak*, 'black-tea'), which comes, as the name suggests, in large bricks wrapped in brown paper. It is made up of mostly stems and coarse leaves, and is closer in flavour to black tea than green. More often than not, a cup of tea was laced with a dab of yak butter that formed a white film on the top and stopped the heat from escaping. The butter was usually rancid, so rancid that it was in a strange way sweet, and I convinced myself it was a good substitute for sugar and milk. Pieces of bread (*gorey*) were broken with morning tea and dipped in the butter floating on top of the tea — indescribable, burst-of-sunlight bliss! It was very bad manners to bite or gnaw a piece of bread, which should be broken off first in a handy piece and then broken with the fingers into bite-sized morsels. In principle, every last skerrick of food was always eaten, either by licking the bowl or using the index finger of the right hand to wipe it clean. Tea, on the other hand, was repeatedly topped up, and often left unfinished.

We often had bread and tea again at noon, but the main lunchtime fare was *tsampa*. *Tsampa* is made by filling a bowl three-quarters full with roasted barley flour (the same flour used to prepare the breakfast porridge), and then adding a little crumbled dried cheese (*chüra*), butter and perhaps a little sugar. (The dry ingredients are usually stored in a compartmented wooden box, or *bokor*.) These are then mixed, using the middle finger of the right hand, with a little hot water or tea. The mixture is then kneaded inside the bowl with the right hand until it forms a firm dough and no dry flour is visible, and then the mixture is pinched in the palm to form cakes, the finished product. When sugar and butter are added it is called *chyemar* ('red flour') — without them it is *tsamnak*, 'black *tsampa*'. *Tsampa* must be one of the earliest inventions of 'instant food', made as it is from a pre-cooked product (roasted barley flour) that keeps well and is ready to eat at any time, simply by adding hot water.

We enjoyed tea and bread throughout the day, especially when friends dropped by. The common word for bread, *gorey*, could be used to cover a large assortment of breads and pastries. There were steamed breads (*gorey langtsö*), deep-fried pastries (*gorey maro*, 'red bread'), oven-baked sourdough (*gorey chakzang*) and pan-baked sourdough (*gorey bama*). All of these could be found in any household's breadbasket, although pan-baked sourdoughs were probably eaten in the largest amounts. Produced in the form of large 'wheels', these could keep for months in the cool dry climate. Baked breads that had hardened could be broken off for eating with tea, or refreshed — just like my own nanna used to do — by steaming. Steamed breads (*gorey langtsö*) must be eaten when still fresh; these are small buns flavoured with rapeseed oil, mustard (a very mild variety) and caraway seeds, all grown locally.

The evening meal was *thukpa*, or noodle soup. The noodles are made fresh with flour and water, the dough rolled out thin and cut into strips. This usually took Kunzang a good half hour or so of kneading. Then diced mutton and spring onions are fried with salt in a heavy wok, water is added to make the soup, and once it is boiling the noodles are added. A quicker way to make much the same thing is to break bits of dough directly into the simmering soup (Tib. *tenthuk*, Ch. *mianpian*). In most households, especially in the upper valleys, it was more usual to make *thukyang*, an entirely meatless noodle soup made with spring onions and Chinese radish (sometimes known in the West by its Japanese name, *daikon*). On special occasions, such as New Year, a more salubrious noodle called *guthuk*, containing meat and a variety of vegetables, is prepared. Vinegar and chilli powder were always served with noodles to add according to individual taste.

These four foods — porridge, *tsampa*, noodles, and bread — formed the greatest part of the Rebkong Tibetan diet. What is added to them, and how often, depends on how well-off a household is. The regular *donmo* that were part of

Sherab's social circle in the monastery ensured there were often more flavourful meals to be had. On special occasions much the same range of delicacies was prepared by village households — these were by no means luxurious, just labour intensive.

I mainly learned about householder life at the home of Sonam and his family. Sonam taught Tibetan at the local training college for Communist Party cadres, and was one of Sherab's closest friends. They met one summer at some hot springs, where both men were trying to recover from chronic health problems. Sonam, his wife Drölma and their three children lived in Sakyi village, a short walk from where Sherab had built his new house. It was not unusual for monks to enjoy open invitations to visit nearby families who appreciated their company. As the weather got colder we would often find ourselves sitting around the stove at Sonam's; sometimes we watched television, but mostly we talked about local history, life's problems and world affairs. Drölma prepared the food, Sonam and the children helped, and everyone had something to say.

Drölma was immensely proud of her abilities as a *chormo*, an expert home economist. Sakyi was in fact Drölma's home village, while Sonam had grown up in a town on the Yellow River, later attending the Northwest Minorities Institute in Lanzhou. Drölma was also a devoted Buddhist practitioner, and was a regular visitor to a large prayer centre run by the village women. She was very highly regarded by her neighbours, and they came to her for assistance with all kinds of matters. Often when we visited she would be helping a neighbour's daughter with sewing a ceremonial gown in preparation for her participation in village festivals. Many Rebkong men are also expert tailors, and it is men who make all the garments for the *lamas*. There were also monks skilled at sewing robes, and Sherab had added a treadle sewing machine to the possessions he now stored in his new house.

While Sherab and his brother Kunzang could manage many of the specialities of Rebkong, those that came from Drölma's kitchen were in a different league altogether. These included *pensi* — small dumplings filled with mutton, suet and chives, not unlike the northern Chinese *jiaozi*, but never made with pork[23] — these burst and fill your mouth with piping hot juices as you bite into them. There were also *tsöma* — round dumplings filled with meat and shredded radish or cabbage, again similar to the northern Chinese *baozi* — consumed a dozen or more to a guest. *Shandrey* — rice cooked with butter and diced meat — was a winter treat. Another winter treat was *othuk*, a thick broth made with flour, suet and milk (also called *jatang*). All of these were enjoyed by townspeople and monks on a fairly regular basis, but for most farmers they were usually eaten only when there were guests, or on festive occasions. Other common celebration fare were *yitsö* (large knots of fried pretzels and other deep-fried breads); *ye* (sausages);[24] boiled joints of mutton (the hind part, *tsang-ra*, is preferred and the tail fat is the most honoured part of all); and much time and delight may be taken over the consumption of an entire sheep's head. Under Sherab's expert instruction I learned how to eat the eyes, the lips and even the skin from under the bridge of the mouth — skills I have since forgotten.

Sherab's kitchen was occasionally supplemented by three foods that came down from the steppe: yak meat, butter, and *tël*. In the winter months there was usually a side or quarter of yak someone had donated drying in Sherab's shed. Sherab was from a farming village, but his mother, like many others, was fond of heading up to the alpine meadows to join her nomad cousins. Most of Sherab's butter arrived in large sheep-stomach bags that she brought down with her. Sometimes she would also bring *tël*, a food made only on the grasslands, produced by nomads as 'road food' (*lamdro*). Like *tsampa*, *tël* could be carried in the pouch (*amdrak*) of a sheepskin coat, the voluminous Tibetan *chuba*, where it was handy when roaming away from home. It was made from an uncooked and highly nutritious mixture of melted butter, dried cheese, sugar and roasted barley flour packed into large enamel or wooden basins to set. A mouthful of *tël* was incredibly rich. It tasted to me like a cross between chocolate and paté, two foods I like very much, but not necessarily in combination. It was a rare and prized treat for the valley dwellers. The highland meadows also supplied farmers with additional supplies of milk, cheese, yoghurt (*sho*) and buttermilk (*dara*). The milk given just after calving, called *dri*, was highly prized for its richness. In summer Sonam and Drölma would served us hot milk with honey and crushed walnuts.

The most highly prized food from the steppe is a tiny sweet potato-like tuber known as *droma*, growing no larger than the little finger and harvested in early autumn or early spring. Restorative and highly nutritious, it was also one of the few sources of sugar, apart from honey, that was native to Rebkong. *Drondrey*, a dish of *droma* steamed with rice, served hot with butter and sugar, was another of the richer offerings I enjoyed as part of Rebkong hospitality. It was only ever served on special religious occasions.

Sherab and his brother occasionally invited me to religious events in their home village of Gyelwo Gang. This was a small upland village of about one hundred and twenty households, about an hour and a half of steep walking from Tongren. Many of the male villagers at Gyelwo Gang were *ngakpa* — or yogins practising Buddhism according to the Nyingma tradition. Their temple was built on a steep spur and stood like a sentinel above the deep, vast valley of the Chutsang River that ran below. Looking up the valley from the village temple to the southeast you could see the peak of one of Rebkong's most imposing mountain gods, Amye Taglung, or Ancestor Tiger Valley. Looking west, back across the Guchu Valley and beyond in the far distance was a *mandala* of snow-capped peaks that gathered around the most senior of all Rebkong's mountain guardians: Amye Chakyung, or Ancestor Garuda (4,767 metres).

Sherab's brother Kunzang once told me a story about Ancestor Garuda and Ancestor Tiger Valley. They were once good friends but had a falling out. To one side of Ancestor Tiger Valley there is a smaller peak, his 'little-woman' Mother Scree (Ama Jomo). Tiger Valley once caught Mother Scree and Ancestor Garuda making eyes at each other (or even something more serious), and he is said to be pushing her back out of sight. For his part, in a huff, Ancestor Garuda has his head twisted permanently westward so he doesn't have to face the anger in his friend. Other villages might have different stories, but this one seems to sum up the tension around finding a mate in Gyelwo Gang and elsewhere. These were tensions that Kunzang himself, already in his mid-twenties, was caught up in.

In his village the roofs of most of the houses adjoin those of other families, and it is almost possible to walk 'in the air' from one side of the village to the other. At night the ladder that gives access to the roof is taken down, preventing the arrival of unwanted trespassers. But there are some young men who, smitten with ardour or with a few drinks under their belts, are adventurous enough to attempt to get down without a ladder. Kunzang apparently tried this once, but he added one flourish too many and somersaulted head-first into the young lady's garden. He broke his collarbone and, even worse, as he howled in pain, he woke up half the village. Needless to say, the girl never wanted to set eyes on him again, and in shame at losing face so dramatically among his neighbours Kunzang had to be restrained from jumping into the gully at the mouth of the Chutsang River.

Kunzang was forever accident prone and a bit dull. He lost the family's best horse by taking it over a ravine during a race. He was lucky to even be alive. His main problem was that he tried too hard, and the ever-judging eye of his older brothers didn't help. There were other strands to the story too: he and Sherab were only half-brothers.

Sherab's father was well liked in Gyelwo Gang for his devotion to the *ngakpa* (householder yogin) tradition and the work that he did for their temple. He was very clear-headed, a skilful handyman, highly literate, and very well read in the fundamentals and *tantras* of the Nyingma tradition. After Sherab's parents separated when he was two his mother married another man in Gyelwo Gang, a peasant who was mostly focused on scratching a living from his land. This was Kunzang's father. His household was one of the least overtly religious in the village, and did not even have a shrine room. He could read neither Tibetan nor Chinese.

As far as I could tell Sherab felt some shame about what was, for him, his mother's disappointing second marriage.

She was from a small village nearer to Tongren and was, like his own father, highly literate in Tibetan, and had even worked as a bookkeeper with the Chinese administration. She had, for her own reasons, decided to return to Gyelwo Gang and live a quiet, hardworking village life. In recent years, as her sons took over the management of their farm, she has spent much of the year living with the *drokpa* (nomadic pastoralists) on the high grasslands between Rebkong and Labrang.

Kunzang struggled with his teacher training, although from what I could gather it was not very demanding. Apart from the political studies class, he was simply consolidating what he had learned in primary school, making sure he could pass it on to the next generation. I think he enjoyed the chores at his brother's house as it was good, uncomplicated hard work like that at home. What Sherab objected to was his inability to do anything much more than simply follow instructions. From what I could see, it may have been this quality that got him over the line and into teachers college. Kunzang was honest, used to hardship and utterly loyal — and these were practical, political necessities for his eventual role serving the government in a cold, windswept hamlet with a broken-down school that could barely pay for its chalk. And the rest of the family were clearly proud of him. They understood that his most embarrassing mistakes were products of his overenthusiasm; his heart was in the right place, but not always his head.

Like so many brothers everywhere, Sherab and Kunzang were each in their way destined to be the antithesis of each other. Akha Sherab would try anything. He had been married, had a son, had made a success of farming, and had won many friends in his village. Then, when Rongwo Monastery reopened, it did not take long for him to decide to enter a monk's life of service. As I watched him from day to day I realised how well he embodied the six transcendent perfections of the Mahayana tradition: generosity, discipline, patience, vigour, concentration and wisdom.

Sherab welcomed everyone to his house with a smile and gave much of his time and hospitality. Old Akha Yeshe, who could be a real nuisance, was visiting us almost every day and Sherab, unlike others, never turned him away. Beggars and the monastery dogs all got something at Sherab's door. For a while we were visited every day by a sick and mangy bitch about to have pups that came by to have a meal and rest in the sunshine of Sherab's struggling garden. This was Sherab's practice of generosity.

Wherever we walked Sherab would clear glass and rocks off the street. He didn't hang around watching TV, play pool or go to the movies at a time when the video parlours near the market got most of their income from Rongwo's monks. Sherab felt a deep sense of obligation to use any resource well, be it firewood or money, fully aware that his livelihood was dependent on others. He treated men and women with equal politeness. This was Sherab's practice of discipline.

He had great hopes for the revival of monastic service in the Rebkong community, but he also knew that this could only be achieved if he and others prepared themselves over time. Service was not about grand projects, but just putting others before yourself. As the great teacher Patrul Rinpoche advised:

Always take the lowest place. Wear simple clothes. Help other beings as much as you can. In everything you do, simply work at developing love and compassion until they have become a fundamental part of you. That will serve the purpose, even if you don't practise the more overt Dharma of prayers, virtuous activities, altruistic works and so on.[25]

I had heard how Sherab had cared unfailingly for one of his teachers, who old age had taken over — feeding, washing and walking him every day for three years. Accepting that the world is not designed with our own hopes in mind, he was never pushy. And despite the difficulties he sometimes had with Kunzang, he rarely raised his voice and never sent his brother away. Cherishing the happiness of others he listened carefully to his fellow villagers when they came to him with their complaints. This was Sherab's practice of patience.

It is rare to find an Amdowa happy doing nothing, although as far as Sherab was concerned there were lots of villagers who were misguided and needed to find more meaningful motivation than simply their own comfort. In fact he blamed the poverty of Rebkong on the pettiness of most of the peasants, including some of their sons in the monastery. He worked on his new house fearlessly. After the painting we started to put glass in the windows. Glass, to be fair, was not a traditional feature of Tibetan architecture. Having only seen it done a couple of times before, Sherab was convinced he could do it himself. After a few practice runs with the glass-cutter he moved on to cutting panes. Zzzup, crack, tinkle. Oh well, try again. Zzzup, crack, tinkle. Oh dear, perhaps the cutter was worn out. I went to the hardware store and came back with a new one. Zzzup, crack, tinkle. 'Well, there seems to be more to this than meets the eye,' Sherab said as we stood on a floor covered in shards of window glass. Eventually we got there, although the windows in his house are now full of places where the glass doesn't quite join. I chickened out though when it came to connecting the electricity — I had burnt my hand once in my Shenyang days, and once was enough. Sherab's confidence and energy never flagged. This was his practice of vigour.

Well aware of his own deficiencies Sherab had little time for gossip and rumour. Living in a monastery close to a bustling town he managed to remain free from distractions. Disillusioned with *samsara*, he focused his life upon the task of establishing a meaningful foundation for future lives. When I first got to know Sherab I wondered why he didn't ever meditate; he couldn't have, he was too busy. I also wondered why he was so busy investing in his house; I didn't need to have a house of my own, why was it so important to all these monks? But I think he understood that a simple residence was a place of refuge from the seeds of bewilderment. Simply opening the gate and walking into a monk's garden could clear the mind, or at least quieten it a little. This was his practice of concentration.

The practice of wisdom for Sherab meant applying his body and mind to tasks within his capacity. Not everyone has access to enlightened teachers, and it is not every monk who is in a position to become a learned scholar or mystic. But if they wish, anyone can begin to develop *bodhicitta*, the mind of enlightenment, just on hearing it explained. Being mindful of the danger of cherishing oneself is the best or even, as many have said, the *only* way to find 'freedom beyond all extremes'. The Tibetan saint Patrul Rinpoche says, 'Worldly preoccupations never end until the moment we die.

But they end when we drop them — such is their nature.'[26] If Sherab had remained in the village he might have become, like Kunzang's other brothers, bored with village life and inclined to run into trouble with the police.

There was something about Akha Sherab's approach to life that was infectious. I was becoming more and more bound up in his life at the monastery, and spending less and less time, I thought, on my research. My daily visits to the monastery were starting to challenge my own understanding of what I was doing.

I once heard that one of the most dangerous things anyone could do in the Buddhist world was 'to make religion an object of academic study' — that is, to get involved in obscure debates about religious topics without actually entering upon the training of a *bodhisattva* — one who is committed to achieving enlightenment for the benefit of all sentient being. I wasn't studying religion, and I trusted that the pursuit of knowledge was a worthwhile thing in itself, but there was something about that phrase that kept nagging at me. Like commerce, agriculture and industry, academia is inclined to involve us in all kinds of projects and distractions, what the Tibetan teachers call the 'eight worldly concerns' — pursuit of gain, pleasure, fame and praise, and avoidance of their opposites. Like most people, the eight worldly concerns were the whole basis of my world, both what I had left behind in Australia and what I carried in my heart. In Rebkong I had entered a very different world. Sharing my days with Akha Sherab, Akha Yeshe and Kunzang, I couldn't help but begin to question my own motivation.

9
Painting magic

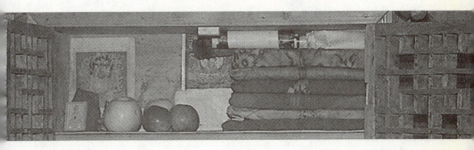

One morning Sherab and I sat in the sunshine on his porch, talking and supping tea. Sherab seemed to hesitate for a moment, and then he asked, as if it had been on his mind for some time, 'Do the Chinese books you have been reading say the Rebkong painters are important people?'

It was clearly an important question. 'Yes, I think they do,' I answered. 'The books say that the painters are very famous, that Rebkong painters are famous throughout the Tibetan Buddhist world. Why? Is that wrong?'

'In our way of thinking, it isn't very good,' was his answer. 'It is embarrassing for us to hear such things about Rebkong. Painters are clever, but in the end they are ordinary people and they shouldn't make Rebkong famous. Rebkong has produced so many great teachers, and they have written many books on Buddhist philosophy. It would be much better if the outside world knew of their fame. In Rebkong we are proud of people like Kaldan Gyatso and Shabkar, great *lamas* who teach enlightenment. Painters don't teach enlightenment. I don't think the Chinese are interested in enlightenment.'

There is no shortage of exceptionally talented painters and sculptors recorded in Tibetan history, and it is clear that many of them were supported by great religious teachers. They are honoured in the *lama*'s biographies, as well as in individual monastery histories. Some feats of artistic creation have even been celebrated in commemorative works composed shortly after their completion. Yet, in the main, Tibetan artists belonged to something akin to a family business, 'artisans who learned their craft from their fathers'.[27] From the point of view of a monk like Sherab, and quite a few ordinary folk too, artists did not deserve the attention they had been getting of late; or at least, any attention they did receive should not be at the expense of true religious goals.

As a 'field' (*thang*) in which enlightened activity is present, a Tibetan painting has value and must be cared for appropriately, but such a function cannot fully begin to occur until it is consecrated. The artist, unless he is a monk, has very little to do with this final step in the completion of a painting or sculpture. And while it would be considered an added blessing to have a great *lama* consecrate a work of art, each consecration, so long as the ceremony was conducted properly, was much the same as another. From a purely religious point of view, once it was consecrated, a painting could not be criticised. In Tibet it didn't make too much sense to evaluate or rank works of art, since after consecration each was completely equal; each work *was* the deity that had been invited to reside within it.

Given my own reflections on my motivation I took Sherab's question as a gentle nudge. I thought I could just walk in and find someone to teach me to paint, but now I was encouraged to think carefully about what I was doing in Rebkong. There was a good chance my work was leading me down the same path as the Chinese authors 'not interested in enlightenment'. Art was important, and the attention it attracted to Rebkong was appreciated, but in the end it really missed the point. I began to realise, as Sherab probably did, that the Chinese focus on art was a way of redefining Rebkong. It was a way of reshaping Tibetan culture in a way that fitted in better with the objectives of the 'four modernisations'. It was also a distraction from the great desecration of Tibetan religious sites that had taken place. Now that the Chinese had stopped destroying monasteries, art could be sold to tourists as part of the 'package' of China's Tibet. That way everyone would be satisfied. Foreigners visiting Tibet (and Chinese for that matter) were blind to its textual heritage, the real market was in colourful images. And art could be promoted, cynically, as a sign that a living tradition continued. It was not a very satisfying scenario from Sherab's point of view.

Perhaps, subtly, Sherab was helping me to take a broader view. I had heard of Westerners who had found painting teachers among the Tibetan refugees in India, as well as among the Sherpas in Nepal. Some had put in decades of training, and some were even responsible for the luminous illustrations I had seen in books on Tibetan Buddhism. When I had first headed off to Rebkong I had been partly motivated by the fantasy of emulating them. But China was a very different place from India or Nepal. After several visits to Rebkong it had become clear just how unlikely the prospect of studying under one of the better known painters was. They were very busy people with their own workshops to run, and passing on their tradition was not something they did lightly. In my scheming I had been hoping that one or two might be attracted by the possibility of international recognition, or opportunities to exhibit overseas, but that was my fantasy. The leading painters already had fine reputations in Xining, Lhasa and Beijing. And besides, there was a good chance that an association with a nosy foreigner might mean more trouble than good, at least politically speaking.

I had resigned myself to the fact that Shawo Tshering was out of reach. Whenever I went to see him he was always busy with visitors or helping with ceremonies at the monastery. And then there was his workshop and apprentices. Since I had first met him he had started a business in Xining making fired ceramic statues of buddhas, *bodhisattvas* and the protectors of religion. His factory also produced a line of gift items: small ceramic 'masks' of fang-displaying *dakinis* (female angels of enlightenment) and bulging-eyed wrathful deities, Tibetan tea bowls, decorated plates and mugs. These were less kitsch than they might sound. His outlet in Xining also traded in painted and embroidered *thangkas* for the tourist market. And his daughter was running a small outlet too, around the corner from my hotel in Tongren; but Tongren was too small, the tourists too few, and that part of the venture soon folded.

Additionally, Shawo Tshering had been earning fame as something of a national treasure. In 1979 he had been chosen to serve as a delegate at the National Committee of Artists and Craftsmen, and in 1984 he had sat on the Ministry of Light Industry's Third National Representative Assembly of Artists and Craftsmen, where he had been awarded the title 'National Master Craft Artist'. I wasn't sure what any of these accolades really meant; they sounded a little to industrial for a man who so well captured the weightless light of Buddhist icons. But what I was learning about Shawo Tshering helped me to arrive at a vision of what I could achieve in Rebkong — how I could shift focus from the technical features of the painting tradition and learn more about what had been happening to Rebkong's artists in the decades since Liberation. How did someone remain a Buddhist painter under a socialist regime?

For Shawo Tshering things hadn't always gone so well. Like many other monks in Rebkong he was forced to leave monastic life in 1958. In that year, the Chinese government was angered by Tibetan resistance to communalisation and moved to eradicate any sign of the 'old society', especially religion. As the army progressed through the valley the monasteries at Sengeshong were vandalised and sealed up. Some monastery buildings were converted to grain stores and animal enclosures, others were pulled down or burned. The most influential Tibetan tribal and religious leaders, many of whom had done their best to work with the government, became victims of the 'Intensified Program to Suppress Revolt'. Many were killed, and others were jailed.

Shawo Tshering, then thirty-six, was sent for 're-education' at the Huangnan People's Commune School, where, along with political indoctrination, he was introduced to oil painting and Chinese watercolour. This was during the period known as the 'Three Red Flags Movement' — when every form of literature and art was required to depict the flag-bearers of the revolution: workers, soldiers and peasants. Shawo Tshering even won prizes, although he never came higher than second, probably because of the fact that, as he now jokes, all his faces came out looking gentle and Buddha-like.

The re-education at the People's Commune School lasted only two years, and Shawo Tshering was soon left without a livelihood. The making of Buddhist art was prohibited at the time, and he was neither used to nor skilled at farm work or other trades. He had been a monk from the age of seven. Then, for a brief period, in 1961, Rongwo Monastery was given approval to re-open. He went there to serve as an assistant in the kitchen and even had ideas of re-entering monastic life. Then the monastery was closed again.

In 1962 he married a girl in his own village; life settled down and they started a family. Quietly, he started to paint again. Then, in 1966, the political madness of the Great Proletarian Cultural Revolution flooded up the Guchu Valley and quickly turned everything upside down. Again things went badly for Shawo Tshering. Traditional forms of art, especially Buddhist art, were attacked under the 'Smash the Four Olds' campaign — really a call for the desecration of old ideas, old culture, old customs and old habits. What was left of the monasteries was vandalised yet again. The Rebkong painters, at least those who had dared to resume their tradition, were attacked as 'ox demons and serpent gods'. Their paintings, brushes, stretchers and pigments were thrown on bonfires and villagers, powerless to act, were forced to watch as they burned. During one 'meeting' Shawo Tshering was dragged through the street wearing the pointed black dunce's cap of a 'bad element'. A *thangka* was suspended from his neck as an example of 'black painting'. As one local government publication put it, the Cultural Revolution was a period when, without exception, elements of traditional ethnic cultures were labelled 'black merchandise', and Tibetan cultural leaders were attacked as purveyors of 'feudalism, capitalism and revisionism',[28] terms that sounded very strange to a Tibetan.

After December 1978, when Deng Xiaoping had finally

settled his score with the Gang of Four and achieved clear command of the Chinese Communist Party, the CCP began to officially redress the injustices perpetrated in the years of the Cultural Revolution. Since Deng himself had been a victim, this was only to be expected, and many who had been attacked during the period were awarded full exonerations. Shawo Tshering's star began to rise again. His appointment to the National Committee of Artists and Craftsmen in 1979 was part of a nationwide process of redressing the wrongs of revolutionary excess.

There is no doubt that Shawo Tshering stands out among the painters of Rebkong because of his consummate skill as an artist. To watch him paint is like magic: the lines appear beneath his brush with such ease it is almost as if they were already there. Under his hand each fine stroke is a single fluid movement. Shawo Tshering was brilliant, but there were other great Rebkong *lhabzo* able to render the worlds of buddhas and *bodhisattvas* with just the same ease. In the paranoid political air of China little happened by accident, and I began to wonder why he was the one who had made it into all the articles I had uncovered.

An important part of the Shawo Tshering story began in 1937, when he travelled with his uncle in a party of monk-painters to Kumbum. They had been engaged to help work on some large-scale renovations and it must have been an exciting time. That very same year the monastery became a base for the search party that had travelled from Lhasa to find the incarnation of the Fourteenth Dalai Lama. For a young artist it was an excellent opportunity to learn about

▲ Butter sculpture: Samantabhadra, 'Offering of the Five Senses' and Jambhala.
◀ Akha Yeshe salvaging the *thangka* I began, in the shade of Akha Sherab's verandah.

▲ Attaching gold leaf to the completed butter sculpture, the 'Offering of the Fifteenth Day'.
▼ The butter-sculptor's palettes, with old work in the background.

▲ Women ready to attend a wedding at Gyelwo Mentshang.
▼ Children at a wedding in the village of Gyelwo Mentshang.

▲ Three *chorten* at Shohong near the monastery of the great Tibetan saint Shabkar.
▼ Me resting with travelling companions, winter, Shohong.

the role of art in a large monastic complex, to swap notes with other painters, and even to show off a little. Shawo Tshering assisted his uncle with the painting of many important *thangkas* and murals. He was also training his hand ornamenting the beams, ceilings and walls of Kumbum's maze of chapels.

At the same moment, behind the scenes, the warlord Ma Bufang was busy frustrating the search for the Dalai Lama, delaying the departure of the boy-candidate, Lhamo Dondrub. Ma refused to guarantee the party safe passage for Lhasa until an exorbitant ransom was handed over, and once that was paid he demanded a second ransom, more than double the first.

Ma Bufang treated Kumbum — like everything else in Qinghai — as his private estate. His meetings with the search party were treated like a picnic, and he often brought along a party of 'friends' from among Xining's gentry. The warlord general, then Governor of Qinghai, also fancied himself as something of a connoisseur and supporter of the arts. The outbreak of war with the Japanese in 1937 offered him the opportunity to indulge his fancy, as Xining became a temporary home for a number from China's illustrious art circles, including the playwright Lao She and the director and actor Zheng Junli.[29]

Among those relocated to the northwest also came one of China's greatest painters of the twentieth century, Zhang Daqian (1899–1983). Early in 1942, with the help of Ma Bufang, Zhang was able to arrange for five *'lama* painters' to join him on his wartime project — making accurate copies of the ancient Buddhist murals in the 'Cave of a Thousand Buddhas' at Dunhuang. The nineteen-year-old Shawo Tshering was one of the monks sent by General Ma.

The Chinese painter relied on the young Tibetan monks for the preparation of pigments, and for brushes and other materials that were in short supply during the war. Despite an enormous language gap they were also able to give him advice on the iconography. Shawo Tshering and the other young Tibetan painters had a unique opportunity to explore some of the earliest works of Buddhist art, early styles of painting that may even have influenced their own tradition. They were also exposed to the ideas and techniques of one of the most progressive and innovative Chinese painters of their time.

Zhang Daqian was then only in his early forties, but his fame as a painter was such that he not only had wealth — he also had good connections and considerable personal influence. The plan to copy the Dunhuang murals, an enormous task, was motivated by patriotic sentiment, and it wasn't too difficult for Zhang to capture the imagination of supporters throughout the country. It was also a way of ignoring the realities of China's descent into civil war. While war raged about them Zhang and his team of monk-painters set up camp on an almost regimental basis, with cooks, supply trucks and a daily schedule setting up the scaffolding, grids, tracing paper and traditional Tibetan materials. They also attracted the envy and suspicion of the local Hui and Chinese gentries, and before the job was over Zhang Daqian was being accused of damaging the murals, and even of slicing off some of the rock carvings — crimes for which he was later cleared. Paradoxically, Zhang was also plagued by local worthies dropping in on the camp in the hope of obtaining one of his valuable Chinese paintings.

After a year of working at the end of a sticky desert road Zhang suddenly seemed to lose interest. Perhaps he had copied as many of the best examples as he felt he needed, perhaps the Tibetan painters had had enough and wanted to go home. So Zhang returned to Sichuan where he had four wives and sixteen children, but he had developed a fascination for things Tibetan and was soon off on painting trips to the nearby ethnically Tibetan province of Xikang. His adventures in Xikang may have even stimulated the later fad among Chinese painters for Tibetan exotica. Even with the civil war raging, Zhang was remarkably free to travel — holding exhibitions in Chengdu, Chongqing, Shanghai and Hong Kong. The Dunhuang paintings created enormous interest, a glimmering record of ancient China's 'Golden Age' appearing right at the moment of his nation's modern crisis. As the certainty of communist victory grew, Zhang managed to fly to Hong Kong and then Taiwan, making his home at various times in Argentina, Brazil and California, and eventually returning to spend his last years in Taiwan.

The Dunhuang adventure ended, Shawo Tshering returned home to Sengeshong, and after about two years further training under his uncle he was allowed to strike out on his own. Soon afterwards, this time accompanied by his own student, he set out on a painting adventure that would take him to some of the most important Tibetan cultural sites of Tibet: Labrang in Gansu, Kantze and Ngawa in Sichuan, Mongolia, and then to the holy city of Lhasa. Following a tradition established by many Tibetan artists before them, the two painters wandered from place to place, living off the earnings from the painting they did for monasteries along their way. In 1951, not quite thirty, Shawo Tshering travelled even further from home, making an excursion to India to visit the Ajanta Caves, Calcutta and Benares. Zhang Daqian may have been in India at the same time, but it is not clear if they met. Again, as at Dunhuang, the young Tibetan painter was able to soak up the secrets of ancient Buddhist artworks.

His association with Zhang Daqian does not seem to have done Shawo Tshering any harm. For the government departments in Xining it is an important link that makes him all that more suitable for writing up in contemporary Chinese history. Any positive co-operation between Chinese and Tibetans needs to be milked for what it is worth. The frescoes at Dunhuang are a convenient way of linking the Chinese and Tibetan traditions of Buddhist art; going back as far as 336, they can be claimed as a source for both, and that strengthens the unity of the 'Motherland'. All of these qualities surrounding this famous *lhabzo* help contribute, in a small but not insignificant way, to China's self-image as a unified multi-ethnic state. They also keep him very busy. Apart from acting as an advisor to the Rebkong Art Gallery he is a member of three or four prefecture and provincial 'consultative committees'. And in a remarkable balancing act he remains a wonderful painter.

Still harbouring a little of my original 'why not become a painter' fantasy, I wondered if I needed to find someone less stretched for time. But time was running out. Sick with frustration I retired to Sherab's porch to sip tea and think. I read the book I had brought along – Joseph Conrad's *Lord Jim* – the nineteenth-century tale of a promising young man who, unable to live with himself after abandoning his sinking ship at sea, tries to escape his guilt by beginning life anew on a jungle island. It had been one of the more promising titles available among the English novels at the New China Bookshop in Chengdu, but it was by far the worst book I could have taken with me at this point.

I started to see parallels between my own and Jim's failures that made me feel ill. Nothing in the field seemed to be going as it should. I wasn't keeping my diary up to date, and that seemed to be related to a total absence of planning. I was frustrated with Sherab, who seemed to have his own plans for me every day. I had even convinced myself it was all the running around I was doing for him that was preventing me from getting interviews and expanding my circle of contacts. He seemed to be jealous of the contact I had with anyone outside his own circle. There was no way out, as fate continued on its sickening course. What was I going to do when I got home without any data? Without a doctorate, what future could I have? What were my head of department and supervisor going to say?

Perhaps I had been a little too ambitious. I had known virtually nothing about Rebkong before arriving — few outside China knew anything. In the late 1980s there were only half a dozen books in Western languages where you might find Rebkong mentioned, and usually it was a bare sentence or two — it was only later that I found out there was a small bunch of young anthropologists converging on this part of Amdo at the same time.

I also began to think about another problem. How 'scientific' was it to go looking for what I thought Tibetan culture should be? I had imagined a Tibetan monastery to be a quiet refuge of well-disciplined men devoted to the pursuit of spiritual goals. I was no longer sure about what I meant by discipline, or, for that matter, spiritual goals. Deep down I suspected I was too shy to do fieldwork. Or was I too afraid of failure to take the steps I needed to take? Telling myself I was reluctant to impose my research agenda on the lives of the people who surrounded me was, probably, just a crafty excuse.

One day I decided I was going to paint a temple scroll myself. I took out a preliminary sketch I had made on paper of the Lord of Wisdom, Manjushri. I set up all the materials on the porch of Sherab's house and started putting together the traditional frame in which the canvas would be suspended. As you might imagine, it was a complete mess. The frame I was binding together was made from rough sticks from Sherab's woodpile. The twine I was using kept snapping as I tightened the corners. And the whole assembly of wood and string wobbled like an old monk's knees. I kept trying, untying twine and tying it again, but with each rebuilding my project seemed more hopeless than the last.

I was just about ready to throw the thing across the yard. Then, as he did most days, Akha Yeshe arrived at Sherab's place. He walked up to where I was on the porch, grabbed the frame out of my hands and started tearing it all apart. It was so sudden and violent I had to jump out of the way. But in the same moment I immediately understood that it was not malicious. Akha Yeshe was acting so just to let me know how much of a stuff-up I had made. He was also letting me know he had decided to take over.

When I had first met Akha Yeshe a year earlier he had been painting Akha Sherab's small reading table, but Sherab had led me to believe that he had refused to paint *thangkas* after the Cultural Revolution. Had I prodded him into a sudden rethink? What had been under my nose the whole time?

The next day one of the painters from the Rebkong Art

Gallery loaned me a prefabricated oil painting stretcher he had adopted for Tibetan painting. At first Akha Yeshe didn't quite know what to do with it, and it took us a long time to work out how to stitch the unprimed canvas inside the frame so it could be used in the traditional Tibetan way. Over the next few days we applied the gesso, smoothing it repeatedly with the shiny surface of a piece of broken china. In my haste, and wanting to have a role in the production of 'my' *thangka*, I got the steps confused, and we almost had to start all over again.

While we waited for the applications of gesso to dry, Akha Yeshe taught me how do draw. First I learned to prepare the *samdra*, a small rectangular writing slate made of wood. It was like a little blackboard, as long and as wide as my forearm — about the same size as a page from a traditional unbound Tibetan book. To prepare it a small amount of butter was smeared evenly over its black face, and then white flour was dusted over the butter. A dusty whiteboard rather than a blackboard, a pin-like wooden stylus was applied to its surface, making black lines appear through the flour. Akha Yeshe was the only person I knew who had one of these.

In the past most monks would have used a *samdra* when they learned to write, and young artists would have used them for their drawing lessons. In recent times the biro and cheap paper notepads had taken over. Akha Yeshe, I was learning, did not like any form of waste. The *samdra* was eminently reusable, and never created piles of unwanted rubbish. It also fitted comfortably in the hand, was firm under the pen, and it could be used sitting cross-legged anywhere. While I watched, Akha Yeshe would draw an example of a deity in one corner of the board and hand it to me, and I would make several copies following exactly the sequence he had shown me.

Akha Yeshe also taught me how to make the charcoal we would use for drawing the preliminary outlines. Unlike pencils, sticks of charcoal did not puncture or score the canvas. Akha Yeshe found suitable sticks and bound them up in a scrap of red cloth from one of Sherab's old robes. The little packet was then given a good soaking in water before being heated in a pile of hot coals. He was a little out of practice, but we got a couple of useful pieces out of it. All of these procedures were really just lessons for my benefit.

Even though I now spent a lot of time with Akha Yeshe I was unable to obtain many of the 'usual' details of his life. For most of his fellow monks he was simply a *nyönba*, or madman, but the more I came to know about him the more I was convinced that he was a living example of the *nyönba* as 'holy madman'. He had no possessions to speak of, sometimes disappeared from view for weeks on end, and would often be seen with a trail of children — including boys and girls from Muslim families — all hoping to eat some of the sweets he had taken from the monastery shrines.

Akha Yeshe's behaviour could be interpreted as evidence for his rejection of ordinary worldly concerns and his transcendence of dualities, particularly those of self and other, but also form and emptiness, and especially 'yours' and 'mine'. The latter he demonstrated most in his love for flowers, which he might pick from any household garden, whether invited or not. Nor did he display concern for ordinary comforts, often choosing not to wear shoes and eating whatever he could scratch together. He combined absolute compassion with total unpredictability. Having insights into reality that others do not have, the behaviour of *nyönbas* is interpreted as being different to ordinary madness, although not everyone always approves of their behaviour. It seems the job of a *nyönba* is to annoy those who take themselves too seriously.

Akha Yeshe was born at Nyenthok in the late 1930s. When he was seven years old he entered Nyenthok Gar and was taken under the wing of his mother's brother, who was an accomplished painter. His brother's family still reside in their Nyenthok home. Like other Monguor in Rebkong his family speak both their own language and Tibetan, and some Chinese.

Akha Yeshe travelled with his uncle to the great monastic university of Labrang when he was thirteen years old. It is possible to walk from Rebkong to Labrang, via the alpine grasslands east of Gyelwo Gang, in about three days. There he continued to learn painting as well as study the usual monastic curriculum. He also gained something of a reputation for his kind-heartedness, devotion and commitment to a true monastic lifestyle — and he is still fondly remembered there.

Akha Yeshe's rash behaviour sometimes stems from his different point of view on life, and sometimes from his bad temper. And sometimes it got him into trouble. He has twice attacked Muslim women in the vicinity of the monastery. One was very poor and lived by selling the milk of her only cow. Akha Yeshe attacked her for selling it inside the monastery confines — and accidentally broke her arm. After that she lived by collecting scraps of meat from butchers and begging from stallholders. While peddlers and hawkers are not permitted in the monastery, Akha Yeshe's actions are still remembered by others as being too extreme, and the woman's continued suffering is a point of some shame. On the other occasion he attacked a woman selling sheepskins on the kerbside beside the monastery, pushing her into a ditch. Again it was something neither he nor the monastery is particularly proud of.

In 1983 he had an argument with a Han-Chinese woman selling *guazi* (Chinese for sunflower or melon seeds roasted and eaten as a snack) on the kerbside in Tongren. He is in the habit of giving the first amount of money he is able to pull from inside his robe, sometimes giving less and sometimes more than what is due. The woman selling *guazi* took offence when he refused to meet the appropriate price. After an argument he kicked the small table, sending everything flying onto the street. This time Public Security pursued the matter and he was locked up for five days. Apparently he has spent longer periods in prison, but the police have now given up because Akha Yeshe does not see it as punishment. Akha Sherab suggested once that a short stay in a gaol cell for Akha Yeshe was just as comfortable as his home in the monastery, the food was tastier and he probably spent most of the time happily in prayer and meditation.

Punishment meted out in the monastery can also be severe, although Akha Yeshe will still often ignore threats, despite his increasing frailty. He often disregards aspects of monastic discipline, especially the scheduled prayer and study sessions. For this he should normally pay fines, but he rarely admits to having money. Sometimes his monthly allowance is withheld, but he knows he can usually rely on Akha Sherab.

One day, during the monastery's Summer Seclusion, Akha Yeshe went to the evening meal not wearing his *dagam*, the formal overcoat worn for more solemn gatherings. When he joined the other monks for the meal he kept muttering and otherwise disturbing those next to him. The *gekö*, or disciplinarian, warned him three times, each time walking over with his iron staff and shouting *da chokge* (Tibetan for 'That's enough!'). Finally, he returned with a leather strap and when Akha Yeshe would still not stop he belted him three times over his freshly shaven head. Akha Yeshe flinched but was not deterred from making an angry reply. He wore red welts for over a week.

In the monastery he is not always treated with respect, and not all the monks respect his special take on life. While monks are normally expected to build and pay for their own housing in the monastery, monastery officials recognised Akha Yeshe's special need and presented him with several rooms — part of a disused Chinese building constructed during one of the periods when Rongwo Monastery was closed down. Not long afterward, some young monks who shared the rest of the building started putting pressure on him to move out. When he didn't get the hint they forced him out, even stealing the timber he had been provided for refurbishing. Blows were exchanged and other monks came to help Akha Yeshe move what they could save. Despite the intervention of a senior *lama*, who confirmed Akha Yeshe's original claim to the rooms, Akha Yeshe remained in possession of only a single small room and makeshift furniture. Without the intervention of the *lama* he would have lost even that.

When it came to painting, Akha Yeshe was also different to other painters. As I was about to find out, he only painted when the proper inspiration struck. He always described this in terms of his eyes being strong or weak. Progress on our Manjushri *thangka* was painfully slow. His eyes were failing, and when working on small details he had to move his face painfully close to his canvas to see what he was doing. But there were also long periods when he experienced crippling depression and was unable to paint. He also paints in secret. Few are allowed to know he is painting and his work is hidden away when he is not working. In this way at least he fits the pattern of what is termed in Tibetan a *trülpey lhabzo*, a 'divinely emanated fashioner of images'. It also explains why I was initially told by other monks that he no longer painted at all. He had in fact been painting all the while, and just before I left China in 1992 he brought out two unfinished *thangkas*, one he claimed to have been working on for nine years, the other for fourteen.

Akha Yeshe did not paint for money, and all his paintings were silently donated to his monastery. Nor does Akha Yeshe make elaborate preliminary measurements beyond an initial division of the canvas using a compass and measuring chalk. Which is not to say that the proper rules of icon-making did not concern him. He was very conscientious regarding proportion, and would mumble measurements to himself as he worked. From what I could see he used the same technique to interpret the changing world, incessantly counting objects around him and remembering them at a later date. He does not physically measure out the iconometric proportions of his paintings because he trusts his own judgement and inspiration.

Thanks to Akha Sherab, I also learned that Akha Yeshe was more literally 'a painter/maker of gods' (*lhabzo*) than other painters I met. There were a number of 'self-manifest' paintings around Rongwo Monastery — revered as having appeared spontaneously in the landscape as 'self-born' expressions of enlightened activity. One of these is an image of the *bodhisattva* Manjushri appearing on a small rock imbedded in the steep rock face behind Kaldan Gyatso's mansion. It is in fact a result of the secret workings of Akha Yeshe. Nevertheless, in Sherab's mind, and increasingly my own, divine manifestation and the work of Akha Yeshe were, more often than not, one and the same thing.

I was learning that there were two traditions of *thangka* painting in Rebkong. Those associated with the state-run Rebkong Art Gallery all belonged to a tradition that could be called 'professional painters'. They were highly skilled and they painted to order. Their painting was rich in gold work and combined fine detail with subtle colour gradations. They lived by their painting, and had been making considerable amounts of money as they painted for the new boom in monastery reconstruction. Some of these painters were among the wealthiest people in Rebkong. Much of the small but growing tourist trade was being met by their apprentices who produced small *thangkas* for sale.

Alongside the professional tradition existed what I would call a 'folk tradition'. 'Folk painters' were also *lhabzo*, but they were not usually able to produce works as fine as those of the professional painters. Their work as painters only supplemented their other income-earning activity. There was one deaf painter I had met at Gyelwo Gang who lived by painting, but he probably also fitted into this category. I had also learned about another type of artist known as *shingtsönpa*, 'wood-colourists', who were hired to do the decorative ornamentation in monasteries and household shrines. The 'folk painters' were a varied group, some painting better than others, some more committed to painting as a way of life than others. Not all of them had the same commitment to the 'right frame of mind' as Akha Yeshe, but it can be said that the conditions under which these painters work have changed less than those of the professionals. Like the professionals they are caught up in the monastery construction boom, but they come to work as craftsmen as they did in the past. They have been untouched by the government's organisation of the professional painters into an institute.

Akha Yeshe was a painter of the folk tradition in terms of the style of his painting, using bold, flat colour and sparingly using gold. Yet he also defied categorisation in terms of his lifestyle and inspiration. I had come to see that his life itself was the art. Spending time with him was certainly colourful, even magical. One of his stories — which he told me just before 'our' painting was completed a full year after it was started — stands out in my mind.

Akha Samdrup was a monk at Rongwo Monastery late last century. His home village was Gyalwo Ngomo. He was well known for his devotion but some also felt his behaviour strange, and called him 'Samdrup the Fool'.

One example of his strange behaviour was the 'ornament' he created for his room in the monastery. Above the window beside his pillow he had prepared a unique package. Two long poles, with a knife and axe between them, were wrapped up with a long rope. Before going to sleep each night he would look up at the parcel above the window, and when he woke in the morning the first thing he did was look up at the parcel and make a prayer of thanks, as well as generating sincere wishes for all sentient beings. The teaching of the Buddha that he cherished most was that death is certain and the time of death is uncertain. He fully believed that death could befall him at any time.

When he passed away, the package above his head was finally put to use. The two poles were bound together with rope to make a stretcher. Two men at each end carried his corpse up the mountain behind the monastery, exchanging positions with other relatives and friends along the way.

Near the top of the mountain is an isolated retreat (ritrö) called White Rock Hermitage, and not far from there is the place where bodies are left for the vultures. The same rope that tied the stretcher was used to tie Akha Samdrup's corpse to a large stone. Soon the birds began to circle down. Like human beings they have their own rules of rank and the chief vulture picks at the body first, opening the stomach and eating the heart. Soon the other birds forced their own way in and picked wildly at the skin and flesh. The large birds kept the younger ones away, greedily picking at the body for themselves.

The knife from the parcel was used to cut flesh off the arms and legs and offer it to smaller birds. Otherwise they had little chance of enjoying the feed. Soon most of the flesh was either picked or cut from the body. Even fingers and toes were cut off to feed the birds, who quickly crushed them between their beaks.

The axe was used to break the legs, arms and larger bones. Once all the body was broken up and prepared it *was distributed to the birds. Some birds swallowed bones whole, others enjoyed them crushed. Last of all the head was crushed using the axe from Akha Samdrup's parcel. The birds poked their beaks in to scoop up the brains.*

The entire corpse consumed, and their hunger satisfied, the vultures wiped their beaks on their wings and walked away to bathe in the sun, the warm rays adding to their pleasure and contentment.

Akha Yeshe took great delight in telling this story, painting the picture with colourful gestures and gruesome sound effects. I wondered if the meaning of art, for this painter, was not something like the life of Akha Samdrup.

The next afternoon, working on the bed I occupied in Sherab's kitchen, Akha Yeshe showed me his technique for making gold paint. Gold leaf from the small pack I had bought in Xining was placed leaf by leaf in a paper bag, and then closing the top of the bag with his fist Akha Yeshe gave it a good shake. Resting a large saucer on my pillow he mixed some water with a binder, and then tipped in the gold powder from the paper bag. Taking my fingers in his hand he said, 'Nice and soft,' and he gave me the job of rubbing the gold into the binder. Each time it turned dry and thick a little more water was added to the saucer, and this process was repeated perhaps twelve times before the paint was fine enough to meet his requirements. That night I truly slept with gold dust on my pillow.

10
Ocean of sacred food

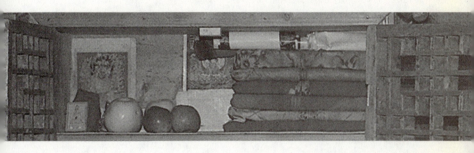

*M*ay the entire realm of space be filled
With the supreme clouds of Samantabhadra's offerings
And with the offerings of gods and humans,
Both those that are physically offered
And those visualised.

— from a Geluk liturgy

Akha Yeshe had taught me many valuable lessons, but the one I most needed to learn was 'surrender and catch'. I had been looking for something, but my looking was about the 'looking', not the finding. Seek and ye shall find? Bah! Just consider these words from the great Persian mystic Jelaluddin Rumi:

> Jesus slips into a house to escape enemies,
> and opens a door to another world.
> Solomon cuts open a fish, and there's a gold ring.
> Omar storms in to kill the prophet
> and leaves with blessings.
> Chase a deer and end up everywhere!
> An oyster opens his mouth to swallow one drop.
> Now there's a pearl.
> A vagrant wanders empty ruins
> Suddenly he's wealthy.[30]

No matter how much searching we have to do, eventually 'finding' is just a matter of having our eyes open — or opened. What does this mean for the anthropologist? For me it meant putting down the template I had brought with me, the template that told me what I should find. I had caught myself playing a game. I had a checklist of things 'Tibetan' I was supposed to find in 'my village'. And I had some very strange ideas about how I should find those things. Where did these ideas come from? Partly they came from the list of things anthropologists assign themselves as part of the 'tradition' of fieldwork. Partly they came from the list of things Tibetanists expect to see confirmed when they read an ethnographic account of Tibet.

The limits of time also shape what anthropologists — and Tibetanists — are doing in Tibet. Until very recently there was little time available (read 'permitted') for anyone to live with Tibetans in a way that would reveal anything about their lives. And so we are often left with rushed collections of information that we reassemble with the help of the pre-fabricated template. When one of my teachers said to me, 'Tibetans? Yes, very interesting, but what exactly about Tibetans?' He was reminding me that academic research was as much about theory as it was about knowledge. He was also reminding me that what I would learn would only ever be a part, a small part, and so I needed to have a good idea of which part. What I wasn't prepared for was the complete phantasmagoria a different society presented; it was not so much impenetrable as 'in your face'.

Towards the end of 1990 I had returned for a four-month stay over winter. Tired of sharing a hotel room with sundry truck drivers, minor officials, occasional drunks and, according to Sherab, a madman who usually lived in an ice cave,

I moved into Sherab's house. At first I had to share the *tsathab* in the kitchen with his brother Kunzang. Once Kunzang returned to Gyelwo Gang I did a lot more of the cooking, rising early to get the fire ready and prepare breakfast, and also doing the shopping. It was the middle of winter and my priorities began to shift from food to keeping warm.

I was learning some interesting tricks. Washing was a problem, but in the cold weather it wasn't a problem to go for a week or two before having a good scrub. Washing clothes was also something I could leave longer than I ordinarily might; I just hoped I didn't smell too unusual. I concluded that if I didn't find anyone else on the nose it was likely that I too was OK. One friend looked over at the grime on my collar and announced that I must have turned Tibetan! I also had no idea you could dry clothes by just hanging them in the winter sun and letting them freeze. While a bit stiff, with one good shake they were ready to wear! In the kitchen I learned to use juniper fronds as a disinfecting scourer, but I still wished for running water, hot or cold.

Akha Yeshe, along with every other painter in Rebkong, was taking a winter break. The temperature rarely rose above $-6\,°C$, and the freezing air played havoc with paint, brush and canvas. Farmers were on their winter break too. The earth was too hard to work, so their main job was simply checking that the livestock were surviving in good shape.

After the harvest and autumn work were finished the ninth lunar month (from around October to November) was largely given over to Buddhist practice. Men and women joined study groups with friends where they exchanged talk about spiritual topics and discussed the life of the village as they turned prayer wheels, read scripture, sang hymns (including variations on the six-syllable mantra), circumambulated temples and *chorten*, or visited nearby holy places and temples. With the onset of the colder weather many of the men would leave for the grasslands to find work assisting the annual harvesting of yak and sheep, and the preparation of carcasses for freezing. Some travelled as far as the banks of Tso Ngönbo — Lake Qinghai, 300 kilometres away. The slaughtering was left as late as possible so the meat froze quickly in the natural freezer of the winter air. But it also had to be timed before the animals began to waste in the colder weather. Finding this kind of work, families with small numbers of livestock were able to acquire amounts of meat that, once dry, would last for many months. A thin slice or two of frozen yak meat is considered one of the winter treats.

The rest of the winter months were spent mostly indoors at home or at gatherings on days set aside in the calendar for Buddhist practice. Buddhist practice in Rebkong is not solely in the hands of the Geluk monks at Rongwo Monastery. Up at Gyelwo Gang, and in nearby upland villages, many of the men belonged to a local tradition of the Nyingma order of Tibetan Buddhism, collectively known as the *ngakpa*, the 'Nineteen Hundred *Phurba* Holding Mantra-Adepts of Rebkong' (*phurbas* being ritual daggers).

One day in the tenth lunar month I walked up to Gyelwo Gang to watch the ritual dance performed by village men during the gathering called *mani drupchen*, Great Accomplishment *Mani*. As I arrived, out of breath and red-faced from the cold, I was whisked into the temple kitchen to keep warm, but the kitchen was full of dust from the hay that fed the fire, and to take my next breath I was forced outside again. The whole village had turned out to support their temple — the dance would re-enact the taming of Tibet's malevolent forces by their 'Second Buddha', Padmasambhava. Inside the *ngak-khang* (the temple used by yogins) wearing the long-haired headdresses of the *dakas* (tantric heroes), were monks from Rongwo Monastery, mostly sons of Gyelwo Gang families, providing musical accompaniment as they led the chanting of the ritual liturgy.

The *ngakmang* — or 'assembled yogins' — of Rebkong are renowned for their devotion to the tradition of Padmasambhava, and are readily recognised by their massive dreadlocks or their single thin braid looped around a shaved head. Visiting each other's villages they gather at the *ngak-khang* to practise the teachings of Secret Mantra and the Great Perfection. Their lineage of the Nyingma tradition has a long history among the communities north and south of the Yellow River, and may even stretch back to the ninth century when monk-refugees arrived in Amdo after the collapse of the ancient Tibetan Yarlung dynasty. Yet its modern form grew out of the Nyingma revival in eastern Tibet and the activities of the 'non-sectarian' Rimé movement in the first half of the nineteenth century. This movement sought to create a freer exchange of wisdom between the various orders of Buddhism. The ongoing coexistence of the Nyingma and Gelukpa traditions in the valley became an important part of Rebkong's place within the Tibetan Buddhist tradition.

The *ngakpa* communities in the villages have gone from strength to strength. Rongwo Monastery and its branch monasteries remain the centres of monastic practice, supported by upland villages with donations of material support and also, traditionally, the 'donation' of at least one son entering the monastic tradition. The upland villagers also maintain their own temples and traditions and these are very much alive today. The *ngakpa* still receive strong support from their proud young members, who, like their elders, do not hesitate to distinguish themselves by wearing dreadlocks wound around their heads.

For the *ngakpa* at Gyelwo Gang, and those who joined them from other villages nearby, the most important aspect of the *mani drupchen* was not the ritual dance, so often celebrated in the accounts of travellers and anthropologists, but the recitation by the assembled yogins of the *mani* mantra. In shifts over several days they recited the sacred syllables of *Om Manipadme Hum* until, it was said, the reverberation took on a life of its own, spreading out from the village temple and throughout the world. And so the ceremony would repeat through one village after another, men and women arriving from neighbouring villages to offer their support. In the evening the village men retreated to their lamp-lit temple to recite the mantra through the night, and every so often one would cup a hand to his ear and share a spontaneous 'song of realisation'.

So the winter break was quite a busy period. When the villagers were not sewing bedding or clothes, repairing fences, grinding snuff, preparing donations, giving service to the monastery or out finding winter work, they were participating in a rich round of religious activities.

The celebrations for Tibetan New Year (*losar*) in Rebkong began towards the end of winter after the three-month lay-off. In the twelfth lunar month villages slowly came to life again as each family began its preparations for the New Year festivities, making sure the house was in order and stocking up on festive items such as candies, biscuits, wine, new clothes and cigarettes. In the monastery all the monks, even including old Akha Yeshe, were kept busy with *losar* preparations too. Every year Rongwo Monastery hosted a series of festivities: a great public prayer gathering, a ritual dance, a street parade and finally, on the first full moon of the year, the 'Offering of the Fifteenth Day' — a festival of lights featuring a giant tableau made of coloured yak butter.

Six degrees below zero was an excellent temperature for butter sculpture, and I was lucky that Akha Sherab invited me along to observe the construction of the tableau. In all it would take four men five days, and they assembled in what used to be Sherab's room by the gate of the *dukhang*. Akha Padma, the 'master', had come down from the slopes of Amye Chakyung to conduct the proceedings. His old friend Wangyal joined him. Both had been monks in the days before Rongwo Monastery was closed; both now had grown-up families. Wangyal's nephew, Tshering, who usually worked at the foundry, was there to lend a hand, and a plump old monk, Kelsang, said to be kind and very learned, also came to help. They sat on the heated bed, catching up on the events of the last year.

When I arrived after lunch there was already a young monk in the courtyard unpacking sheep-stomach bags filled with fresh yak butter. He split one open, emptied the ball of butter — the size of a man's head — onto a large board, and began kneading. At first it was hard and he strained with all his weight, but soon the sun began to help him. The smoother the butter became the paler it got, until it was almost pure white. Nearby stood a whole sheep carcass — our lunch and dinner for the next five days.

Once a ball of butter was smooth it was taken inside and distributed to the four artists. Each took a large handful and shaped it into a bowl. Into the hollow they tipped amounts of coloured poster-paint powder, folded the 'bowl' up and began stroking the butter much like one might stoke a cat. The colour appeared through the butter in deeper and deeper streaks, until finally it was kneaded and divided into four or five small cones. These were then lightened with white butter or combined with other primary colours.

Nearby there were four pine boards to be used as palettes. Once a cone of coloured butter had been finished it was placed on the palette, until after about two hours there were twenty-two tones and hues. One board held all the pinks and reds, another orange and yellows, a third a whole range of greens, and on the last there were several shades of blue. Akha Padma asked for a pot beside the stove, turned it upside down, and began dabbing a ball of butter over its charred base. Soon he had a cone of black to add alongside the blue, while the uncoloured butter provided white. I was reminded of a Tibetan saying that gave advice for choosing friends: 'Walking around a *chorten* some white rubs off, walking around an old pot some black rubs off.' The palettes of coloured butter glowed, translucent and luminous.

Everything happened without fuss, everyone was familiar with the established pattern. I wondered at the tapering cones of butter, shaped that way so that fingers reaching for one colour would not knock another. Keeping the colours pure was essential, otherwise the whole rainbow-coloured tableau about to be constructed could end up being dull and grey. Cornstarch on wet fingers helped, and to stop the butter softening as they worked each of the artists had a basin of iced water to keep his fingertips cold!

That first afternoon the four men looked over the remains

of the previous year's tableau, picking out sections of previously used butter that could be used again, and wooden backings that could be salvaged. The old butter was stripped off the supports and saved to use as foundations for the modelling of the New Year's tableau. At about four-thirty it was tools down and the artists all headed home.

I arrived before the others the next morning. In the *chöra* in front of the Assembly Hall the *akha chungchung* and some of their little mates swept and picked up rubbish, supervised by a monk in his sixties. Soon they were joined by elderly women on their rounds of circumambulation. One by one the artists arrived, and we started the day with tea and bread, also given to the working bee as they finished their sweeping.

The monk Kelsang started work first, nimbly shaping dozens upon dozens of leaves as he pressed pieces of green butter into a wooden mould. The others assembled spatulas, needles and other wooden tools used in their art. Sitting on an L-shaped *dzongthap* (a heated sitting-platform or bed) they formed a half-circle, the coloured butter arranged in the middle to share between them. Each had his own bowl of iced water and a work board resting across his lap or on the bench surrounding the *dzongthap*. The two older men reworked the coloured butter, while the youngest, Tshering, got a head start on modelling the deity Samantabhadra (Forever Good), known in Tibetan as Kuntuzangpo. As he practised shaping the butter he regularly asked for advice from the older men.

The basic form of Samantabhadra from the previous year's tableau was already attached to its wooden supports, 'his' head removed and carefully placed to one side. The rim of the board would later define the arc of his halo, but first he had to be given a new layer of skin, a skirt over his crossed legs, silk ribbons, and many other adornments. These were all assembled in rudimentary form as small pieces on Tshering's work board, then later pressed onto the waiting figure and reshaped.

Like most other elements of Tibetan religion, Samantabhadra signifies a number of 'values'. At one level he is one of the *bodhisattvas* known as the 'eight close sons of the Buddha', at another level he is a buddha representing primordial awareness beyond all taint of delusion. In his *bodhisattva* form, as depicted in the 'Offering of the Fifteenth Day', he sits in the lotus position supported on a lotus throne. His naked torso is golden yellow and draped with a red sash and ribbons of green silk, his skirt is deep blue, his leggings crimson. His hands meet at his heart: the right hand in the *mudra* of fearlessness, the left holding a gem representing his ability to multiply all offerings. His eyes are half-closed, and on his head he wears the golden five-faceted 'crown of victorious concentration', each facet inlaid with precious gems.

All of these features had to be made visible in a coloured butter image 20 centimetres high. Piece by piece, Tshering assembled all of the *bodhisattva*'s attributes out of butter, sometimes pressing it into thin sheets, sometimes building up jewels from the tiniest balls, sometimes rolling butter into thin lines. At one stage he pulled a thin thread of maroon cotton from a monk's robe to recreate the line of Samantabhadra's serene, meditating eyes.

At first the others began the day making flowers. These decorative flowers were made from a thin stick of dowel (the stem) topped with a head shaped like a champignon to be covered by butter petals. At an easy speed the artist pinched a piece of coloured butter between his fingers and then rolled it, pressed it flat, and attached it to the head of the flower. These petals were repeated in rows and each row would be made a lighter hue than the last, until the head of the flower was a mass of shimmering light. Using these basic techniques the old monk Kelsang was able to make roses, chrysanthemums, peonies and dahlias, and the lotus petals for the deities' thrones.

After lunch on the second day the artist Wangyal began work on the figure of Jambhala, or as the Tibetans call him, Dzamser, the Golden God of Material Blessings. He too was depicted seated on a lotus throne, the colour of his body and ornaments were much the same as for Samantabhadra, but he was corpulent, sat with one leg forward in the posture of 'royal ease', had dark hair draping over his shoulders, and displayed much more jewellery. In his right hand he held a blue fruit, and with his left he patted a dark-blue jewel-spitting mongoose sitting in his lap. Rainbow-coloured jewels lay around his seat, a stand of red coral beside him to his left. His eyes were large and open, gazing straight ahead.

Again these elements were attached to a pre-made foundation on a circular board. Wangyal had soon caught up to Tshering, and they began to work in unison: when Tshering was working on the hands and fingers of Samantabhadra, Wangyal was working on those of Jambhala and so was Sonam; when Tshering worked on Samantabhadra's head, Wangyal picked up Jambhala's head and applied his face — like fitting a mask.

Up until this point Akha Padma had been largely occupied supervising the whole procedure. But he now began work on the Emblem of Manjushri, a flaming sword standing atop the loose-leafed book known as *The Perfection of Wisdom in Eight Thousand Verses*. This figure, and those of the two deities, are, like the full-sized statues found in the temples, surrounded by intricate haloes of light and flame — lots of orange, yellow and red. Akha Padma first worked on its foundation, shaping the halo that surrounded the sword like a pointed arch. All of the details were made in butter, but the effect was just as elaborate as any 'real' statue I had seen.

Akha Padma was constantly interrupted for advice, or to help with details required on smaller *torma* for the offering tables inside the *dukhang*. At one point he flattened white butter into a long sheet along a board. Using a template he cut the butter into an elongated diamond and then, using a wooden stylus, in a single line he drew a series of arabesques. Taking one corner of the butter in his fingers he lifted it and in one stroke took away all the unwanted butter to leave a long tongue of flame in butter filigree. After this miracle the piece was taken into a cold storeroom to harden and then transferred to a stick — again in one movement by turning the work board upside down. While 'pretty' is perhaps not appropriate to the seriousness of the *torma* offering that it surmounted, that is the only way I can describe it. And yet 'prettiness' is somehow not a concept completely out of place.

This was a form of 'cake-decoration', an art with a long and deeply symbolic function within world folklore. On one level the *torma* is the very deity to which it is being offered, in which case it should be given serious respect; but at another level it is a food offering to the deity, and this means it must be presented in a delightful and pleasing manner. And given that the deities embody a drama leading us out of our habitual illusions, they have very diverse proclivities and tastes.

Akha Padma turned again to work on the rainbows that

twist around the Lord of Wisdom's sword. The other two were using matchstick-sized twigs to attach crowns to their deities. Soon dinner was being readied and the artists were visibly tired. Tshering showed me how the length of a hand should be the same as the distance between the dent in a figure's chin and the hairline. The hands too are added with the help of tiny sticks. Just as Akha Padma flipped another filigree flame on to its support stick, everyone started singing the grace for dinner.

That night over our noodles Akha Padma told us he once knew a family of five Americans who had lived for a time in a valley nearby. After 1949 they went to live in India at Kalimpong and I was only the second *yinji* he had ever seen.

On the third morning I was enlisted to help the teenage monks to move a giant-sized *torma*, or ritual 'offering-cake', out onto the steps of the *dukhang*. Made of *tsampa*, it was tall — about a metre and a half high — with a rounded top and covered in dust. We cracked open its crust and peeled it away. Inside was the core, the 'life-tree', made of conifer branches wrapped in gauze-like 'felicity scarves' (ceremonial scarves). This was saved and after the dry dough around it had been dusted off the monks smoothed sticky handfuls of fresh *tsampa* over it. Renewed, the *torma* was given a coating of red butter, and we took it back inside and set it up in a position just left of the main throne. This was the main offering, a 'cake' as well as the 'body' of the deity, and it had wooden 'arms' that would support the panels of coloured butter 'offerings' the artists were to fashion over the next days.

In all, three sets of offerings were modelled by the team. Two were 'sets of eight'. On the right of the *torma* the 'Eight Auspicious Emblems' would be arranged in pairs: a parasol and a pair of golden fish; a vase and a lotus; a conch shell and a mystic knot; a victory banner and a wheel. On the left of the *torma* the 'Eight Precious Offerings' would be arranged in pairs on four 'golden' dishes: the mirror and white mustard; curds and sacred grass; *bilwa* fruit and a conch; and minium and bezoar. The third set, the 'Offering of the Five Senses', consisted of a mirror (sight), a lute (hearing), a conch filled with incense (smell), peaches (taste), and a length of cloth (touch), and added to these was a sixth, a tiny red *torma* (purely mental phenomena). Again, these were modelled in every detail with coloured butter, all except for the strings of the lute — those were made of real cotton thread. The six '*external* sources of perception' would eventually be arranged together on a lotus base and displayed at the very centre of the giant *torma*.

There are a great many explanations concerning the function of the various offerings (*chöpa*) associated with the practice of Buddhism in Tibet, from the point of view of both the Tibetans themselves and the outsiders attempting to understand Tibetan religion. The centrality of the altruistic attitude in Tibetan religion has brought a unique complexity to the notion of offering. If prayer is central to Christianity, offering has a similar role in Tibetan Buddhism, and is central to spiritual development.

One view classifies offerings into three types or aspects: namely, the 'outer offerings', the 'inner offerings' and the 'secret offerings'. In some traditions a fourth level of offering is included, known as the 'Offering of Ultimate Actuality'. This last involves the seemingly paradoxical task of presenting undifferentiated reality to undifferentiated reality itself, a concept one may understand after reaching the heights of Tibetan Buddhism.

The outer offerings consist of objects thought pleasing to various deities or protectors — as in the two sets of eight offerings included in the set made at Rongwo Monastery. In the Indian tradition of *puja* there have usually been ten kinds of offering: flowers, garlands, incense, ointment, food, cloth, ornaments, umbrellas, victory banners and flags. In Tibet, water has been considered especially appropriate as a symbol of clarity and other important qualities. Atisha, an early Indian teacher in Tibet, said that water was one of the best offerings: it does not generate attachment, and, although it is only water, when it is properly offered the buddhas regard it as ambrosial nectar.[31]

Besides material objects, music, song and dance — and even a fresh share of one's own food — may also be offered. Whatever is offered, if it is prepared with mindfulness, pure motivation and care for the purity of the offering, the benefits are immeasurable:

> *An offering placed on one's altar*
> *Becomes a constant offering to all the Buddhas.*
> *By that gift great merit arises, and with the merit*
> *The supreme accomplishment is soon achieved.*[32]

The 'supreme accomplishment' is enlightenment and the inner offerings comprise symbolic 'substances' such as the six senses, or certain 'essences' of the physical body. The six senses may be offered in the way just described, but in some contexts they can also be presented in far more potent form in the shape of what is called 'the flower of the senses'. This is a 'gruesome, if formal arrangement of human eyeballs, ears, tongue, and so on — all crafted from dough and butter ... set in a real skull'.[33] Offering these six '*internal* sources of perception' brings about a lessening of attachment to the body.

Finally, the 'secret offering' harmonises dualistic emotions in an encounter analogous to a physical embrace, surrendering the egocentric mind and its attachment to this situation or that. The 'objects' offered are the very attachments that are subdued by the practice. The offering of ultimate actuality, or the 'definitive' offering, recognises the non-dual nature of reality: the offerer, the offering and the recipient are completely identical.

At another level still, the 'Offering of the Fifteenth Day', as well as the other rituals enacted at Rongwo Monastery over the New Year, contribute to ensuring that the hard-won well-being of the community is protected. The sublime powers of distance and altitude are constant elements in the life of communities hemmed in by bitter snows and precipitous mountainsides. The home, the people in it and their material resources need to be protected from misfortune, especially the threat of supernatural or invisible forces such as *dön* (evil spirit bringing disease and bad luck), *drey* (demons that enter humans), *düd* (demons that interfere with the positive influence of religion), and *meyti* (goblins that bring poverty). Also, far more than their cousins on the high pasture, Rebkong's farmers are at the mercy of natural disasters such as frost, blizzard, drought and infestation. In this they share a tendency towards animism with agricultural communities throughout Asia. For many in Rebkong the most immediate meaning of these and other rituals held in monasteries and at home is their protection from natural disasters, but other religious aspects are not forgotten or unknown.

Over breakfast the next day, day four, Akha Padma, 'the

master butter-sculptor', told the story of how he ended up lame. Malicious spirits had been troubling his village, and the previous year they had a hand in crushing his leg under a small tractor. Then they harassed him for two days while he was unconscious in hospital. The leg wouldn't straighten and now he walks with an awkward hobble, and has to rest after every ten steps or so. All the same, he remained one of the busiest people in the whole valley, helping with art work on temples throughout Rebkong. During the lead up to New Year he moved from one monastery to another to help with the construction of the 'Offering of the Fifteenth Day'. His generosity and devotion meant he was also in demand as a sculptor and painter. I wondered if a good man like this was not an obvious target for *dön* spirits and *düd* demons.

His old friend Wangyal couldn't resist taking a jibe. Might not the problem be, he suggested, that Akha Padma was being punished for taking a new wife thirty years younger than himself? Akha Padma was mortally embarrassed, but everyone thought it was very funny. 'Why blame it on spirits when you are just worn out trying to keep up with a young lady,' Wangyal added. This got an even bigger laugh. For the first time after days of non-stop chatter Akha Padma had nothing to say.

Religious duties (*chöley*) might involve all sorts of symbolic and spiritual complexity. But whether it was butter sculpture or sewing new buntings for a monastery hall; preparing tea or enjoying a 'feast'; sweeping the courtyard or bringing donations; when people came together, for whatever reason, the monastery glowed with warmth. Surrounded by the bitter cold of mid-winter, the workroom united us with a single good purpose, and joviality prevailed. Sometimes the conversation turned to the crimes of the Cultural Revolution, or the news of His Holiness the Dalai Lama, or the institution of population control among the villages of Rebkong, or tension in the Persian Gulf. In the warmth of the workroom stove, however, the underlying mood was definitely a pervasive optimism.

By the afternoon of the fourth day all of the major offerings that would decorate the *torma* were complete. We fixed wooden support panels to the giant *torma* — one either side of it for the two sets of eight offerings, and one on top for the Emblem of Manjushri, its flaming sword tip pointing to higher planes. On the body of the *torma*, just below Manjushri's sword, was Samantabhadra, the main 'host', and below him the 'Offering of the Five Senses' surrounded in a gleaming rainbow of butter buttons. Below that, lending his weight to the whole arrangement, was the golden, corpulent form of Jambhala, God of Material Blessings — at ease, but immovable. With dinner on the stove, work stopped early.

On the last day everyone got to work finishing the dozens of flowers and myriad leaves that would surround the whole tableau. Every butter flower demanded enormous concentration, no matter how many times it might have been made before. Some had pointed petals, some were flat and some were tiny tubes formed by rolling a flat circle of butter between the thumb and index finger. All had to be arranged in concentric rows of even size, gradually getting smaller towards the centre. Some flowers sported layers of two or three colours.

As the flowers and leaves were inserted into the support boards surrounding the offerings, I realised that each flower had its identical twin, that the flowers on the two sides of the giant *torma* were arranged symmetrically. What was taking shape was truly a feast for the eyes. Suddenly the flowers were like stars in the night sky. A shimmering, luminous vision floated in the dim butter-lamp light of the monastery hall.

Once everything was in place Wangyal stood on a chair, and from his hand took leaves of pressed gold to sprinkle over the entire apparition. Breaking into slivers, the gold leaf stuck readily to any butter it touched, half attached, half floating on the slow currents of freezing *dukhang* air. The application of gold finished, Wangyal stepped down and we all stepped back to admire the team's work, letting out a long sigh of *yaaaaamtsen*, wondrous!

Dinner was ready early. The work finished, time was taken to enjoy the boiled mutton, dipping it in chilli flakes and vinegar. The mutton broth, steaming hot, was consumed bowl upon bowl. After dinner, just before leaving, the laymen in the team were each presented with two large packs of brick-tea and a *khatak* (felicity scarf). They were also invited to attend a party the next day, but in the event they were either too modest or too busy. They were needed at other monasteries down the valley. Instead, in the evening, all the monks who had been involved cooked up the remaining meat and bones, making sure that nothing allotted to this year's preparations was wasted.

11
Cross-currents

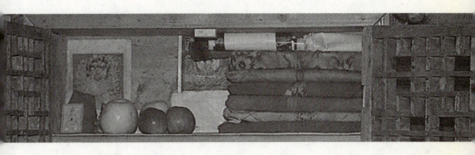

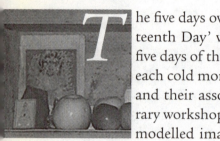

The five days over which the 'Offering of the Fifteenth Day' was produced were also the first five days of the Gulf War, in January 1991. Early each cold morning I would join the five artists and their assorted young helpers in a temporary workshop in a monastery room while they modelled images that represented the peace, grace and luminosity of complete and perfect insight. Each evening, back at the hotel in the television room, I joined another group of Tibetans who were transfixed, along with the rest of China, by a 'lightshow' in a desert 10,000 kilometres away. These images provided the inspiration for meditations on power, justice and heroism, and, more pertinently, for questions on why such a lightshow could never be created in the cause of Tibet's own independence.

Edmund Carpenter, a colleague of Marshall McLuhan, published a book many years ago called *Oh What a Blow that Phantom Gave Me!* It was an odd little book, a rather disjointed collection of stories and happenings from both the centres of cultural power and the backwaters. Collectively the brief narratives provided examples of how we have begun to favour mediated images over more direct forms of perception; how mass communications, by their very size, have overtaken direct experience as the measure of authenticity. Carpenter asked the question, 'What happens when the power of electronic media spreads beyond the culture in which it had its origin, and confronts worlds that are completely unprepared for it?' He found that electronic representations have the power to create enormous confusion. The more time I spent in Rebkong the more I began to perceive how mass communication can confuse fiction and reality, and how the mirages we create can return to haunt us.

From January 1991 to January 1992 I made a total of seven trips from Chengdu to Rebkong and each time I arrived the changes that had taken place surprised me. Before I came home in 1992 the streets of Tongren were awash with the noise of video parlours: these had replaced the official din of the town's increasingly decrepit PA system. The town had a new arcade, a veritable 'Crystal Palace' with restaurants, beancurd sellers, electrical goods, whitegoods, Chinese fashions, music and video-cassette stores, and a long line of pool tables that were in continual use throughout the day.

New media such as film, television and video have introduced new forms of visual experience. The concept of fiction is still in its infancy in Rebkong. Images of robots and spaceships compete against Buddhism's 'wrathful deities' and 'rainbow bodies'. Images created as fiction, such as robots, are accepted by many as real. This is at least partly because in the past all media images — temple scrolls and statues — were always understood to be depicting reality, no matter how fantastic they might appear to ignorant non-Buddhists. Until the arrival of the Chinese revolution in Rebkong there was no category of fiction; all images were accepted as portraying actual beings, objects and events, the reality of which was unquestioned. There was no fiction in Tibetan art or literature, and little conceivable need for it. Perhaps this distinction could never have occurred in a philosophical culture where our closest 'realities' are described as illusions, *maya*. When I looked through dictionaries for the Tibetan word for fiction the word I found meant 'lies'. It is, then, an irony that 'fiction' appeared in Tibet as the Chinese delivered Tibet's 'liberation' in 1950.

With the sudden arrival of Hollywood and Chinese action films, there has been a shift in consciousness that is yet to stabilise. One day Sherab's brother, Kunzang, who was at least twenty-five, came to ask me if robots could really fly. His doubt was significant, but he was not doubting the existence of robots. To be fair to the Tibetans, there was also a Chinese university student in Shenyang who burst into a friend's room one night. He told us that he had to get to America because he had just seen a film called *Mr No-Legs* — at least that was the Chinese title — where a crippled police detective hunted down criminals in a wheelchair that was equipped with an assortment of hidden guns and knives. 'It's just fantastic what you Americans can do!' he pleaded. And he wasn't referring to film-making.

Kunzang's teachers college was doing little to develop his sense of sceptical inquiry; the monastic education system seemed to be doing a little better. Akha Sherab said he wanted to visit a large Chinese city because he was curious about whether or not they were as big and advanced as the television images claimed, or whether it was all propaganda bombast.

Early in May 1991, Sherab visited me in Chengdu; he came with old Akha Yeshe as no one back at the monastery would accept responsibility for him. At first we were able to find them a room in a guesthouse in the Sichuan University campus, but the first night Akha Yeshe caused such a commotion we were forced to look further afield.

In the city Akha Yeshe was a handful. He refused to get used to the idea that cars, buses and bicycles were unlikely to stop if he got in front of them. And he played his usual tricks with money, giving five dollars for a fifty-cent map, and then giving five dollars for a twenty-five dollar pair of pink runners. And he got away with it — the map-seller was happy and the shoe vendor just shrugged his shoulders.

Sherab was not much better, trying to kill himself several times as he raced me around the Chengdu ring-road on a bicycle. I now wonder whether the two of them weren't perhaps affected by the excess oxygen they were getting at sea level. Ostensibly, Sherab was on a shopping trip for the monastery, and had to report back on the prices of various religious paraphernalia, as well as precious objects like red coral and gold. He was also worried about liver problems and wanted to have a medical check-up. I took him to the best hospital in town, and they sold us tickets for about twenty specialists. We went from room to room where he was prodded, poked and otherwise measured. It took several days to complete the visits and get the results. But, not unlike a wide-eyed kid at a fairground, Akha Sherab was having a great time. He is the only person I have ever seen get up from a stomach examination with a beaming smile on his face.

But the city did have its shocks. When we came across a vendor gutting eel nineteen to the dozen on the head of a nail, old Akha Yeshe froze. His eyes blinked as he tried to process what was going on. A string of quietly hummed mantras followed, then he grabbed my hand. He was shaking.

Rushing out of the market he took us to a nearby bridge. He then reached inside his robe and took out a bag of crumbly *tsampa*, dipped his hand in, and sprinkled it into the river below. He might have appeared off with the fairies most of the time, but when he wanted to Akha Yeshe could summon the utmost clarity.

As we made our way around town the citizens of Chengdu were mostly curious, but sometimes there was genuine fear. On our visit to Wenshu Monastery in the north of town Akha Yeshe got his pen out and started adding decorations around the border of a large notice on one of the walls — a list of regulations regarding proper conduct in the monastery grounds. No one seemed to mind, and before he had finished a couple of old Chinese matrons came up to touch him. Complete strangers, for some reason they believed he had healing powers. One said she had a problem with pain in her shoulder, and Akha Yeshe, unable to suppress a cheeky smile, obliged with a few short prayers mumbled under his breath. In those days *qigong* was all the rage through China, and in the minds of many Han-Chinese I met it was their single item of interest in Tibetan Buddhism.

When we found Akha Yeshe and Akha Sherab a hotel room near the university they had to share it with a couple of peddlers. I overheard the two Chinese men worry about whether they might become victims of the monks' magical powers — the next day they had arranged a new room.

At Wenshu Monastery, Akha Yeshe wandered off while we were sitting in the teahouse. After an hour searching for him we knew the rooms of Wenshu Monastery inside out, but still there was no Akha Yeshe. There was no choice but to give up and go back to the university. He was there waiting for us. By some magic he had run into the Tibetan curator of the university's museum walking down a side street near the centre of town; she had brought him back.

Then he got lost again on the way up Mount Emei. Well, not lost exactly, more like left behind. I made the mistake of letting the pair of them travel unaccompanied to the sacred Buddhist mountain, 160 kilometres out of Chengdu. I suspected that if I went I wouldn't be able to keep up. Getting to the top meant climbing 30 kilometres up and down endless series of steps in sub-tropical humidity. Sherab quickly got tired of Akha Yeshe's tendency to dawdle: he was in a hurry to get back and complete his shopping for Rongwo Monastery. Solution? Go on ahead and leave Akha Yeshe to find his own way home. I almost lost my temper when Sherab arrived back in Chengdu without him. What was the likelihood of him running into a nice Tibetan lady like the curator from the museum? Two days passed and I was getting ready to call the police when finally he turned up, ready to give Sherab an earful. I didn't ever find out how he found his way back — I began to wonder if Akha Yeshe perhaps had a better command of Chinese than he had previously let on. But then again it might have been his own special magic.

One afternoon when Akha Yeshe was still missing on the slopes of Mount Emei, I was sitting in the lounge room of my university flat and came across an interesting story in *The Guardian Weekly*. I told Sherab about it. It was only a brief article. Two brothers had been arrested in Guangzhou (Canton) for serving *char siew bao* (steamed roast-pork buns) in their restaurant, in this case stuffed with human flesh. One of the brothers was employed at the neighbourhood morgue and had been carving meat from the thighs of the corpses — to supply his brother's kitchen. The lean pork fillets used to make *char siew bao* are very expensive, and so the brothers, without telling anyone, decided to cut corners, so to speak. Their strategy worked. The restaurant soon gained a reputation for the tastiest *char siew* buns in town.

Sherab listened, swallowing the story with interest. And when I had finished he said, 'Yes! We have a woman like that in our valley.' At first I didn't quite get what he meant, and then I sat up in my chair and listened. He proceeded to tell me about an old woman who lived upstream from his village in the Guchu Valley whom everybody knew ate children. I think he called her a *gimijimi*. Many years earlier one family had lost five children in the nearby forest but the fifth child escaped and told everyone. When his family went back with the child, he was unable to find the house where the woman lived. For as long as anyone can remember children have continued to disappear when they stray into one particular wood.

This was the kind of story I was used to reading in collections of folktales, and the themes are familiar the world over. Needless to say I have never bothered to go looking for the *gimijimi*. On the other hand, I did accept *The Guardian*'s story as plain truth, and certainly that was the way I translated it for Sherab.

As it happened, after returning home to Australia, I ran into someone else who had read the cannibal-dumpling story in *The Guardian Weekly*. What I didn't know, however, was that it had been an April Fool's Day prank. Because *The Guardian Weekly* had arrived in Chengdu well after publication, April Fool's Day had never crossed my mind.

Certain events made me realise that I had a strange relationship with the place I had been visiting. Part of it had to do with the strained relationship that exists between China, Tibet and the Western world; part of it had to do with how I had put Tibet away in its own little part of my mind. Moving between Rebkong and the 'outside world' often caught me off-guard.

On a return trip to Rebkong in 1995, I was taking photographs in a last-minute attempt to document recent changes. I took shots of price boards out the front of shops, street scenes with the popular new 'West Lake' imitation of a Yamaha motorcycle, a new row of shops leading up the highway almost to the monastery gates. Inconsequential things, I thought, that might be useful to have when I got home. It was a way of dealing with the feeling I often had that I hadn't seen or learned enough.

One of the images I brought home with me was of the billboard outside a video parlour not far from the market. The covers of the video of the day or week could be displayed above the program written in chalk (of course this was only in Chinese). When I was reviewing the slides back in China I was stunned to see that one of the movies showing that day in Rebkong was a film in which I had played a part. It was called *Kuang* ('Crazed', released outside China as *Ripples Across Stagnant Water*), and I had been involved in the filming during a break in Sichuan in 1991. It was a speaking part and I had played a priest baptising a convert in turn-of-the-century Chengdu. The once-famous director Ling Zifeng had hoped the film would be China's answer to Kurosawa's *Ran*, but that was not to be.

It was a real surprise to find this photo; what stunned me most was the realisation that I had failed to notice it at the time I had aimed my camera. I had looked through the lens and taken a shot, without anything registering. Thinking back, something else set my head spinning just a little. A day or so before taking that shot I had been walking down the road from the monastery into town when a young monk I vaguely knew greeted me with, 'Hey, you're the man in the film.' 'Sorry, no I'm not!' I said, and I wondered why he would say something crazy like that out of the blue. I wrote it off as another crazy comment among the many other strange remarks I might get on an almost daily basis as a foreigner in Rebkong. As it turns out, a lot of dud movies find their way to video parlours in China's out of the way places (although *Kuang* later appeared on Australian television, twice).

For me the big question remaining was why, when I could very well have been (and was) 'the man in the film', I was not prepared to acknowledge that the young monk had seen me as such. Certainly I had no idea at the time that 'my movie' had been showing in town — otherwise I would have rushed to see it. (At that time I had not seen it myself, and I had more or less accepted that I might never see it.) Nor am I an actor, and so I don't normally think of myself as 'the man in the film'. But I suspect there was something else behind my blindness.

My response to the monk's recognition was to deny it immediately — not even a glimmer of doubt crossed my mind. I had been 'a man in a film', but something had prevented any memory of *Kuang* from surfacing. More than that, a day or two later I had aimed my camera and taken a photograph of a billboard with my film plastered all over it, and still I hadn't seen it when it was right in front of me. While in Rebkong I seem to have been blind to those parts of myself that were in 'the outside world', or to put it another way, I had cut Rebkong off entirely from the outside world. As an anthropologist I had fallen into the habit of wanting the place vacuum-sealed!

Kuang was not the only film in which I acted during my period of fieldwork. About a year earlier, I had also played a priest — that beard again! — for a short video production made by the Chengdu Military Region Drama Troupe located in Chengdu. This particular military division is heavily involved in China's control of the Tibet Autonomous Region. Many of the crew had lived or worked in Tibet. As the make-up artist applied an ageing agent (talcum powder) to my hair I even suspected she might be Tibetan, but she said she wasn't.

Our short film was written around the theme of a soldier helping the needy, describing the generous spirit of a local armoured-tank driver who had looked after an old and childless widow (cleaning her house, providing coal, sweeping snow, visiting at New Year etc.). As the story progresses, it is revealed that the widow had not originally been childless. In her younger years she had been forced by the loss of her husband during the Japanese invasion to give up her only daughter to the care of a church orphanage. My role as a priest was to come down the stairs of the orphanage, take the girl from her mother, give the mother some money to help her on her way, and lead the girl away. The scene was probably meant to be ambiguous; to Chinese audiences I could be buying the child. The girl, about nine years old, screams through tears for her mother as she is led away.

About two weeks after filming I received another visit from the film crew, who came to ask if I would like to take another role in their production, this time to play God. It was quite a promotion, and of course too interesting to resist. All this theology was a real innovation in socialist film-making; I could have been making history.

For the part of God my hair was doused in even more liberal applications of talcum powder and I was draped in pink tulle — looking, I hoped, something like Aristotle, but probably more like a very strange ballerina. On a stage spread with dry-ice 'clouds' my role was to orchestrate a heavenly reunion of the widow with her husband and daughter. For her many years of faithful devotion to her lost family the widow was finally rewarded. Confucianism, socialism and Christianity all wrapped into one twenty-minute blockbuster I never got to see. I tried to see it, but I was stopped at the entrance to the theatre. It was in a military film competition and foreigners were not allowed. No matter how long my 'co-stars' pleaded, I wasn't allowed in. By definition my film was classified material.

Not long after filming had finished I was invited to attend a dinner with my co-stars and crew. It was quite a grand affair, upstairs at a famous beancurd restaurant in a northern suburb of Chengdu. There were lots of top-notch dishes I couldn't usually afford, and lots of *baijiu*. As the night went on and we'd had quite a bit to drink the subject of conversation turned eventually to my work in Tibet. Crew and cast had all spent some time in Tibetan communities and were keen to show off the Tibetan words they had picked up, like *chang thung* (Drink your beer!), *tsampa*, and *sha* (meat).

'Why are you so interested in Tibetans?' they asked. (This question always seemed to imply that Tibetans didn't deserve anyone's time or interest.) I began to tell them something about what I thought I was doing, and why the West found Tibetan Buddhism interesting. Then the make-up lady who had transformed me into a priest — and then into God — suddenly said three words that left the whole table silent: 'I'm a Tibetan.' This left me surprised and a little confused, because when I had asked her this question only a few weeks earlier she had said she wasn't. Her colleagues were equally stunned. It seems she had managed to hide her identity for more than thirty years, and pass as a Han-Chinese. One of the men even asked her if her Chinese husband knew, which he did. There were a lot of embarrassed looks at the table.

She had spent thirty years denying her Tibetan identity. I think tears came to my eyes when I thought I might have had a role in her choosing her moment to 'come out'. But the role of the anthropologist is all too easily exaggerated. I am quite certain that the nostalgic theme of the film we had made must have played no small role in influencing Li — her Chinese name is the only one she uses now — to take off her mask. The time for her patience to be rewarded had also come. True to her profession she chose, I think unconsciously, a wonderfully theatrical moment to do it. Or the moment chose the time for her. By interjecting when she did, Li cut in just as the anthropologist was about to take on the responsibility of representing her culture; the moment the fantasy of Tibet was about to arrive in the hallucinatory space of the restaurant.

12
Many paths

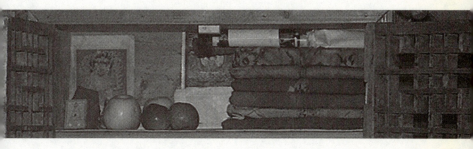

*I* returned to Australia at the beginning of 1992. It took a long time — three years facing down the black dog of depression — but in the end I realised I had got what I wanted. I had enough material to scrape my thesis together, thanks mainly to Akha Sherab. But what I had brought home wasn't what I had expected. I had come to learn that the stories of cultural contact and crisis I had found were more significant than the museum-piece picture of Tibet I had started out with; I still wonder what Akha Sherab got out of it. I continue to visit Rebkong every few years, mainly just to keep in touch, and I keep promising myself I'll get back there to do serious work on a number of projects I have in mind.

Every visit to Rebkong reveals so much, and Sherab especially continues to surprise me. Before one of my visits, in 1995, he produced a short biography that revealed something of his own trajectory before our first meeting. The original document had been dictated orally in Tibetan. Karma, a young man whose family had not long returned from decades of exile in Sikkim, had written it out in English. There is no written version in Tibetan. I was asked by Sherab to rewrite it for him into a hardcover notebook using my best composition and handwriting skills. I was also given permission to copy it into my own notebook for use in my work. I think it has much to say about the context in which our exchanges took place, and he also reveals that the workings of *ley-wang*, the power of karma, may be leading in a more unusual direction still.

I was born in the late 1950s at Rebkong Gyelwo Gang. My father's name was Tashi, and the name of my mother was Dechen Kyi. Gyelwo Gang, my family's village, is located on a hill near the great mountain known as Amye Taglung. About 120 families live there. They are all engaged in farming, and usually each family also has a few cattle. It has always been the custom of our village to take pity on others, helping everyone in need of help, as well as avoiding sinful conduct. There are many Nyingmapa practising the Buddhist religion. After my birth I was given the name Katub Gya.

When I was only two years old my parents separated. I was left in the care of my mother and we soon moved to her mother's home. Not long afterwards, in 1958, the land fell into severe famine, and all the children between three and seven years old were taken to nursery homes. By Chinese and Tibetan reckoning I was three years old and so I was now taken away from my mother too. In the nursery perhaps one in three of the children died of hunger and sickness. Then, after three years, the famine ended. The nursery homes were closed and I was reclaimed by my mother.

A few years later the Cultural Revolution began, and lasted for three years. When I was eight years old my mother began living with a new husband. I was left in the care of my mother's mother and my uncle, but it wasn't long before they sent me to live with a woman living alone who had no husband or children. I was really like a servant in her house, and she often beat me. I was still very small and the work was too hard. After a year I ran back to stay with my grandmother. At that time a village school had opened. I first went to school when I was ten years old.

When I was eleven I was given away again. This time I went to live with a nomad couple. They were old and had no children of their own. Really I was luckier this time. They treated me much like their own child, but after attending school I yearned for learning, and life on the high pasture was lonely and hard for me at that age. Then my grandmother came and took me back into her home. I didn't know what to expect. I wondered how long it would be before I was given away again. But they were happy to have me back and even asked me why I looked so worried. When my grandmother said she would look after me I pleaded with her that she never give me away to anyone ever again, and I made a promise to never burden them when I was older.

I was eleven when I returned to the village school, and I kept studying there until I was seventeen. At that time we only had to study what we were told to, there was no distinction between pass and fail, and there were no divisions into elementary and high schools. When I finished school I joined others working in the fields. That was the only work people did at that time. Nobody worked in offices. Everyone was working in the countryside. That was the system then.

I worked with a shovel for nine years, supporting myself as well as my grandmother's family. The farm work taught me much — particularly that one should not harm others, especially not the poor.

Around 1980 things started to improve as China opened

up. Tibetan culture and religion were allowed again after being banned for many years. With the aim of helping others I became a monk at the age of twenty-five. Entering Rongwo Monastery I took the name Gendün Sherab, although the name on my identity card is the same one I was given at birth. After entering the monastery I began to meet foreign travellers. The first was Margaret Causeman, a German. She spoke Tibetan and I was able to learn a little English.

Only after a long time did I have another opportunity to study English. An Australian man studying in Sichuan came to the monastery and spent a long time learning about Tibetan life. We became friends and later I travelled to Chengdu. There I realised that our Tibetan standard of living was low, but that our spiritual achievement was high.

Later I met a man named Winkler who invited me to Beijing. There I met Mr Lambert Kohl in 1993.

So ends Sherab's short biography. While it provided only the bare bones of his life history, it made me aware of the many ways in which his life has been shaped by the forces that surround him. It was also a very Buddhist presentation of his life, a moving illustration of one of the defining doctrines of Buddhism, the 'three marks of existence': impermanence, suffering and no-self. Wherever we are on the Wheel of Life, whether we have risen high or low, nothing remains as it is, it is hard to find anything reliable, and even our 'own' life will be taken away. And impermanence is only one of many forms of suffering, as we are separated constantly from whom or what we hold dear, and continually haunted by what we fear. And over the years I have come to understand that the doctrine of no-self does not only mean that there is no essential 'me', that as I live I am constantly being redefined, but also that the world does not co-operate as 'mine', it resists my will — 'the world' is impersonal.

Sherab's story is imprinted with all the 'three marks'. As a child he witnessed other children die around him. For a long time he had no home or family to speak of, passed from one guardian to another, wondering where he belonged. And the events of history ground on around him, reminding us of the invisible complexity that shapes any one individual. His life so far has straddled a remarkable period of Tibetan history. It also tells us of many other issues in contemporary Tibetan culture: the remarkable flexibility of Tibetan families in Amdo; the ambiguous social position of children and the weight of cross-generational authority; the presence of mountain ancestor cults in the lives of Tibetan communities; the ability of people to resist domination and to revive a religion that has been systematically destroyed; and that some roles in a community, like monks, are more open to the outside world than others.

The arrival of Western identities in Sherab's life deserves comment. Margaret Causeman is, I believe, a German ethno-linguist who has published on the dialect of Nangchen, a Khampa region in the far south of Qinghai. The 'Australian man studying in Sichuan' was me. My notes on Winkler mention only that he was from Switzerland, and Mr Kohl …

A year or two after returning to Melbourne I received an overseas telephone call from Akha Sherab — at 3:00 am. He called to tell me he was in Zhengzhou, an important city in northern China, and was going to Shaolin Monastery, the temple famous for its *kungfu*, the next day. And then he casually informed me that he would be flying to Beijing and on to Switzerland. He asked me if I wanted to speak to his German friend, Ge Lou. It was a very short conversation; I hadn't had time to take it all in. But after hanging up I concluded that 'Ge Lou' must be one of those eccentric German students that seem to be everywhere in China. In fact, as I later found out, 'Ge Lou' was Mr Kohl, an engineer and a representative for a large German earthmoving equipment firm, who worked from an office in the exclusive Beijing Hotel, and moved between Germany, Switzerland, Cyprus, Beijing and, apparently, Rebkong.

Back in Rebkong in 1995 I got to see the latest photos in Sherab's album. During his stay in Beijing he had resided at the five-star Jianguo Hotel, partied at the Swiss embassy, become a personal friend of the Swiss ambassador and many other diplomats, and holidayed with the foreign diplomatic and business community in Xiangshan, the 'Fragrant Hills' resort area in the mountains west of Beijing. (His family and fellow monks were somewhat perturbed by the holiday snaps of Sherab lounging by the pool in swimming attire!) He then ran into passport application difficulties that neither Kohl nor the ambassador were able to fix — and he did not make it to Switzerland. Not that year, anyway. Eventually he did — two times and counting.

Most of the prominent names in the history of Rebkong and Amdo have travelled a variety of paths. Many of them had to make the important journey to Lhasa if they wanted to pursue higher studies in Buddhist philosophy. Some went further, visiting the holy places of India, like the great yogin Shabkar or the modern revolutionary Gendün Chöphel. Some went through China too, visiting pilgrimage sites; or, as quite often happened, they were invited to study or teach in the Chinese capital. While Sherab may not be remembered as one of the most prominent Rebkong Tibetans, his travels mirror many of those by Tibetan Buddhists, as they explore their opportunities for spiritual development.

When I left Rebkong in 1992, among the things I was given to bring home by Akha Sherab's brother Kunzang was a short essay by a young local writer named Dondrup Gyel, published in the important Tibetan literary journal *Gentle Rain*. Part autobiography, part short story, 'A Threadlike Path' was a meditation on nostalgia and cultural revitalisation. Running through it is the image of the path from his home village, and what such paths may mean for small villages — not only in Rebkong but throughout Tibet. The only link to the outside world, 'the threadlike path' has endured the battering of centuries of snow and rain; it has sometimes suffered under the feet of countless generations, and sometimes it has become stronger as villagers have strained with the climb. But as far as Dondrup Gyel could see, the venerable elders of the village today could only boast about their family ancestors who blazed the trail or fight over which legendary figure had the greater hand in it.

None of this equalled the love he developed for the path on his way to school for the first time: the air full of early mist, the ground soft underfoot, the path descending through one wood after another as it writhed dragon-like down the mountainside. As he progresses he picks up on the legends that the old folk are endlessly talking about, and realises that their stories reveal a heroic spirit that might have been lost. It was once a path that showed the way to the glorious cultural achievements of the Tibetan people and how these spread to the four ends of the world.

When they were not trying to bask in their ancestors' glory, the old folk cursed them for leaving them such a paltry thoroughfare. And even good monks, ever mindful of their mantras, seemed to have little thought for the track under their feet. Passing along the path every day none lifted a hand to improve it. Tibetans rode on mules while around them there were people travelling all over the world, over land, through the air and across the seas.

One year the path was washed out by a torrent spilling down the mountain and still no one lifted a finger. They were too busy arguing about who really owned it, or worrying about how the local spirits might react. After 1949 great highways had been blasted through the valley, broader than anyone had ever seen before. These highways had their own faults: they had treacherous bends and they wound back and forth so much before they could get to the pass. They were murder to walk on and they created two classes of people — drivers and basket carriers, who would endlessly abuse each other.

Weighing up his thoughts, his fondness for his people and his homeland tearing at his heart, Dondrup Gyel comes to what he describes as an irreversible decision, and he turns and walks onto the new highway.

When I first read his story I thought that Dondrup Gyel's decision was a decision in favour of 'progress', in particular the Chinese version of 'progress', since the broad highway clearly represents the arrival of not just a new technology but a new power. Yet now I do not think that is what he was saying, at least not exactly. He did not mean to suggest that Tibetan ways are irrelevant and ready to be superseded or forgotten. There is deep fondness for his homeland and its traditions at every turn in the story. What he may be saying, in turning towards the new highway, is that as a Tibetan he is ready for a new and even greater kind of wandering. He invokes the heroic spirit of Tibet's original trailblazers and this enables him to take what might have been a raw symbol of external domination and transform it into a means for 'self-liberation', in Tibetan *rangyel*, which he took for his favourite *nom de plume*. This fits well with the tantric tradition of Tibet, the path of transformation where poison becomes *amrita*, the 'elixir of life'. The new highway through Rebkong provides for the rebuilding of ancient monasteries as well as entry into the global debate concerning human rights and diversity. It also leads out beyond the limiting dualism of China–Tibet relations. Tibetans have more to contend with than just China.

In 1985, just a year after 'A Threadlike Path' was published, its author, Dondrup Gyel, ended his own life, aged just thirty-two. In one version of events it was said that he had already been depressed when he got word that the PSB were planning to seize him. One night, before they could arrive, he drank himself into a stupor and then let his room fill with the fumes of burning coal from the stove that kept it warm.

Dondrup Gyel had been a leading light in Tibetan intellectual circles. At the Central Nationalities Institute in Beijing he had completed a brilliant Masters' thesis under one of the most prominent Tibetan scholars of the old generation. By any standard he should have been given a university post, but back in Qinghai he was sent to teach in a middle school in a small town well out of harm's way. He had spoken out too boldly, both against the government and against conservative or ineffectual leaders in Amdo. The highway had run into a dead end.

On an early spring morning on my last visit back to Rebkong in 2001, I walked once again up to Gyelwo Gang. There was still no road, although I could see by the tracks that someone was taking a jeep up there every so often. Stepping through the gate of Kunzang's father's house, I found his father resting barefoot in the sunshine on the porch. Kunzang was down in Tongren doing some shopping, so I sat down with his parents and their grandchildren to have a cup of tea. Their courtyard was tidier than I had remembered it, and under some hay beside the stock pen I could see they had a new mechanical threshing machine. It was a gift from Mr Kohl.

As evening began to fall, the light of the sun shifted across the porch. The air started to chill, crystals of dew forming in the air. The whole village glowed as golden light spread out from behind the faraway peak of Ancestor Garuda. Up above, the sky was on fire with flames of magenta and emerald. I begged my hosts' pardon, picked up my camera and went out into the village lane. A mule was heading home, unattended, with a load of briar twigs. Across the village's northern spur the temple was red, neon, ochre. On the eastern horizon, hovering above the dark crevice of the river, clouds like pale-blue lotus leaves cradled the rising moon. Children headed home, their backs laden with casks of water. The deep valleys around us were pure space, aqueous in opal light.

Kunzang, hurrying home, came up the path, cheeks flushed, and we walked back to the house in the dark. He had brought Chinese chives to make dumplings for dinner. Always doing his utmost. Back inside, the kitchen-room glowed with the heat of the hearth fire. As Kunzang chopped the meat his father took his usual place in the warm alcove above the stove, soon to be joined by his seven-year-old granddaughter, Drolma Tsö, who was the daughter of one of Kunzang's brothers. Under a naked light bulb she reviewed her *Chinese Reader*, much to the pleasure of her granddad. I asked if I could look at it, and, showing off, I read her a few lines — stories about butterflies and good children. She followed me, or rather anticipated my every word, reciting her lessons from memory.

That night in Kunzang's room we watched a Tibetan movie on the new video player, another present from Mr Kohl. Made in Chinese at the Shanghai Film Studio, and later dubbed in Tibetan, *Red River Valley* (or *A Tale of the Sacred Mountain*) was the latest big thing, and everyone was very excited about it. Drolma Tsö and a few other kids joined us. The video player whirred and the show flickered to life. What unfolded in front of us was China's answer to *Seven Years in Tibet*. There was a tragic love story between a beautiful Chinese girl and a tall, dark and handsome Tibetan hero, but it was hard to tell if the love story was the background to the British massacre of Tibetans at Gyantse in 1904, or if it was the other way around. At one point a central tenet of the Chinese Communist Party's policy on human rights was neatly announced by a Tibetan leader: 'China and Tibet are one family, and no one should meddle in China's internal affairs.' If the movie had a take-away message, the audience was left in no doubt that this was it. The film has since become a cornerstone of China's international propaganda tour, 'China Tibetan Cultural Week'.

Drolma Tsö knew the whole dialogue by heart. It was exciting, it was big and colourful, and it was sad too. But every line? As we watched she recited the actors' lines a fraction of a second before they leapt from the actors' mouths. We could have switched the sound off and let her fill in the entire dialogue; Drolma Tsö was no doubt a prodigy. Clearly too, this family had watched *Red River Valley* many times over. It was one of only a small handful of movies that described Tibetan culture in any way, and it had been supported by a decent budget and produced with all the quality of a major motion picture. In Rebkong the neighbourhood video library is two hours walk away; when a movie like this comes out in Tibetan it finds a hungry audience. As men with beards and long noses shot down unarmed Tibetans I squirmed in my seat. Fortunately, this was not one of the movies I had played in.

The next morning Kunzang took me on a trek to the village at the end of the valley where he was one of the two teachers at the primary school. It was two hours away, skirting around the base of Ancestor Tiger Valley. The air was eye-watering cold. On the way we happened upon two weddings, including one that was, as it happened, for Akha Sherab's son. As he was a monk, Akha Sherab did not attend, and had not even mentioned it. We were grateful for the chance to warm up with *baijiu* and noodles before heading on again.

Behind a high wall Kunzang's school stood on a hillside. Two small classrooms faced a sloping square. In the square was a bare flagpole. It was holidays. Up the hill were the teachers' quarters — two rooms, one for each teacher. Each room served as living quarters and office. There was not a single toilet — not for the teachers, not for the children. The teachers' rooms were in bad repair, the classrooms were worse. Most of the windows were broken, and half of one door was missing. From the state of disrepair it was clear the damage had been accumulating over a long time. Repairs had to be initiated by the teachers, with the funding collected from the villagers. Funding was the real rub, and Kunzang had learned that a repair project might have the unhappy consequence of diminishing his already paltry salary. It looked like nothing had been done since the school was first built in the late 1970s.

Leaving the school and heading out of the village Kunzang and I started on the three-hour walk down to Tongren on the other side of the gorge. Not far along, at a spot where the mountainside dropped away into a massive valley, I noticed a bunch of sticks tangled up in wool just off the road. It was a thread-cross, or *namkha*. Made from two crossed wooden sticks wound with coloured wool, *namkha* are a device as old as culture itself — used by shamans and *lamas* to net malevolent spirits and other invisible dangers and hurled out into the elements, usually at a crossroads, where they are left to slowly dissolve. The two crossed sticks represent a person's life, and perhaps also time and space — for it is from their conception, a perfectly unique point in time and space, that each individual springs. The coloured threads represent the network of elements through which we grow. It is such a strange thing, the life that appears in space around us.

My thoughts went back to Kunzang's brilliant little niece, Drolma Tsö. And to the brilliant writer Dondrup Gyel, and his first walk to school along the threadlike path, and his lonely death on the floor of a squalid schoolhouse. I also thought of the struggle that Akha Sherab had to find a warm home as a boy, let alone a path to school.

How things had changed. Drolma Tsö was the apple of

her grandparents' eye. When they watched her recite from her *Chinese Reader* I swear I could see the pride and love swell in their hearts. Everyone in the village had been surprised by the appearance of this jewel. But what will fate have in store for a bright little Tibetan girl hidden away in her ancestral mountains? Where will the threadlike path that winds up to her village lead her? Will fate find her a highway?

Epilogue

One of the things I dreaded most in China was packing parcels at the post office. No matter who you were, you had to pack your overseas parcels in the post office in front of the staff. In the past this had meant taking along rolls of brown paper, packing twine, scissors and your own glue. On the day before I flew home I gritted my teeth, loaded up my backpack, got on the bus and headed off to the post office in Wangfujing, Beijing's central commercial avenue.

It was the middle of the morning and the streets were as crowded as only Chinese streets can be. It took me a long while, carrying a very full pack of books, to find the post office. I didn't know it was down a crossroad. Then, just as I approached the post-office door, I recognised the back of the head of the person in front of me. I don't know why. I hadn't ever met him before. But the impression was so strong I yelled out to make sure he heard, 'Lambert! Lambert Kohl!' I had never seen him before, except in Akha Sherab's photo album. How I recognised Kohl from the back of his head I will never understand.

With joy and disbelief we stood in the street out the front of the post office and looked at each other. Kohl knew who I was straight away. Although we had not met each other before, Sherab's *ley-wang*, as well as our own, had finally guided us towards each other in one of the most crowded cities in the world. Even more remarkable, it was my last day before flying out of the country. Kohl had been moved back to Switzerland and was only travelling through Beijing after finishing some business in the far northeast. We arranged to meet in the evening and go out for a beer.

That night in his hotel room Kohl told me his life story. I can't remember all the details, but what I do remember is startling enough. Before joining the earthmoving equipment company he had been a very successful businessman. But in 1979, after the shah was overthrown, he was gaolled in Iran. Either he or his partners were accused of some kind of embezzlement by the new government of the Islamic republic. He was released after seven months and the charges were never substantiated.

He easily climbed up the ladder of success again, and he and his wife enjoyed the best Europe had to offer. Then she contracted cancer. The two travelled the world looking for a cure, but in the end the disease took her from him. Her death was devastating. Soon afterward he went blind, probably from grief, and he returned to live with his mother. Nothing the doctors did helped. Still blind, he travelled to Hungary to work in soup kitchens run for the homeless. Then, just as suddenly as it had disappeared, his sight returned.

Starting from scratch he studied engineering, got a new profession, and was posted to Beijing for seven years. There, in 1993, he met Akha Sherab, who was staying with friends from the Swiss embassy. They immediately became firm friends. I was so happy to meet him, finally closing the loop that had formed between us. And after I heard about the life he had led I was even more amazed. I also knew that Sherab was in very safe hands on his trips to Europe.

When I got to my room at the hotel another gentleman had arrived to take the other bed. He was Australian: Anglo-Indian. His father had been an officer in the Indian army. And everything he said convinced me he was mad. I think I still have his business card somewhere. He called himself 'Mr Planet'. He was only staying one night — an Ethiopian friend had found somewhere much cheaper, and he really only needed the bath. And he did need a bath. Mr Planet was travelling around the world, for the seventh time, on his shoestring mission to visit every single country. He could achieve this, and survive, he said, because he was a master of disguises. He showed me some of his photos from Africa to prove it. He was also a master at bribing border officials, and was in China to attempt a visit to North Korea.

Mr Planet reminded me of the strange world I was going back to, where images are circulated purely to fascinate or momentarily entertain. Perhaps by now his story has been told to the tabloids and on the midday shows, and then forgotten. In Rebkong images had always been made to be treasured, and no one was quite sure about what to do with the new kinds of images arriving from the outside world. Perhaps, after his travels in Europe, Akha Sherab will be better placed to interpret the phantoms our world creates. Or perhaps when I next get back to Rebkong Akha Sherab will no longer be there.

Glossary

Note: Most terms are defined where they are initially used in the text. The words listed here are those of particular significance or those that are used repeatedly. Approximate Rebkong pronunciation for Tibetan words, where radically different, is indicated by 'Reb.' Also, Tib. = Tibetan; Ch. = Chinese; Skt = Sanskrit.

ache lhamo   Tib. a dramatic art developed by Thangtong Gyelpo in the fourteenth century; Tibetan opera.
akha   Tib. term of address for monks in Amdo, often added before a monk's name. It is also used like 'Uncle' before the name of a man senior to oneself.
alak   Tib. honorific term of address in Amdo for important *lamas*, Reb. *ah-lok*.
Amdo   Tib. the northeastern province of Tibet, also called Domey.
amrita   Skt ambrosia, the nectar of immortality.
Avalokiteshvara   Skt a sublime manifestation of the compassion energy of the buddhas, Avalokiteshvara has a special relationship to the history and culture of the Tibetan people.
baijiu   Ch. strong distilled spirit.
bardo   Tib. 'the in-between', the intermediate state between life and death; states of psychological transition.

Glossary

bodhicitta   Skt a mind set on enlightenment; altruistic intention.

bodhisattva   Skt 1) a person who has committed to achieving enlightenment for the benefit of all sentient beings; 2) a deity embodying one or several aspects of enlightened mind.

Bön   Tib. the native pre-Buddhist religion of Tibet, later much influenced by Buddhist thought.

buddha   Skt 'the awakened one', a fully enlightened being.

char siew bao   Ch. (Cantonese) a steamed bun filled with a sweet mixture of diced roast pork and onions, a delicacy from the Cantonese cuisine.

Chengdu   Ch. capital city of Sichuan province.

chöley   Tib. religious activities.

chöra   Tib. literally 'religious enclosure,' monastic courtyard, debating ground.

chorten   Tib. (Skt *stupa*) a monument, usually a white dome topped with a spire, containing relics of the Buddha or other important Buddhist teachers.

Cultural Revolution   a period of ultra-leftist upheaval (1966–76) that began with an attempt by Mao Zedong to regain control of Communist Party policy and re-establish his own ideal of the complete revolutionisation of the masses. The result was ten years of political chaos and vast human misery.

daka   Skt a male angel of enlightenment.

dakini   Skt a female angel of enlightenment.

Dalai Lama   Tib. the temporal and spiritual leader of Tibet (since the seventeenth century). Emanations of Avalokiteshvara, the Dalai Lamas are the most important and revered series of reincarnate *lamas* in Tibet. The present Dalai Lama is the Fourteenth.

danwei   Ch. work unit, place of employment.

demo kyi   Tib. farewell, Reb. *demo chee*.

dharma   Skt the teaching of the Buddha.

Domey Chöjung   Tib. a religious history of northeastern Tibet, researched, written and published by the monk Konchog Rabgye in the nineteenth century.

dön Tib. bad luck spirit, Reb. *hdon*.

donmo Tib. feast or party, Reb. *doonmu*.

drokpa Tib. nomadic pastoralists.

düd Tib. spirit interfering with the positive influence of religion, Reb. *dil*.

dukhang Tib. assembly hall, main hall of a monastery, Reb. *nderkang*.

dzongthap Tib. heated bed/sitting platform, Reb. *êdzong-tev*.

fentang Ch. soup with bean-flour noodles.

gakhyil Tib. whorl of delight, pinwheel pattern, Reb. *ga-chee*.

ganban Ch. egg-noodles with lamb mince, vegetables and gravy.

Gang of Four a group of four political opportunists implementing Mao Zedong's policies during the Cultural Revolution. They included Mao Zedong's wife, Jiang Qing. All were arrested after trying to gain control of the Chinese Communist Party following Mao's death in 1976.

gar Tib. an outpost or encampment monastery, a term often found in the names of Nyingma monasteries or monasteries based near communities of nomadic herdsmen.

garuda Skt a giant bird of Indian myth, symbol of primordial wisdom in the Nyingma tradition, Reb. *(shya-)choong*.

gekö Tib. proctor responsible for discipline and organisation in a monastery, Reb. *gef-kee*.

Geluk Tib. literally 'the tradition of virtue', one of the four main orders of Tibetan Buddhism, associated with political power in much of Tibet since the seventeenth century.

Gesar Tib. the legendary king of the kingdom of Ling, and hero of Tibet's great epic of the same name.

gompa Tib. literally 'place of seclusion', a monastery or centre of religious life.

Glossary

gonchen Tib. a large monastery.

gondag Tib. the 'Lord' of the monastery, the supreme spiritual head of a monastery, usually the monastery's chief *trülku*.

gonyer Tib. temple doorkeeper.

gorey Tib. (loaf or bun of) bread, Reb. *go-ree*.

gyang Tib. stamped-earth walls, Reb. *jyang*.

Han Ch. the ethnic Chinese.

Huangnan Ch. Tibetan Autonomous Prefecture including the Tibetan tribal region of Rebkong.

huaquan Ch. drinking game.

Hui Ch. a Muslim ethnic group widely distributed through China.

Jambhala Skt a god of wealth.

jataka Skt tales recounting the previous lives of the Buddha.

Je Tib. a term of address, 'Lord'. An epithet of Tsongkhapa.

kang Ch. a heated bed/sitting platform.

karma Skt literally 'action', but usually implying actions and their effects.

Kham Tib. the eastern province of Tibet.

khatak Tib. ceremonial scarf, Reb. *kaptag*.

labrang Tib. monastic mansion, Reb. *la-trang*.

Labrang Tib. important monastic university in Amdo.

lama Tib. spiritual master, religious leader. Originating as an equivalent of the Sanskrit term guru, the title *lama* is applied to highly qualified religious teachers, and by custom also to incarnate *lamas*, or *trülku*.

laowai Ch. nickname for 'foreigners'.

ley-wang Tib. the manifestation of past deeds, the power of karma, Reb. *ley-reng*.

lhabzo Tib. master painter of icons.

lhakang Tib. temple or shrine room.

lhatse Tib. a cairn marking a power place, especially those associated with mountain gods.

liumang Ch. lout.

losar Tib. New Year.

Mahayana Skt the Great Vehicle, a system of Buddhist practice emphasising compassion together with social orthodoxy.

Maitreya Skt 'the Loving One', the buddha to come, the buddha of a future age.

Malho Tib. name of Huangnan Tibetan autonomous prefecture.

mandala Skt a sacred circle.

mani Skt in Tibet, the mantra *Om Manipadme Hum*.

mani drupchen Tib. a celebration of the *mani*.

Manjushri Skt the sublime manifestation of the wisdom energy of the buddhas. Usually depicted as a handsome youth sitting cross-legged, Manjushri holds a sword aloft with his right hand and at his heart his left hand holds the stem of a lotus flower supporting the Perfection of Wisdom Sutra in its petals.

mantou Ch. steamed bread.

mantra Skt a set of spoken or written 'sounds' which when repeated have the power to transform consciousness and, by extension, situations.

Mantrayana Skt the Secret Mantrayana, see Vajrayana.

Mao Zedong (1893–1976) Chinese Communist Party founder.

mo Ch. baked unleavened bread.

momo Tib. meat-filled dumplings.

Monguor An ethnic group related to Mongolians and located in eastern Qinghai province.

mudra Skt sacred hand gesture.

namkha Tib. thread-cross, a ritual scapegoat.

nang Ch. the same word as *nan* in Central Asia, meaning unleavened bread. A 'oan word' of some antiquity in Chinese, it is a word used only by particular Muslim communities in China.

nangso Tib. the tribal leader of the Twelve Tribes of Rebkong, Reb. *nang-zo*.

ngak-khang Tib. village temple used by *ngakpa*, Reb. *ngêk-kêng*.

ngakmang Tib. literally 'many yogins', the 'Nineteen Hundred *Phurba* Holding Mantrins of Rebkong', Reb. *ngêk-mêng*.

ngakpa Tib. practitioner of Secret Mantra, in Rebkong, mantra-adept of the Nyingma order leading the life of a villager, Reb. *ngêk-hwa*.

nirvana Skt liberation from the endless cycle of suffering.

Nyenthok Gar Tib. name of Geluk monastery in Rebkong, just north of Tongren, Reb. *Nyên-thug*.

Nyingma Tib. order of Tibetan Buddhism venerating the teachings of Padmasambhava, Reb. *Nyêng-ma*.

nyönba Tib. crazy person, crazy yogin.

Om Manipadme Hum Skt 'Om O Jewel-Lotus Hum', the mantra of the enlightened being Avalokiteshvara, sublime manifestation of compassion.

Padmasambhava Skt name of a great master and mystic active in Tibet in the eighth century, also known as Guru Rinpoche.

phurba Skt ritual dagger, Reb. *pherwa*.

PLA People's Liberation Army.

pönpo Tib. head of a nomad group or of a village, Reb. *hwen-bu*.

PSB Public Security Bureau.

puja Skt a ritual offering.

qigong Ch. literally 'inner-energy (*qi*) techniques', qigong includes the manipulation of inner energy for curing or fighting in traditional Chinese medicine and martial arts.

Qinghai Ch. province in northwestern China, capital Xining.

qingzhen Ch. 'pure and true', *halal*.

Rimé a nineteenth-century non-sectarian movement in eastern Tibet that included many Nyingma, Sakya and Kagyü masters.

rinpoche Tib. literally 'precious one', honorific title for *trülku* and occasionally other respected teachers.

ritrö Tib. mountain retreat.

Glossary

Samantabhadra Skt 'Forever Good', the name of a buddha or *bodhisattva* with special significance in the Nyingma order.

samdra Skt a small, rectangular, hand-held blackboard.

samsara Skt cyclic existence, the repeated and relentless confusion and suffering experienced by sentient beings under the spell of self-centredness, see also Wheel of Life.

Shakyamuni Buddha The historical Buddha (c.541–c.461 BCE), usually referred to in Tibetan as Shakyatubpa. The enlightened founder of the Buddhist tradition.

shimkhang Tib. residence of an important *lama*.

Sichuan Ch. a province in southwest China, capital Chengdu.

siddha Skt an adept of yoga who has acquired higher insight and supernatural abilities.

Sri Kalachakra Tantra Skt the *Glorious Wheel of Time Tantra*, the central text of the 'Wheel of Time' system of *tantra*.

stupa Skt see *chorten*.

sutra Skt a text containing the Buddha's teachings.

tantra Skt a presentation of methods, usually rich in symbolism, for achieving fully enlightened buddhahood.

TAR Tibet Autonomous Region, the administrative region of Tibet as currently defined on Chinese maps.

Tara Skt in Indo-Tibetan Buddhism a female *bodhisattva* and 'mother of the buddhas' (i.e. the matrix of compassion), represented in iconography as a young maiden, 'the saviouress'.

thangka Tib. a Tibetan scroll painting.

thukpa Tib. noodle soup.

Tongren Ch. name of Chinese administrative county in Rebkong.

torma Tib. an offering-cake that features in many Tibetan rituals.

trülku Tib. literally 'emanation body', a reincarnate *lama*, recognised (usually in childhood) as the rebirth of a predecessor and empowered to act in the capacity of the previous *lama*. Great Buddhist masters, important historical figures, and sometimes even those closely associated with them, have been catalysts for lineages of *trülku* in Tibetan history. Reb. *strêgê*.

tsamkya   Tib. the flour ground from parched barley, Reb. *dzam-chya*.

tsampa   Tib. parched barley flour mixed into cakes with a little hot water (or tea) and butter, Reb. *dzam-ba*.

tsathab   Tib. a heated bed/sitting platform, Reb. *tsa-tev*.

Tsongkhapa   Tib. (1357–1419) the founder of the Geluk order. Born in Tsongkha, Amdo. Reb. *Dzong-ga-ba*.

tsowa   Tib. a local settlement or group, a tribe.

tubazong   Ch. a title given to Monguor headmen.

Twelve Tribes of Rebkong   A confederacy of twelve farming and nomad tribes in Rebkong, loyal supporters of Rongwo Monastery.

Ü-Tsang   Tib. the two provinces of Central Tibet surrounding the Tibetan capital, Lhasa, Reb. *wee-tsang*.

vajra   Skt the king of stones, the diamond, or an adamantine thunderbolt. Symbol of compassion, decisiveness and insight. Also a symbol of the Vajrayana.

Vajrayana   Skt 'Diamond Vehicle', a branch vehicle (or path) of the Mahayana employing *tantra* as a rapid means to enlightenment.

Vinaya   Skt 'discipline', the Buddhist codes of monastic discipline and ethical guidelines.

Wheel of Life   a diagram showing the arising of cyclic existence (*samsara*), divided into the two upper realms of gods and humans, and the three lower realms of animals, hungry ghosts and denizens of hell. At its centre it is driven by the energy of greed (symbolised by a pigeon or cock), hatred (a snake) and ignorance (a pig), each chasing each other in an endless circle. The aim of Buddhist enlightenment is to escape from the suffering found in all forms and all realms of cyclic existence. Reb. *shepi-khorlo*.

Xining   Ch. capital of Qinghai province.

yamtsen   Tib. Amazing! Incredible!

yinji   Tib. foreigner, European.

yoga Skt in the context of Tibetan Buddhism, union with (or return to) the real or natural state.

yogin Skt a practitioner who is pursuing the realisation of *yoga*.

yum cha Ch. literally 'drink tea'. In Cantonese cuisine of southern China, an array of snacks taken as morning tea or lunch.

Recommended reading

David-Neel, Alexandra and Lama Yongden. *The Superhuman Life of Gesar of Ling*, Shambhala Publications, Boston, 1987.

A bold tale of magic and adventure, recounting the life of Tibetan literature's warrior-king.

Doga, Geshe. *Inner Peace and Happiness: The Path to Freedom*, Lothian Books, South Melbourne, 2002.

A gentle, contemporary teaching on the path from self-centredness to more open ways of approaching life.

Ekvall, Robert. *Tents Against the Sky: A Novel of Tibet*, Gollancz, London, 1954.

A novelised account of Ekvall's experiences as a missionary in Amdo.

Heller, Amy. *Tibetan Art: Tracing the Development of Spiritual Ideals and Art in Tibet, 600–2000 AD*, Jaca, Milan, 1999.

A thorough and accessible history of Tibetan art that incorporates an account of its historical and social context. Highly recommended, but still not strong on Rebkong.

Recommended reading

Jackson, David. *A History of Tibetan Painting: The Great Tibetan painters and Their Traditions*, Verlag der Österreichischen Akademie der Wissenschaften, Wien, 1996.

A masterful history of the great masters of Tibetan painting and the movements they inspired, with good information on Rebkong.

Nietupski, Paul. *Labrang: A Tibetan Buddhist Monastery at the Crossroads of Four Civilizations*, Snow Lion Publications, Ithaca, New York, 1999.

A very readable introduction to this famous monastery and its role in regional tensions in the first half of the twentieth century, much of it based on missionary accounts.

Patrul, Rinpoche. *The Words of My Perfect Teacher*, trans. Padmakara Translation Group, HarperCollins Publishers, San Francisco, 1994.

A classic, traditional presentation of the foundations of Buddhist practice by a great nineteenth-century master of meditation.

Ricard, Matthieu. *The Life of Shabkar: The Autobiography of a Tibetan Yogin*, State University of New York Press, Albany, New York, 1994.

A lively autobiography of a nineteenth-century yogin, beautifully translated by a French Buddhist monk, that is full of spiritual insights and cultural detail from old Tibet.

Rock, Joseph. *The Amnye Ma-chhen Range and Adjacent Regions*, Is. M.E.O., Rome, 1956.

An early geographical survey of the Amdo region, including information on Rebkong and good maps. Usually available in larger university libraries.

Sogyal, Rinpoche. *The Tibetan Book of Living and Dying*, revised edition, Rider, London, 2002.

> A contemporary introduction not just to the Tibetan teachings on life and death, but also to the nature of mind.

Traleg, Kyabgon. *The Essence of Buddhism: An Introduction to its Philosophy and Practice*, Shambhala Publications, Boston, 2001.

> A comprehensive, clear introduction to the deeply transformative practices of the 'three paths' of Tibetan Buddhism.

Yeshe, Lama. *Introduction to Tantra: The Transformation of Desire*, Wisdom Publications, Somerville, 2001.

> An introduction to tantra in the Tibetan tradition, which demonstrates how everyday life can become the path.

Websites related to the themes of this book

An excellent place to start exploring the diverse world of Buddhism on the Internet is Buddhanet, run by the Buddha Dharma Education Association Incorporated, Sydney:
<http://buddhanet.net/>

An excellent place to start exploring the world of Tibetan Studies on the internet is Dr Matthew Ciolek's Asian Studies WWW Virtual Library where you may find the Tibetan Studies WWW Virtual Library:
<http://www.ciolek.com/WWWVL-TibetanStudies.html>

Another well-linked site is the homepage of the Australia Tibet Council:
<http://www.atc.org.au/>

Recommended reading

There is also a website introducing Dokham, or Eastern Tibet (combining Amdo and Kham) at:
<http://mdokhams.gmxhome.de/index.htm>

Bibliography

Barks, Coleman. *The Essential Rumi*, Harper San Francisco, San Francisco, 1997.

Birrell, Anne. *The Classic of Mountains and Seas* (Shan hai jing), Penguin, Harmondsworth, 1999.

Eliade, Mircea. *The Myth of the Eternal Return*, trans. Willard R. Trask, Pantheon Books, New York, 1954.

French, Rebecca. *The Golden Yoke: The Legal Cosmology of Buddhist Tibet*, Cornell University Press, Ithaca, 1995.

Ganze Zanghua editorial group. *Ganze Zanghua* [*Tibetan Paintings from Kantze*], Sichuan Nationalities Publishing House, Chengdu, 1987.

Gladney, Dru. *Muslim Chinese: Ethnic Nationalism in the People's Republic*, Council on East Asian Studies, Harvard University, Harvard University Press, Cambridge, Mass., 1991.

Huangnan gaikuang editorial group. *Huangnan Zangzu Zizhi Zhou Gaikuang* [*A Survey of the Huangnan Tibetan Autonomous Prefecture*], Qinghai Renmin Chubanshe, Xining, 1985.

Jackson, David. *A History of Tibetan Painting*, Verlag der Österreichischen Akademie der Wissenschaften, Wien, 1996.

Kohn, Richard. *Lord of the Dance: The Mani Rimdu Festival in Tibet and Nepal*, State University of New York, New York, 2001.

Lopez, Donald. *Prisoners of Shangri-la: Tibetan Buddhism and the West*, University of Chicago Press, Chicago, 1998.

Mullin, Glen, trans. *Path of the Bodhisattva Warrior: The Life and Teachings of the Thirteenth Dalai Lama*, Snow Lion Publications, Ithaca, New York, 1988.

Patrul Rinpoche. *The Words of My Perfect Teacher*, trans. Padmakara Translation Group, HarperCollins Publishers, San Francisco, 1994.

Smith, E. Gene. *Among Tibetan Texts*, Wisdom Publications, Boston, 2001.

Smith, Warren. *Tibetan Nation: A History of Tibetan Nationalism and Sino-Tibetan Relations*, Westview Press, Boulder, 1996.

Tibet Information Network. *A Poisoned Arrow: The Secret Report of the 10th Panchen Lama*, Tibet Information Network, London, 2000.

Tucci, Giuseppe. *To Lhasa and Beyond: Diary of the Expedition to Tibet in the Year 1948*, Snow Lion Publications, Ithaca, New York, 1987.

Wang Yao. 'Tibetan Operatic Themes', in Barbara Aziz and Matthew Kapstein, eds. *Soundings in Tibetan Civilization*, Manohar, New Delhi, 1985.

Wang Yao. *Tales from Tibetan Opera*, New World Press, Beijing, 1986.

Notes

1 A mantra is a 'spell' — a set of spoken or written 'sounds' which when repeated (verbally or by turning prayer wheels) have the power to transform consciousness and, by extension, situations. *'Om Manipadme Hum'* ('Om O Jewel-Lotus Hum') is the mantra of the enlightened being Avalokiteshvara (who in iconography holds a crystal rosary and a lotus). A sublime manifestation of the compassion energy of the buddhas, Avalokiteshvara has a special relationship to the history and culture of the Tibetan people. On the varied interpretations of this mantra, Tibetan and non-Tibetan, see Donald Lopez, 'The Spell', *Prisoners of Shangri-la*, pp. 114–34.
2 Tibet Information Network, *A Poisoned Arrow: The Secret Report of the 10th Panchen Lama*, p. xiv.
3 Lopez, *Prisoners of Shangri-la*, pp. 175–7.
4 My translation.
5 The Han make up approximately 90 per cent of China's population, with fifty-six minority nationalities making up the remainder. While the minority nationalities (including the Tibetans, Mongolians, Muslim Hui, Turkic-speaking Uighurs, and Koreans) are officially celebrated as part of China's 'unified multiethnic state', in practice the term 'Chinese' (Ch. *zhonguoren* [de]) is almost always used to refer to the Han people and their interests.

6 In Tibetan, a Tibetan inhabitant of Kham is known as a Khampa, and an inhabitant of Amdo is called an Amdowa.
7 *Ganze Zanghua* bianweihui (1987) *Ganze Zanghua* [Tibetan Paintings from Kantze]. Chengdu: Sichuan Nationalities Publishing House.
8 The Hui are one of China's many Muslim minorities.
9 The Chinese name Ta'er Si means 'Monastery of the Pagoda (or *chorten*)'.
10 The painters of Rebkong are concentrated in five villages in a single valley. This is a term used only by Chinese writers.
11 Traditional Chinese painting was divided into two broad categories: 1) *gongbihua*, a meticulous, detailed realism, and 2) *xieyi*, an impressionist style, in later dynasties sometimes bordering on abstraction.
12 Donald Lopez, *Prisoners of Shangri-la*, p. 152.
13 Dru Gladney, *Muslim Chinese: Ethnic Nationalism in the People's Republic*, pp. 26–7.
14 With 13.7 per cent of the population registering as Hui in 1982, Qinghai came second only to Ningxia Hui Autonomous Region (31.6 per cent), see Gladney, *Muslim Chinese*, Table 2, p. 28.
15 Anne Birrell has recently shed new light on the strange mythogeography of early China in her translation of *The Classic of Mountains and Seas* (Shan hai jing).
16 The term *buddha*, 'awakened one', was not originally meant to apply to any one individual. The Buddhist tradition (as we know it) begins with the historical Buddha, usually referred to in Tibetan as Shakyatubpa (Skt Shakyamuni), the great sage of the Shakya clan, Siddhartha Gautama (c.541–c.461 BCE). As a guiding teacher a buddha attracts in us an intuition of our own potential for spiritual awakening. Over many aeons there have been innumerable 'awakened ones', but in Buddhist symbolism and art the dynamic nature of an individual's evolution towards

awakening is depicted through images of a number of symbolically potent 'awakened ones', or buddhas, each represented as appearing in the field of space-energy in divine form.

17 Giuseppe Tucci, *To Lhasa and Beyond*, p. 90.
18 David Jackson, *A History of Tibetan Painting*, pp. 96–8.
19 E. Gene Smith, *Among Tibetan Texts*, pp. 161–2.
20 Glen Mullin (trans. and ed.), *Path of the Bodhisattva Warrior: The Life and Teachings of the Thirteenth Dalai Lama*, p. 263. My emphasis.
21 'Pastoral Areas of Tsinghai [Qinghai] Province in the Great Revolutionary High Tide' (1 October 1958), cited in Warren Smith, *Tibetan Nation: A History of Tibetan Nationalism and Sino-Tibetan Relations*, p. 409. My emphasis.
22 See Robert Desjarlais, *Sensory Biographies: Lives and Deaths Among Nepal's Yolmo Buddhists*, University of California Press, Berkeley, 2003.
23 In Central Tibet they are known as *momo*, but in Qinghai *momo* or *mo* refers to baked and steamed breads made mostly by Muslim bakers.
24 Sausages are of four main kinds: those made with meat (*shaye*), *tsampa* (*tsamye*), blood (*trakgyu*) and flour (*chyegyu*); the chief spice added to these is *yerma*, Szechuan pepper. Sausages are not normally made by men and are therefore not often eaten in the monasteries.
25 Patrul Rinpoche, *The Words of My Perfect Teacher*, pp. 209–10.
26 Ibid. p. 246.
27 Lopez, *Prisoners of Shangri-la*, p. 150.
28 *Huangnan gaikuang*, p. 69.
29 A member of the 'Second Generation' of Chinese filmmakers.
30 Coleman Barks, *The Essential Rumi*, p. 40.
31 Glen Mullin, *Path of the Bodhisattva Warrior*, p. 157.
32 Ibid. p. 161. From *Fifty Verses on the Guru*, by Asvagosha.
33 Richard Kohn, *Lord of the Dance*, p. 120.

Index

ache lhamo, masked drama 112–13
Achung Namdzong Hermitage 79
Amdo xvii, xviii, 6, 36, 39, 40, 42, 52, 54, 66, 75–80, 113
 food in 150–7
Amye Chakyung 157–9, 196
Amye Taglung 157–9, 225
anthropology xi, 9–10, 13, 144–7, 191–2

Bao'an 82, 84–5, 115
Beijing 6, 12–20, 26, 149, 229, 232, 239–40
Bithang Palden, eighteenth-century painter 123
Bonan nationality 85
British, invasion of Lhasa 39
Buddhism, Tibetan xviii–xx, 5, 7, 16, 28–30, 58, 60, 74, 79, 109, 168, 193, 203, 214, 221

Carpenter, Edmund 210
Central Asia xix, 58, 70
Chaksam 111
Chakyung Monastery 74
Chendza (Ch. Jianza) 78–9
Chengdu 28–45, 211–21
Chengdu Military Region Drama Troupe 219
China Tibetan Cultural Week 234
Chinese Communist Party 6, 12, 17, 67, 106, 121, 172, 234
Christianity 203, 220
Confucius 103–6
crazy-saints 118, 126, 182–7
Cultural Revolution 7, 34, 54, 91, 119–23, 171

Dalai Lama 37–8
 First 112
 Fourteenth 6, 15, 17, 28, 41, (birthplace) 71, 94–5, 172
 Fourth 118

Index

Third 37–8
Thirteenth 39, 122–3
Deng Xiaoping 7, 28, 34, 54, 114, 171
Dentig 74–5
Derge 43–4
Domey Chöjung, history of Amdo 126
Dondrup Gyel 236–9
drokpa, nomadic pastoralists 161
Dunhuang 176–8

Eliade, Mircea 124

folktales 189, 222–3
Four Fortresses 131–2

Gang of Four 174
Gansu xvi, 87
Geluk order xix–xx, 5, 16, 37, 54–5
Gendün Chöphel 229
Gentle Rain (Sbrang char), journal 229
Getag *Rinpoche* 48
Gobi Desert 20
gold leaf 188, 208
Golden Valley of Rebkong, see Sermojong
Golmud 18–25
Gomar 128
Gönlung Monastery 119

Guangzhou 215
Guchu Gorge 80–3, 84–5, 113–15
Guchu River 114, 119
Gulf War 210
gya-ma-wö, between Chinese and Tibetan 128
Gyantse 234
Gyelwo Gang 158–9, 181, 192–5

Huangnan 60–1
Huangshui River 51, 69, 71, 72
Hui nationality 50–1, 52, 72, 75–6

India 175
Intensified Program to Suppress Revolt 170

Jambhala, God of Material Blessings 200–7, *passim*
Jataka tales 100, 101
Jishi Shan Range 73

Kadampa order xix
Kagyu order xix, 113
Kalachakra Tantra, Sri 121
Kaldan Gyatso, Shar *Rinpoche* 5, 94, 143, 166, 185
Kasar 128
Kham xviii, 6, 36, 39, 40–2, 113
Khenchen Lama 119
Khubilai Khan 38

Kuang (Ripples Across Stagnant Water) 217–18
Kumbum Monastery 54–7, 172
Kundun 71–2
Kunlun Ranges 74

Labrang Monastery 111–12, 183–4
Lang Darma, Tibetan king 79
Lanzhou 14
Lao She 175
Lhalung Palkyi Dorje 79
Lhasa 4, 39, 42, 133
Li Bai 34
Lo Dorje Drak Monastery 79
Longwu Zhen (Lung-wu chen) 134
Lord Jim (Joseph Conrad) 179

Ma Bufang 5, 52, 54, 98, 175
Maitreya 55, 89, 112
malevolent spirits 236
Manchu nationality 35, 38
mani drupchen, ritual 197–9
Manjushri 55, 122, 180, 187, 205
Mao Zedong (Mao Tse-tung) 6, 18, 28, 34, 91, 121
Marx-Leninism 58, 121
mass communications 216–18
McLuhan, Marshall 216
Mencius 106–8
Migot, André 52–3

Mongol nationality 35, 37–8, 121
Monguor nationality (Ch. Tu) 87, 127–32, 183
Mount Emei 221–2

namkha, thread-cross 242–3
nang, flatbread 76
Nangra 78
nangso, pan-tribal leader 151
ngakpa, yogins 159, 161, 197–9
Nyenthok Monastery 121–7, 183
Nyenthok 120–8, 131, 183
Nyingma order xvii, 197–9

Ocean of Sacred Food, *see* 'Offering of the Fifteenth Day'
'Offering of the Fifteenth Day' 200–13
offerings (*chöpa*) 207–10
Om Manipadme Hum 3–4, 199

Padmasambhava xvii, 74, 198
Panchen Lama 15–18, 94
Patrul Rinpoche 160–1, 165
People's Liberation Army (PLA) 5–6, 22
Ping'an 68–9

Qing dynasty 38, 40, 121
Qinghai xviii, 13, 24, 40, 128

Index

Qinghai Provincial Museum 52–4
Qunke 75–6, 110, 115

Rebkong art 28–9, 58–9, 61, 91–2, 98–104, 126–7, 187–9
   gallery 90–2
   see also Huangnan; Tongren
Red River Valley (Tale of the Sacred Mountain) 240–1
Rimé, non-sectarian movement xx, 194
Rock, Joseph 148
Rongwo Monastery xviii, 5, 90–6, 126, 134–5, 142–5, 200
Rumi 190

Sakya order xix
Sakyi village 132
Samantabhadra (Kuntuzangpo) 198–208, passim
Sengeshong 98–104, 128, 131
Sermojong, Golden Valley 84–5, 114
Seven Years in Tibet 234
Shabkar xvii, 166, 229
Shadzong Hermitage 71
Shawo Tshering 96–102, 169–76
Sichuan xvi, 14, 28–45
six perfections, the 162–5
Smash the Four Olds Campaign 173

Smith, Patti 70
Songtsen Gampo, Tibetan king 98, 100

Ta'er Si, see Kumbum Monastery
Taklamakan Ranges 20
Taktser 71
Tashilhunpo Monastery 114
Tenzin Ching Wang 119
Thangtong Gyalpo 110–13, 115, 125
The Highland Barley Prince 44–5
Thonmi Sambhota 42
Three Learned Men of Tibet 75, 79
three marks of existence 233–4
Three Red Flags Movement 172
Tiananmen Square 12, 14, 34, 104
Tibet Autonomous Region (TAR) xviii, 13, 19, 36, 40, 219
Tibet
   art 28–30, 45–8, 58–60, 168–71, 180–2, 186–91
   geography xviii
   language xv, 42
   political history xx, 6–8, 17, 37
Tibetan Government-in-Exile 36
Tibetan Paintings from Kantze 45–8
Tongren 60, 86, 115–16, 134–7
Tri Songdetsun, Tibetan king 74
Tso Ngönbo (Lake Qinghai) 197

Tsongkhapa, Je xix, 16, 54–5, 73, 110
Tsultrim Gyatso, *Siddha* of Danma 118
Tucci, Giuseppe 111–13
Twelve Tribes of Rebkong 5, 60, 82

video parlours 160, 211

Waiting for Godot 82
Wangchen, modern warrior headman 78
Wencheng, princess 98, 101
Wenshu Monastery 30–1, 214–16
Wheel of Life 121–4, 127, 136, 227

Xikang 40, 175
Xining 24, 50–62
Xunzi 104–6

yak butter 196–7
Yarlung Dynasty xix, 194
Yellow River 51, 72–4, 77, 113, 126
Yunnan xviii

Zêkog 134–7
Zhang Daqian 173–6
Zhao Erfeng 39
Zheng Junli 173
Zhou Enlai 54
Zhu De 48